# An Introduction to the Logic of Psychological Measurement

Joel Michell
*University of Sydney*

1990
LAWRENCE ERLBAUM ASSOCIATES, PUBLISHERS
Hillsdale, New Jersey Hove and London

Lawrence Erlbaum Associates, Inc., Publishers
365 Broadway
Hillsdale, New Jersey 07642

**Library of Congress Cataloging-in-Publication Data**

Michell, Joel.
An introduction to the logic of psychological measurement / by Joel Michell.
p. cm.
Includes bibliographical references.
ISBN 0-8058-0566-4
1. Psychometrics. I. Title.
BF39.M54 1990
150'.28'7—dc20 89-77406
CIP

Printed in the United States of America
10 9 8 7 6 5 4 3 2 1

# Contents

# Preface

Plato suggests in his *Sophist* that corresponding to each productive activity there is a form of sophistry, a pretence or imitation of that activity. If measurement is the assessment of quantity then S.S.Stevens' famous definition of it as "the assignment of numerals to objects or events according to rule" is an incitement to sophistry if ever there was one and the practices called "psychological measurement," which presently lean heavily upon Stevens' definition for legitimation, are, perhaps, nothing more than a pretense.

It would be harsh, indeed, to dismiss such practices simply because a doubt has been raised. Science needs speculation as much as it needs criticism. However, a doubt raised lives until resolved, and doubt about the status of quantitative practices in psychology has a long history. If measurement is the assessment of quantity then there is only one way to resolve this doubt and that is by showing that the psychological variables involved actually are quantitative and that the procedures which psychologists use in the hope of measuring them enable quantitative relations between their values to be assessed. This book addresses the first of these issues.

To show that a variable is quantitative is to show that it has a definite kind of structure: its values stand in ordinal and additive relations to one another. This does not mean, as the physicist and philosopher N.R.Campbell mistakenly thought, finding empirical analogues of numerical addition. However, it does mean finding evidence in favor of underlying additive structure. How that may be done in psychology is now becoming clearer, thanks largely to the work of R.D.Luce and his associates on the theory of conjoint measurement. As Richard Feynman stressed in his lectures on physics, "whether or not a thing is measurable is not something to be decided *a priori* by thought alone, but something to be decided only by experiment." The theory of conjoint measurement lights the way to the relevant experiments.

Although expositions of the theory of conjoint measurement have been in the literature for more than a quarter of a century, the thinking of psychologists about their quantitative practices has not been greatly changed (outside of psychophysics, that is). There are two reasons for this. One is that expositions of this theory have been highly technically mathematical. Most psychologists are not trained as mathematicians and so this literature is largely inaccessible to them. However, the essential features of the theory can be understood with only a minimal mathematical background (i.e., high school algebra). Therefore, I have sought to provide what is for the most part a non-technical introduction. The second reason is that the radical implications of this theory have not been expounded by its originators. They have remained within the confines of the representational theory of measurement, a theory which I regard as false. The theory of conjoint measurement shows how non-extensive forms of measurement can be incorporated within a single, neo-traditional conception, one which has number as part of the empirical realm. In this book I have sought to present conjoint measurement as part of such a theory, one consonant with the development of quantitative science and consonant with an empirical realist theory of number. According to such a theory the distinction between the quantitative and the non-quantitative is absolute and empirical, and so the issue of where psychological variables fall becomes explicit.

This book is written as a text for a one semester course introducing students to the foundational issues involved in psychological measurement. It is not intended to compete with traditional textbooks on psychometrics, but rather to supplement them, by bringing to students in a critical way some of the recent advances made in our understanding of measurement by theorists such as S.S.Stevens, P.Suppes and R.D.Luce. It is not possible to have a balanced perspective on the practice of psychological measurement without exposure to this foundational material.

In undertaking this book I was stimulated, encouraged and constructively criticized by many people, to all of whom I extend my gratitude. I make special mention of J.P.Sutcliffe, who, as teacher introduced me to the issues surrounding measurement, and as supervisor and later as colleague, encouraged me to inquire into these issues; of G.W.Oliphant and L.Stankov, who commented valuably upon earlier versions of various chapters; of J.R.Maze, who expounded a version of Anderson's empirical realism which I came to accept as a vantage point from which to view psychology generally and measurement theory in particular; of D.M.Armstrong, who encouraged me to believe that the empirical realist account of number and quantity is not as outrageous as many adjudge it to be; and of R.D.Luce, whose writings on measurement theory inspired my vision. Over many years of teaching this kind of material to undergraduate, honours year and postgraduate students, I have been privileged to know many perspicacious minds, from whom I have learnt much. Without naming them I wish nonetheless to thank them for their criticisms, their energy and their interest. The University of Sydney has not only provided me with times and places to teach, it also granted me leave from teaching for a year, without which time completion of this book would have been all the more difficult; provided me with the typing assistance of S.Brooks and A.Cook, who at different times contributed with dedication their excellent skills; and met the cost of the illustrations (splendidly drawn by Greg Gaul). Finally, I thank my family and friends who have sustained and encouraged me, generously as ever, especially Anne, Sarah and David, who, simply in their being, were partial causes of my writing this book.

*Joel Michell*
*Sydney*

# Part I

# Theory

*. . . number is, of all conceptions, the easiest to operate with, and science seeks everywhere for an opportunity to apply it.*
*—Bertrand Russell*

# Section 1

# Some History

*We must measure what is measurable and make measurable what cannot be measured.*
*—Galileo*

# Chapter 1

# Making the Myth of Mental Measurement

## THE QUANTITATIVE IMPERATIVE

Quantitative concepts possess power, simplicity, and beauty. So the temptation to suppose that the fundamental structure of all natural processes is quantitative is strong. It has been thus since science began. Pythagoras was the first to yield: "All things are made of numbers," he is said to have taught. Plato ingeniously developed the same theme in the *Timaeus*: all things were composed out of the four basic elements, earth, fire, air, and water; they, in turn, were thought to be made up of certain regular polyhedra; the polyhedra, he said, were made of triangles; and, as is well known, triangles can be reduced to lines and angles and these to numbers. Such flights of mathematical fancy were to shape the course of science.

Aristotle disagreed with this reduction of all things to quantity. Naturally, he recognized that there were quantities (numbers, lengths, areas, volumes, angles, weights, etc.). But alongside these he thought that there were *qualities* as well. These were the nonquantitative properties of things, like color or temperature, so he said. The distinction he took to be an observational one. Properties that were quantitative possessed an additive structure. Those that were qualities did not. Imposed upon this distinction was his prejudice that the *essential* properties of things were qualities, not quantities. This affected his theorizing and he developed a fundamentally qualitative physics.

In medieval Europe interest in science reawakened about the 11th century. This coincided with the rediscovery of Aristotle's scientific works, which had been preserved by the Arabs after the barbarian invasions. The struggle between quantitative and qualitative conceptions of nature resumed. From the 12th to the 17th centuries Aristotle's nonquantitative physics dominated scientific thinking.

But the Platonic–Pythagorean tradition lived on. A portion of the *Timaeus* had been preserved in the Augustinean monasteries. Its influence sparked the beginning of modern quantitative science. The 13th-century English bishop, Robert Grosseteste, not only rediscovered the experimental method; he proclaimed the fundamentally quantitative structure of the universe: "All causes of natural effects can be discovered by lines, angles and figures, and in no other way can the reason for this action possibly be known" (*De Lineis, Angulis et Figuris*, cf. J. McEvoy (1982), p. 168).

Galileo echoed these sentiments four centuries later when he wrote that the "book of nature" (by which he meant the universe itself) ". . . is written in mathematical language, and the letters are triangles, circles and other geometrical figures, without which means it is humanly impossible to comprehend a single word" (*Il Saggiatore,* cf. S. Drake (1957) pp. 237–238). These Platonic sentiments were shared by his great contemporaries, Kepler and Descartes. But, more than anything else, it was the victory of Galileo's physics over its Aristotelean rival that caused this theme to dominate the future of European science. Quantitative science had triumphed over nonquantitative.

Out of this success was born the quantitative imperative, encapsulated in the quote from Galileo that heads this section. Its impetus was strengthened by the work of Newton and it culminated in the 19th century with the successful extension of quantitative theories to the study of most physical phenomena, including electricity, magnetism, and heat. Again the philosophers taught it. Kant wrote that ". . . a doctrine of nature will contain only so much science proper as there is applied mathematics in it" (1786, p. 7). The 19th-century British philosopher of science, W. S. Jevons, concluded that there was ". . . no apparent limit to the ultimate extension of quantitative science" (1873, p. 274). Even a philosopher as unlikely as Nietzsche considered that ". . . knowledge has become scientific to the extent that it is able to employ number and measure" (1968, p. 378).

However, it was that great 19th-century physicist, Lord Kelvin, who gave it its most forthright proclamation:

> I often say that when you can measure what you are speaking about and express it in numbers you know something about it; but when you cannot measure it, when you cannot express it in numbers, your knowledge is of a meagre and unsatisfactory kind; it may be the beginning of knowledge, but you have scarcely, in your thoughts advanced to the stage of *science*, whatever the matter may be. (W. Thomson, 1891, pp. 80–81)

This saying became a favorite of the quantitative movement and versions of it abound (cf. Eysenck, 1973; Hacking, 1983; Kuhn, 1961; Merton, Sills, & Stigler, 1984; Pearson, 1978; Yule & Kendall, 1911).

Into this intellectual milieu modern psychology emerged in 1860 with the work of G. Fechner. No discipline can free itself from the methodological presuppositions of its time. Modern psychology was no exception. As a 19th century invention it conformed to 19th century conceptions of the nature of science. It conformed to Kelvin's dictum that science had to be quantitative. Indeed, the mere fact that modern psychology is taken to have begun with Fechner's contribution confirms this judgment. He began his scientific career as a physicist and established his reputation measuring direct currents. Later, he became preoccupied with issues of a psychological kind, and sought to establish the reality of mental phenomena, attempting to measure the intensity of sensations. Doing so he developed psychology's first quantitative methodology. Without this contribution, Boring (1929) wrote, ". . . there would . . . have been little of the breath of science in the experimental body, for we hardly recognize a subject as scientific if measurement is not one of its tools" (p. 286). So it was ". . . as a consequence of Fechner's contribution that psychology advanced from prescience to science" (H. E. Adler, 1980, p. 13).

Fechner was not the first to think of measuring psychological variables. That honor belongs, I think, to the 14th century scholar, Nicole Oresme. Later, J. F. Herbart (1816) was to propose a quantitative psychological theory. But Fechner proposed *methods of measurement* and that is why modern psychologists date their science from his work.

In the minds of the founding fathers the issue was paramount. Francis Galton wrote, ". . . until the phenomena of any branch of knowledge have been submitted to measurement and number, it cannot assume the status and dignity of a science" (1879, p. 147). His one-time assistant and one of America's first professors of psychology, James McKeen Cattell, wrote, "Psychology cannot attain the certainty and exactness of the physical sciences, unless it rests on a foundation of experiment and measurement" (1890, p. 373).

The founder of the factor analytic method, Charles Spearman, wrote that

> . . . great as may be the potency of this [the experimental method], or of the preceding methods, there is yet another one so vital that, if lacking it, any study is thought by many authorities not to be scientific in the full sense of the word. This further and crucial method is that of measurement. (1937, p. 89).

The early American structuralist, E. B. Titchener, thought that there was ". . . no question but that, in some way or other, mental processes are measurable" (1905, pp. xxi-xxii). Kulpe, the founder of the Wurzburg school was equally confident that ". . .the universal validity of psychological results is guaranteed by the measurability of mental phenomena" (1895, p. 11). And Hermann Ebbinghaus, the first to attempt to measure the "higher mental processes" wrote, "The brilliant results produced in natural science by measurement and calculation suggested the idea that something similar might be done for psychology" (1908, p. 13).

Wilhelm Wundt, said by some to be the father of modern experimental psychology, felt it necessary to refute Kant's claim that psychology could not be a science because it could not be quantitative. Wundt concluded that, "Our inner life . . .

has at least two dimensions which implies the general possibility of expressing them in mathematical form" (1873, p. 6). E.L. Thorndike, the American functionalist, attempted to justify the quantitative imperative with Pythagorean dogma (in an oft-quoted saying, cf. Eysenck, 1973; Johnson, 1936; & McCall, 1923): "Whatever exists at all exists in some amount. To know it thoroughly involves knowing its quantity" (quoted in Eysenck, 1973, p. x). Freud, also, was victim to the same doctrine: he wrote that ". . . science recognizes only *quantities*" (1895, p. 309).

The early years of modern psychology's development are largely the history of psychophysical measurement (in the work of Fechner, Wundt, Titchener, and others); of mental chronometry (Donders); of the attempt to measure learning and memory (Ebbinghaus); and of the attempts to measure mental abilities (Galton, Spearman, and their followers).

Few who took seriously the claim that psychology was a science questioned the idea that it could be quantitative. Too much seemed to be at stake. Psychology's credentials as a science, both in the eyes of its founders and of the wider scientific community, depended on its development as a quantitative discipline.

One who did have a more relaxed attitude about this matter was Franz Brentano, the founder of Act Psychology. While going along with the prevailing view that psychology was, as a matter of fact, a quantitative science, he recognized the contingent nature of this situation. The general issue he saw as follows: "Mathematics appears to me necessary for the exact treatment of all sciences only because we now in fact find magnitudes in every scientific field. It there were a field in which we encountered nothing of the sort, exact description would be possible even without mathematics" (Brentano, 1874, p. 65).

Uncharacteristic as it is of its age, Brentano's view has an Aristotelian ring to it, as does much of his work. If, as Aristotle argued, the distinction between quantity and quality resides in the structure of the variable involved (quantitative variables being additive, qualitative ones being nonadditive) then it is possible that some sciences may be purely qualitative, precisely because the variables studied within them are qualitative variables. Measurement need not be a universal characteristic of science. Instead, what characterizes science is the method of observation. And it is only through observation that the structure of any variable can be known. The structure cannot be determined a priori. On this matter at least, Aristotle and Brentano were correct. The only way to decide whether or not the variables studied in any particular science are quantitative is to put that hypothesis to the test. This essential step is missing in the development of modern psychology and this fact has put the pursuit of psychological measurement on the defensive. In its turn this defensiveness has helped shape psychologists' thinking about psychological measurement. As will be shown, they have been led to adopt some curious views.

Until the 1930s the development of psychological measurement was relatively untroubled. Certain variables were taken to be quantitative and various methods were hypothesized to measure them. The presumption that these speculations delivered the substance of measurement was not seriously challenged. Then in 1932 a committee was established by the British Association for the Advancement of Science, its purpose being to enquire into the status of psychophysical measurement. Some serious criticisms were made of these supposed methods of measurement and this, by implication, raised questions about the entire enterprise of psychological measurement. The impact on psychology was catastrophic. Psychologists responded by redefining the concept of measurement, in the end accepting a definition so inflated as to rule out none of their methods. That this devalued the concept was ignored, for at least it gave the appearance of conformity to the quantitative imperative.

Of course, such a response inhibited serious interest in the issue of psychological measurement. The irony is that such redefinition was not the only way to justify attempts at psychological measurement. The psychologists of that period were not only in the grip of the quantitative imperative, they were also deeply confused about the nature of measurement. Had this concept been properly understood the crisis could have been resolved satisfactorily. The source of confusion about the concept of measurement was ignorance about the history of the concept prior to the 20th century.

## HISTORY OF THE CONCEPT OF MEASUREMENT

Psychologists are not alone in ignoring the classical treatments of the concepts of measurement and quantity. Modern treatments of the topic read as if serious thinking about measurement began with Campbell (1920), Helmholtz (1887), Holder (1901), and Russell (1903). Occasionally reference is made to an earlier, "traditional" view (e.g., Ellis, 1966, Fraser, 1980) but only to dismiss it, never to understand it. Such 20th century arrogance, with its ahistorical insinuation that no clear thinking was ever done prior to this century, is not compatible with a serious interest in a topic as ancient as measurement. Its origins cannot be dated but the ancient Greek mathematicians and philosophers thought deeply about the subject. Their views sustained the practice of measurement from their time until the late 19th century. The theories of measurement which then developed, the representational theories of Helmholtz, Russell, and Campbell, need to be understood as the outcomes of interactions between this classical theory and other influences. They should not be taken as either the first or last word on any aspect of measurement or quantity.

A coherent theory of measurement and quantity is to be found in the writings of Aristotle and Euclid. The following summary takes ideas from both writers, and I take it to be a fair appraisal of what these concepts meant then and, with some modification, continued to mean for more than 2,000 years. Indeed, the view of the modern layman and scientist uninfluenced by philosophy is still remarkably close to this ancient view.

Aristotle took quantity to be one of the fundamental categories of reality. He divided it into discrete and continuous. The discrete quantities were the natural numbers (i.e., the numbers 1, 2, 3, . . . ) by which he meant, not the elements of some formal system, but the properties common to certain classes or collections. The *number 2*, for example, was thought to be that which is common to all pairs of things. The continuous quantities Aristotle called *magnitudes*, by which he intended to designate variables like length, time, weight, volume, and so forth. What he though distinguished quantities from qualities was the fact that any particular quantity (i.e., any natural number or any value of a magnitude, say, a particular length) is additively composed of parts. In the case of natural numbers the parts are *ones*. In the case of magnitudes the parts are smaller magnitudes of the same kind. For example, every length is additively composed of smaller lengths. Hence, magnitudes must be infinitely divisible and this is part of what Aristotle meant by calling them *continuous*. Pairs of quantities of the same kind (homogeneous quantities) stand in a relation of *ratio* (i.e., relative magnitude) to one another. For example, the magnitude of a yard relative to that of a foot is 3. More generally, let $A$ and $B$ be any two homogeneous magnitudes (e.g., 2 lengths) then the ratio of $A$ to $B$ ($A/B$) $\leqslant n/m$ (where $n$ and $m$ are natural numbers) if and only if $mA \leqslant nB$ (where $mA$, for example, is that magnitude entirely composed of $m$ discrete parts each identical to $A$). Then two ratios of magnitudes, $A/B$ and $C/D$, are equal if and only if for all natural numbers, $n$ and $m$,

$$A/B < n/m \text{ if and only if } C/D < n/m,$$

$$A/B = n/m \text{ if and only if } C/D = n/m \text{ and}$$

$$A/B > n/m \text{ if and only if } C/D > n/m.$$

So not only was the concept of relative magnitude well understood but so was the idea of a ratio of nonnumerical quantities equalling or not equalling the ratio of two natural numbers. As was also well understood by the time of Aristotle and Euclid, some ratios of magnitudes equal ratios of numbers and some do not. Those that do not are incommensurable pairs of magnitudes (like the lengths of the side and the diagonal of a square). If $A/B = n/m$ then $n/m$ is the *measure* of $A$ in units of $B$. If $A$ is incommensurate with $B$ then the measure of $A$ in units of $B$ is only *approximated* by a numerical ratio, though as was known by Euclid, in principle it may be approximated to any degree of precision.

As it stands this theory copes admirably with all of the then recognized quantities. These are some of those that are now called *extensive quantities*. Length may be taken as the paradigm. The fact that lengths are additive, and therefore quantitative, is readily seen in the behavior of some objects possessing lengths. A pair of rigid, straight rods may be combined end to end in a straight line, the length of the joined rods equalling the sum of their separate lengths. In such a case the operation of combination reflects the additive structure of the length variable in a simple and direct fashion. This is the way with all extensive quantities. But it needs to be emphasized that the classical theory is about the structure of quantitative variables and not about the behavior of objects possessing values of such variables. This aspect of the classical theory was not emphasized by the ancient philosophers and mathematicians. The only magnitudes they knew of were extensive and so there was little need to make the point.

However, modern science, in contrast to ancient, deals with many quantitative variables that are not extensive. Temperature is a good example. Combining two liquids does not generally produce a liquid whose temperature is the sum of their separate temperatures. In this case there is no operation that simply and directly reflects the additive structure of the quantity. Such quantities are called *intensive*. They differ from extensive quantities not in their inner, additive structure but only in their external relations to the behavior of objects manifesting them. These relations are less direct and more complex, hence, so is the evidence for these variables being quantitative. Despite this, the classical theory still describes the structure of the variable involved.

This capacity of the classical theory to cover both extensive and intensive quantities was first made explicit by the 14th century French scholar, Nicole Oresme. His insight sprang from what began as a theological problem. For some time prior to Oresme, theologians had argued over how they should conceptualize the fact that the virtue of charity could increase or decrease within the same person. Eventually the problem was generalized to that of whether *any* qualities admit of quantitative increase or decrease in intensity and if so, how this fact might be conceptualized. Oresme's solution was as follows:

> Every measurable thing except number is imagined in the manner of continuous quantity. Therefore, for the mensuration of such a thing, it is necessary that points, lines and surfaces, or their properties be imagined. For in them (i.e., the geometrical entities), as the Philosopher has it, measure or ratio is initially found, while in other things it is recognized by similarity as they are being referred by the intellect to them (i.e. to geometrical entities). . . . Therefore, every intensity which can be acquired successively ought to be imagined by a straight line . . . For whatever ratio is found to exist between intensity and intensity, in relating intensities of the same kind, a similar ratio is found to exist between line and line and vice versa . . . . Therefore, the measure of intensities can be fittingly imagined as the measure of lines. (*De Configurationibus* I, i, pp. 165–167)

In this passage it is Oresme's suggestion that the quantitative structure of the length variable (lines and their properties) is the paradigm or model of all quantity, extensive and intensive alike. Indeed, to give it authority he attributes this suggestion to Aristotle ("the Philosopher"). According to this view, length is the model for measurement and to describe a variable as quantitative is to attribute to it a structure similar to that of length. Therefore, measures of any such variable may be conceptualized by analogy to lines and their ratios one to another. Oresme was thus enabled to speculate about the measurement of all manner of variables, many hitherto considered nonquantitative. These included not only physical variables like velocity, but psychological ones as well, such as pleasure and pain. In so doing he became, in theory at least, the first psychometrician. His solution, obvious to us because of our facility with graphical methods, freed the classical concepts of magnitude and measurement from their ancient exclusive attachment to extensive magnitudes and broadened them to include the intensive ones as well. This proved important in the ensuing scientific revolution and its aftermath.

Considered in the light of this extension of the classical theory, the attempts at quantification made by the founding fathers of modern psychology were perfectly proper. To suggest that variables like mental ability or the intensity of sensations are quantitative is to speculate that they possess an additive structure akin to that of length. It is perfectly meaningful to speculate thus, even though the evidence supporting the speculation is thin. Furthermore, if procedures are suggested for the measurement of such variables then the hypothesis is that they *measure* them in the classical sense of that word. Of course, validation of these measurement procedures may be a long way off. The next step is to develop the means of testing these speculations and hypotheses. One cannot properly boast of measurement at this early stage. However, it is a necessary stage and progress comes in science through finding ways to test new hypotheses.

Now there is every reason to believe that the founders of modern psychology accepted the classical theory of measurement. Not that many of them explicitly defined the concept, the classical theory being taken too much for granted then. But those who did, did so in a way consistent with the classical theory. For example, Fechner (1860) wrote, "Generally the measurement of a quantity consists of ascertaining how often a unit quantity of the same kind is contained in it" (p. 38). E. B. Titchener (1905) defined it similarly: "When we measure in any department of natural science, we compare a given magnitude with some conventional unit of the same kind, and determine how many times the unit is contained in the magnitude" (p. xix). And the entry under "measurement" in Baldwin's (1902) *Dictionary of Philosophy and Psychology* states: "In order that a concept may be measured as a mathematical quantity without ambiguity, it is essential that the special attribute by which we measure it should be conceivable as made up of discrete parts, admitting of unambiguous comparison *inter se*, with respect to their quality or difference of magnitude" (p. 58).

So in their acceptance of the quantitative imperative, and in their speculations that their own special variables were measurable they presumed the classical theory of measurement and quantity. In doing so they courted quantity at the end of an era. The classical theory was soon to go.

The classical theory has it that ratios of magnitudes may equal (or be approximated by) ratios of numbers. Now magnitudes, like for example length, are *empirical* properties or relations. That is, they belong to the spatio-temporal world of experience. On the other hand, the empirical character of numbers has always been a matter of debate, even in ancient times. However the classical theory, in asserting the existence of relationships between ratios of magnitudes and ratios of numbers, implies that numbers must have an empirical character.

This could have been Aristotle's view (cf. J. Lear, 1982). Nevertheless, it was a view lacking wide support at the dawn of the 20th century. One factor causing its eclipse was the critique given by the German philosopher, G. Frege, of the empirical view. In his *System of Logic*, John Stuart Mill had proposed an empirical theory of number. Frege (1884) mercilessly attacked Mill's thesis. Since then few have followed Mill's or any other empirical theory of number. A second factor was the development during the 19th century of the theory of noneuclidean geometries. Their appearance was taken to imply that the science of mathematics generally possesses a nonempirical subject matter. Then late in the 19th and early in the 20th centuries nonempirical theories of number were proposed. The time was ripe for a new theory of measurement, one compatible with nonempiricism about numbers.

The second intellectual development weakening the classical theory was *verificationism*. This is the tendency to confuse the meaning of a proposition with the observational conditions that would verify it. Within the classical theory the fact that a variable is quantitative is distinguished from the observational evidence supporting that fact. For example, length and density are both taken to be quantitative variables (i.e., to possess additive structure), although the kinds of observations supporting each are quite different. In the case of length, the behavior of rigid rods directly reflects the hypothesized additive structure. In the case of density the evidence is less direct, being via the relation of density to mass and volume. There are, as will be shown in the following chapters, a number of different ways in which the hypothesis that a variable is quantitative may be tested. The laws that characterize the structure of a quantitative variable are what might be described as *uniformities of coexistence* (to borrow a term from J. S. Mill, 1843). In themselves they do not license any predictions, they simply state how values of the variable are related to one another. For example, one such law is the following proposition: $A + (B + C) = (A + B) + C$ (where $A$, $B$, and $C$ are any three values of the variable and the relation $A + B = D$ means that value $D$ is entirely composed of the two discrete parts $A$ and $B$). Laws like this only license predictions in conjunction with other laws relating not only to the character of the objects involved but also to our capacity to operate on them and to make observations. Because these other laws may vary from one situation to another, even though the laws of quantity are invariant, there may be no limit to the number of different ways in which quantitative structure may be manifest in the behavior of objects.

Verificationists have little patience with such subtleties. In the context of measurement they attempt to reduce quantitative structure to a specific set of observations, most often to those that directly reflect it. That is, they tend to reduce the concept of quantity to that of extensive quantity, making the existence of the latter a necessary condition for all measurement.

The theory of measurement put forward by N. R. Campbell (1920) satisfied both of these tendencies. He distinguished two kinds of measurement: *fundamental* and *derived*. Fundamental measurement requires the existence of a physical analogue of numerical addition, such as the combining of two rods end to end in a straight line. Given that this physical operation satisfies properties similar to those of numerical addition, numbers (or numerals) may be assigned to the objects so as to reflect their physical addition. For example, if rod *c* is the same length as rod *a* combined with rod *b* then the number assigned to *c* should equal the sum of the numbers assigned to *a* and *b*. In this way numbers and the relations between them may be used to represent empirical, non-numerical relations of order and addition. Thus Campbell's theory involves no commitment to numbers as empirical entities, as does the classical theory. It is indifferent to their ontological character. On this view numbers are a mere tool enabling ". . . the powerful weapon of mathematical analysis to be applied to the subject matter of science" (Campbell, 1920, pp. 267–268). Campbell's theory of fundamental measurement also satisfies the requirements of verificationism, for it ties quantity to fundamental measurability. To be a fundamental quantity a variable must be related to an operation of physical addition formally similar to the operation of numerical addition.

However, according to Campbell this is not the only way that quantity is manifest. In derived measurement the fact that a variable is quantitative is manifest through its relationship to fundamental quantities, thought Campbell. When a set of fundamental measures reveals a system of constants, then the constants may be taken as derived measures of another quantity. For example, relative to each different kind of material the ratio of mass to volume is a constant and this constant is taken to be a derived measure of that kind of material's density. Because derived measurement depends on fundamental measurement (a derived measure being a numerical function of fundamental measures), for Campbell the concept of quantity is still tied to that of fundamental measurement and fundamental measurement is the first, necessary step along the road to quantification.

Campbell's theory had enormous influence, particularly on psychologists. From 1935 onwards a series of articles and books appeared within psychology (and associated disciplines) relating Campbell's theory to attempts at psychological measurement (c.f. Bergmann & Spence, 1944; Comrey, 1950; Johnson, 1936; McGregor, 1935; Reese, 1943; Smith, 1938; and Thomas, 1942). Initially, attempts were made to reconcile psychological procedures with Campbell's theory, but this was not possible. Already, in 1934, E.G. Boring had correctly followed the logic of Campbell's theory to the conclusion that "Psychology lacks true measurement . . . because there are not additive units" (Newman, 1974, p. 138).

Eventually, all agreed that psychology lacked fundamental measurement in Campbell's sense because it possessed no additive operations for its supposedly quantitative variables. This conclusion was made quite public in the Final Report delivered by the committee of the British Association for the Advancement of Science. One of the psychologists on the committee wrote: "If all measurement must conform to the Laws of Measurement enunciated by Dr. Campbell, and, in particular, if the second law can only be satisfied by the physical juxtaposition of equal entities, then sensation intensity cannot be measured" (Bartlett, 1940, p. 423). Of course, what was here concluded of psychophysical measurement applied equally to all psychological measurement. Without fundamental measurement there could be no derived measurement and so, according to Campbell's theory, psychology was without measurement. What is more, the task of locating analogues of numerical addition pertinent to psychological variables seemed hopeless and thus the prospects of psychological measurement appeared grim.

This dismal situation, combined with acceptance of the quantitative imperative appeared to place psychology in an intolerable position. To be a science in the full sense of the word psychological measurement was thought to be necessary, however, the requirements held to be necessary for measurement were absent from psychology and seemed unattainable. The obvious conclusion, nevertheless, was totally unthinkable. The tension was resolved by the American psychophysicist, S. S. Stevens. He had a special interest in the report of the British committee, because his *sone scale*, for the alleged measurement of sensations of loudness, had been singled out for examination. However, for a long time he had been considering the plight of attempts at psychological measurement. He was at Harvard University with E.G. Boring and so he was, no doubt, aware of the latter's critical stance based on Campbell's theory. In an autobiographical article Stevens wrote, "My own central problem throughout the 1930s was measurement, because the quantification of the sensory attributes seemed impossible unless the nature of measurement could be properly understood" (1974, p. 409). The theory of measurement that he came to propose owed much to Campbell's, but it also owed a lot to what was then a fledgling philosophical movement, *operationalism*.

Operationalism was a homespun, American philosophy of science, presented by the Nobel prize-winning physicist, P. W. Bridgman (1927). His concerns centered around the then recent revolution in physical theory, the replacement of 19th century physical theory (what is sometimes called "Newtonian" theory) by Einstein's theory of relativity. Bridgman hoped to show that the fault with "Newtonian" theory was the inadequate definition of its terms. His proposal was for a program of conceptual reform based on a system of what he called *operational definitions*. It was really a blend of verificationism and pragmatism. According to Bridgman, ". . .the true meaning of a term is to be found by observing what a man does with it, not by what he says about it" (1927, p. 7). Thus, the meaning of supposedly theoretical terms had to be reduced to observations (verificationism) and the relevant observations were those relating to scientific practice (pragmatism). His pivotal slogan was that, "In general we mean by any concept nothing more than a set of operations; *the concept is synonymous with the corresponding set of operations*" (1927, p. 5).

Operationalism's iconoclastic rejection of traditional concepts and methods and its promise of a fresh-start appealed to the generation of American psychologists who had already broken with the older mentalism and taken to behaviorism. In particular, S. S. Stevens was a leading spokesman for the psychological arm of the movement throughout the 1930s (cf. Stevens, 1935a, 1935b, and 1939), the same period during which he was struggling to find a new theory of measurement.

Operationalism implies a theory of measurement. This was made explicit by the British operationalist, H. Dingle, who defined measurement as ". . . any precisely specified operation that yields a number" (1950, p. 11). Obviously, according to operationalism, what such a number measures is "synonymous with" the "precisely specified operation." The issue of whether the number relates to a quantitative variable is, on this view, a nonissue. One has a procedure and the procedure generates a number, so one must have "measurement." Stevens' starting place was Campbell's theory and not the operational theory of measurement. However, he developed those aspects of Campbell's theory that led in Bridgman's direction. He finished up with a theory that, whether he realized it or not, was indistinguishable from Dingle's operational theory of measurement. He did this by developing Campbell's *representationalism* at the expense of his emphasis on additivity.

The concept of additivity is an essential part of the classical theory of measurement, for without additivity one cannot have ratios of magnitudes and without ratios of magnitudes there is no measurement. Campbell, however, logically detached the use of numbers in measurement from the existence of additivity. He still insisted on additivity, although not because this was thought to be logically necessary for the use of numbers. He replaced additivity as the basis for measurement by the concept of representation: numbers are used in measurement to *represent*. Reading this shift of emphasis quite accurately, Stevens recognized that other relations apart from additivity could be represented numerically and given this new emphasis such representations had an equal right to be included within the concept of measurement.

Numbers could be used to represent identity or difference with respect to some attribute. For example, if people are classified by sex and all males assigned 1 and all females 0 then one has the numerical representation of a nonadditive empirical relation. The relation is that of *being the same sex as* and $A$ is the same sex as $B$ if and only if $A$ and $B$ are assigned the same number. This assignment rule gives what Stevens thought of as the simplest variety of measurement, the *nominal scale*.

Or, numbers could be used to represent order relations between things. Students' essays, for example, fall into the set of ordered categories: high distinction, distinction, credit, pass, fail. Numbers may be assigned to essays to represent this ordinal information. Then the empirical relation represented is that of *being at least the same quality as*, and essay $X$ is at least the same quality as essay $Y$, if and only if the number assigned to $X$ is at least as great as the number assigned to $Y$. This assignment rule gives what Stevens called an *ordinal scale*.

Thirdly, the numbers assigned may be used to represent equality and order of differences between things with respect to some attribute. Suppose, for example, that the volume of a certain liquid expands linearly with increases in temperature. Let $X$ and $Y$ be two samples of the liquid, equal in volume but at different temperatures (temperatures $A$ and $C$ respectively). Suppose that they are heated to new temperatures, $B$ and $D$ respectively. Then a judgment can be made via the change in volume as to what temperature difference is the greater, $B - A$ or $D - C$. In this case the relation is that of one temperature difference being at least as great as another temperature difference and numbers may be assigned so that temperature $B$ − temperature $A$ is at least as great as temperature $D$ − temperature $C$ if and only if $n_B - n_A \geqslant n_D - n_C$ (where $n_A$, $n_B$, $n_C$ and $n_D$ are the numbers assigned to the temperatures $A$, $B$, $C$ and $D$ respectively). Such an assignment rule produces what Stevens called an *interval scale*. Finally, Stevens recognized, that empirical, additive relations could also be represented numerically, producing what he called a *ratio scale*.

These are Stevens (1946, 1951, 1959) four general types of measurement scales and although he sometimes mentioned others (e.g., the log–interval scale), he seems to have believed that these four were the most important. The completed theory distinguished them one from another by classes of admissible scale transformations and prescribed for each scale–type a class of permissible statistics. This latter aspect of his theory always remained controversial within psychology, though it would seem to be a trivial point that numbers used to represent different kinds of empirical information could not all be treated in the same way. In particular, rules would have to be devised to ensure that only conclusions already entailed by the empirical information alone, could be drawn from the numbers assigned. Stevens' "measurement" scales are really instances of numerical coding, the purpose of the coding being to allow inferences to be made by numerical means.

Of course, these four types of scales are not the only ones possible. Every empirical relation, no matter what its character, can be represented numerically. Again, this is a fairly trivial observation. As is well known, any relation can be defined set-theoretically as a class of ordered $n$-tuples. That is, each binary relation is a set of ordered pairs, each ternary relation a set of ordered triples, and so on. Now, let $R$ be any binary empirical relation which we wish to represent numerically. Let each object in the field of $R$ be assigned a different number, any number. If $x$ and $y$ are any such pair of objects then there exists a binary numerical relation, $S$, such that

$$<n_x, n_y> \in S \text{ if and only if } R(x,y)$$

(where $n_x$ and $n_y$ are the numbers assigned to $x$ and $y$ respectively, a set described by "<" and ">" is an ordered set and $R(x,y)$ means that $x$ stands in the relation $R$ to $y$). $S$, being a set of ordered pairs of numbers, is a numerical relation and it represents the empirical relation, $R$. A similar relation exists for any ternary relation or for any relation of any degree. So it follows that if measurement is nothing more nor less than numerical representation then *all* variables can be measured and any consistent assignment of numbers to objects measures *something*. Of course, such measures may not generally be very useful, but the important point is that they exist.

Whether Stevens grasped this point or not is unclear. However, from 1946 onwards he always defined measurement as, ". . . the assignment of numerals to objects or events according to rules" (1946, p. 667, 1951, p. 1, and 1959, p. 19). In 1959 he added the comment that ". . . provided a consistent rule is followed, some form of measurement is achieved" (p. 19). So it seems he may have. If so, then he took the representational theory as far as it can go, making it equivalent in practice to the operational theory. On both views, any "precisely specified" operation for making "consistent" numerical assignments to things is "measurement."

In being brought to this destination the concept of measurement is virtually emptied of all content. Not only are all variables measurable and all consistent numerical assignments measurement, but also the ancient distinction between quantity and quality is dissolved. Whether a variable is quantitative or not simply becomes a pragmatic issue, one determined not by the character of the variable itself, but by the decision of the researcher. This point was acknowledged recently in the context of multidimensional scaling by F.W. Young, who noted that ". . . the distinction does not reside in the observation circumstances, but is in the mind of the observer" (1984, p. 56). Thus to say of a variable that it is measurable by a certain procedure is not to say anything about it nor about the procedure (other than that it is number generating). It is simply to say that some one wants to treat the variable numerically.

Precisely because it was so emptied at the hands of Stevens, the concept of measurement came to encompass all of the quantitative and pseudo-quantitative techniques existing within psychology. And it was because it so obviously promised to do this that Stevens' definition of measurement was rapidly absorbed into psychology's storehouse of conventional wisdom. Not only that, it was also made to appear as if this definition was all that measurement had ever meant. By 1954 Coombs, Raiffa, and Thrall were referring to it as the "classical measurement theory." Even Stevens was surprised by that (cf. his 1959, p. 21). Also in 1954, J. P. Guilford, in the second edition of his famous text, *Psychometric Methods*, quoted it (p. 5). He remarked with some satisfaction that now the concept of measurement was wide enough to include psychological procedures. Then he endorsed Stevens' definition strangely attributing it, not to Stevens, but to Campbell. A similar kind of error was also recently made by the historian of psychology, H. E. Adler, who wrote that "Fechner understood the essential nature of measurement as 'the assignment of numerals to objects or events according to rule' " (1980, p. 14). As already indicated, Fechner did no such thing: he endorsed the classical theory of measurement! These mistakes suggest a tendency to bury all other views on measurement beneath Stevens' definition.

Guilford's textbook was not the only influential authority to endorse Stevens' definition. It was also endorsed by most of the major reference books of the time within psychology. Stevens' own *Handbook of Experimental Psychology*, of course, contained his (1951) treatise on measurement, which, for many psychologists over the next 30 years, "stood like the Decalogue" (Newman, 1974). B. F.

Green (1954), in his article on attitude measurement in Lindzey's *Handbook of Social Psychology*, also quoted it, attributing it not only to Stevens but, to add to the weight of authority, also to "Lorge (1951) and others." Whoever the "others" were, it is not difficult to guess from whence they obtained Stevens' definition. In the case of Lorge a guess is not necessary. His article had appeared in another widely used reference book, E. F. Lindquist's *Educational Measurement*, and he explicitly attributed the definition to Stevens.

Thus, there was within the psychology of the 1950s an almost immediate consensus about the meaning of measurement. Stevens' definition produced a collective sigh of relief. Since then, more than a generation of psychology students have been trained in the belief that this definition states what measurement really is. The misconception is now firmly entrenched. As a consequence, it is now accepted within psychology that mental tests measure abilities, that multidimensional scaling measures perceptual attributes, that magnitude estimation measures the intensity of sensations, and that summated rating scales measure attitudes and personality traits. In each case the justification for these beliefs resides in Stevens' definition. To illustrate this, consider Norman Cliff's justification of rating scales as a method of psychological measurement: "Crude as they are, rating scales constitute a workable measurement technology because there has been repeated observation that numbers assigned in this way display the appropriate kinds of consistency" (1982, p. 31).

Prior to the acceptance of Stevens' definition few psychologists would have been so bold on behalf of their quantitative methods and least of all on behalf of this "crude" method. As already indicated, Boring had concluded in 1934 that psychology lacked measurement and he was referring to psychophysics, which had until then been regarded as the jewel in psychology's quantitative crown. From then until the acceptance of Stevens' definition, treatments of psychological measurement were full of doubt. Stevens' definition allowed the illusion of quantification to persist in the face of Campbell's critique.

Stevens' definition is mistaken because it confuses two quite different practices: measurement (in the classical sense) and numerical coding. As will be made clear in chapter 3, measurement involves the discovery of empirical facts of an intrinsically numerical kind. Numerical coding on the other hand is simply a useful cosmetic in the analysis and presentation of what is otherwise nonnumerical information. To confuse these two is to confuse how things are, with the use of a symbolism for representing them. For measurement involves an ontological commitment to quantity and number as part of the furniture of the universe, whereas numerical coding is simply a notational device for the symbolic representation of facts. Any theory that confuses these two is a hindrance to scientific progress for it obscures important factual issues that need to be addressed.

This chapter has shown why psychologists were prepared to accept this confusion. They were obsessed with the implementation of a quantitative program within their science. Such an obsession would permit scientific progress only if the variables studied actually were quantitative. Thus, the logically prior task was that of finding out whether or not these variables were quantitative. The mistake of the psychologists was to be more interested in the pursuit of their quantitative program than in the pursuit of the underlying facts. They steered this course because they believed that all science must be quantitative. Campbell's theory of measurement, inadequate as it was, challenged psychologists to examine the underlying factual issues. They declined to meet this challenge and took instead the apparently easier way offered by the acceptance of Stevens' definition. However, this definition gives nothing more than the illusion of measurement. It has not served psychology well, for the underlying factual issues still need to be addressed. What is needed to replace Stevens' definition is an understanding of how these issues can be tackled. Clearly, Campbell's approach via his concept of fundamental measurement is too narrow. A wider range of methods is needed in order to test whether or not any given variable is quantitative. Then those methods that can be applied to psychological variables may be used to settle the matter.

# Section 2

# And Philosophy

*what has philosophy got to do with measuring anything?*
*—Galileo*

Chapter 2

# The Theory of Measurement in Psychology

Before considering in some depth the question of what quantity and measurement really are, I want to consider two conceptions of measurement now widely accepted within psychology: operationalism and representationalism. The preceding chapter traced the emergence of these two theories of measurement from the older, classical theory. It is important to recognize that the history of a theory is logically independent of the issue of its truth. Even granting that these later conceptions of measurement were accepted within psychology *simply* to save the preconception that psychology had to be quantitative, it still may be the case that one or the other of them is true. Other arguments must be presented in order to show them to be false. That is the aim of this chapter.

These two conceptions, operationalism and representationalism, will be treated separately, first, because they are distinct doctrines and, second, because they are motivated by quite different spirits. This is not to say, of course, that they cannot be welded together into a single view of measurement, as in Stevens' case. But even in this case, his theory of measurement was predominantly a representational theory. It was his definition and his practice of measurement (consider for example his method of magnitude estimation), which showed the influence of operationalism.

Operationalism, as a general methodological doctrine, is motivated by the fear of being mistaken. Its aim is to restrict scientific claims as far as possible, to a mere description of scientific observational practice. It is against speculation. Of course, such a spirit is not scientific. Anyone who fears being mistaken and for this reason seeks a "safe" or "certain" scientific method, should never enter upon any scientific enquiry. To do science is to speculate about how things work and to follow up one's speculations with observations.

Representationalism, as a theory of measurement, is motivated by a quite different concern. It is motivated by the belief that numbers are not part of the furniture of the universe. Its aim is to explain how, given this premise, numbers find their way into the practice of measurement. Whatever the philosophical motivations for this view about numbers (and the motives are many and varied), it is mistaken. There is no place in science for entities thought to be outside of space and time or for "convenient" fictions. When we speculate in science, our speculations are about real things located in the same spatio-temporal universe as ourselves. In chapter 3 an attempt will be made to explain just where within the universe the numbers found in measurement are located.

In the first section of this chapter it is argued that operationalism is logically incoherent. It involves the deliberate confusion of *what* is being measured with *how* it is being measured. It attempts to define what is being measured solely in terms of the relations into which it enters (viz. the operations involved in its measurement). This is logically impossible because something can only stand in a relation (to other things) if it has an existence independent of that relation. Operationalism denies an independent existence to that which is being measured.

In the second section it is argued that although the representational theory of measurement is logically coherent, it is, as a matter of fact, a false theory of measurement. It is false because it fails to allow for a realist interpretation of measurement statements. Such an interpretation of measurement statements is part and parcel of scientific practice and a theory of measurement that conflicts with that cannot be accepted.

## OPERATIONALISM

Bridgman's reasons for putting forward his doctrine of operationalism were quite different to psychologists' reasons for accepting it. As already mentioned, his sprang from the, then recent, revolution in physics. He was disturbed by the fact that the Quantum and Relativity theories involved the revision of concepts (like space and time) fundamental to "Newtonian" theory. This fact conflicted with Bridgman's inductivism. On this view, scientific knowledge accumulates bit by bit, with only minor adjustments being made to laws and theories from time to time. The overthrow of "Newtonian" theory was no minor adjustment and so could have been seen as an indictment of inductivism, but Bridgman concluded, instead, that the fundamental concepts involved in "Newtonian" theory were to blame. They had been improperly defined in the first place, being laced, he thought, with more than a dash of metaphysics.

Bridgman's solution was a far-reaching program of conceptual reform. Scientific concepts were to be purged of their metaphysical content through being reduced completely to the kinds of operations scientists use. A scientist may, for example, say that he takes the word "length" to refer to a property of objects. In his laboratory practice, however, the use of the word is tied to the operations he performs with certain measuring instruments. It is these operations, says Bridgman, that really show what he means by the word and not any verbal formula he might give. Bridgman goes on:

> The concept of length involves as much as and nothing more than the set of operations by which length is determined. In general we mean by any concept nothing more than a set of operations; *the concept is synonymous with the corresponding set of operations*. (1927, p. 5, Bridgman's italics)

An early reviewer of Bridgman's book, L.J. Russell (1928), noted how ill this view accords with the actual usage of scientific terms. Often one operation is spoken of as being better than others for the measurement of some quantitative variable. No such comparison is allowed by Bridgman, for if "the concept is synonymous with the corresponding set of operations" then each different operation defines a different concept and such comparisons are no longer possible. Quantitative concepts as they are used in science generally transcend the operations used in their measurement. Although length may be measured in different ways, each different procedure is generally held to be measuring the same quantity, namely length. Bridgman's operationalism shatters the conceptual unity of properties such as length, leaving a multiplicity of splinter concepts, one for each different procedure. This only proves, however, that Bridgman's principle is not a description of how things are done in science. He never intended it to be: Bridgman came to prescribe, not to describe.

Many psychologists accepted his principle, using it as a rod with which to beat mentalism, which they saw as a kind of metaphysics. This ignored Bridgman's view that mental operations could be used to define mental concepts. Their operations were invariably of a physical public kind, such as depriving an animal of food for 10 hours or measuring the time it took to run a maze. So they took operationalism to imply that all theoretical concepts used in psychology must be defined in terms of such operations (cf. Bergmann & Spence, 1941). Not only the behaviorists, but also many psychometricians, found this construal of Bridgman's principle agreeable. They were attempting to measure variables like intelligence, attitudes, and the intensity of sensations, variables that had been thought of as mentalistic. The issue of whether or not the procedures they used actually measured such variables lay unresolved in the background, not often addressed, but nagging. Operationalism appeared to solve their problems in one fell swoop. The concept measured could be defined in terms of the procedures used. As Boring was to put it for the concept of intelligence: "Intelligence is what tests test" (1945, p. 244).

It was left to the British operationalist, the physicist H. Dingle, to draw out of Bridgman's operationalism the theory of measurement implicit within it. He defined measurement as "any precisely specified operation that yields a number" (1950, p. 11). Not all concepts so defined will be of equal scientific interest, he notes:

> I think the reason why we make some measurements and not others can be understood only in terms of the ultimate object of science, which is to find relations between the elements of our experience. If we passively accept experience as it comes the problem is far too difficult, so we establish artificial conditions that yield results more easily related with one another than natural occurrences are. (pp. 11–12)

Dingle's view captures the operationalist spirit that has pervaded attempts at psychological measurement from the 1930s to the present. On any other view it is a real issue whether or not any number-generating operation is a genuine measurement procedure. Only operationalism makes this a matter of definition. So, if operationalism is refuted, this theory of measurement is refuted as well.

Bridgman's principle, if taken seriously, makes all concepts, and all operations, unknowable. If the meaning of a concept is the set of operations by which it is determined, then knowing the meaning of the concept is dependent on knowing the appropriate set of operations. "Unless one knows the operations one does not know the meaning" (Bridgman, 1938, p. 116). However, recognizing, or knowing operations must in turn depend on knowing concepts. So which comes first, knowing concepts or knowing operations? For example, all cases of length measurement by ruler will have something in common in virtue of which they are just operations of that kind rather than some other. This something must be some set of properties or relations involved in the operation. Identification of the operation requires recognizing them. In this case the relevant properties or relations may be the property of being a ruler, the relation of being placed along side of, and counting, which involves relating the names of the natural numbers (numerals) to things. The operation can only be recognized as being of the right kind if these concepts are recognized. However, according to Bridgman's principle, recognizing these concepts must involve recognizing the operations by which they, in turn, are identified. So, to know a concept is to recognize an operation and to recognize an operation is to know further concepts, which requires knowing further operations and so on *ad infinitum*. In practice this infinite regress does not occur because there are some concepts that are known directly, unmediated by any prior knowledge of operations. However, the regress follows from Bridgman's principle and so proves it unworkable.

Operationalism is not saved by the reply that observation itself is an operation and, hence, that knowledge of concepts by direct observation is knowledge based upon operations (cf. Stevens, 1939, p. 233). It is true that observation is an operation, in the sense that it is something that we do. Stevens calls it science's "fundamental operation." This attempted reply overlooks the distinction between *performing* an operation and *knowing* it. For example, in our seeing that X is red, what we know is that X is red and not that we are seeing that X is red. That is, the seeing operation itself is usually not known while we are performing it. So, clearly, the concept (red) may be known even though the operation by which it is determined (seeing) ordinarily goes unrecognized.

Even if this was not true, operationalism would still fail. For if in seeing that

X is red, the concept of red is reducible to the operation of seeing, then the concept of red would be indistinguishable from that of blue, or any other visible quality. They, likewise, would be completely defined by exactly the same operation. In so linking concepts to the operation of seeing them, the operationalist arrives at a position not unlike Berkeley's subjective idealism. Bridgman was happy with this and in a later publication (1950) made his subjectivism explicit. To psychologists, however, subjectivism was anathema, and few followed him to that destination.

Operationalism served quite a different purpose within psychology. It was not applied in psychology with the same rigour as was used by Bridgman in applying it to physics. It was never applied in psychology to those concepts that are able to be directly perceived and so the regress from concepts to operations to concepts and so on *ad finitum* was avoided. Operationalism was only applied to, so-called, *theoretical concepts* and was seen as a means of purifying them of "surplus meaning." The aim of this more dilute operationalism was to reduce all theoretical concepts to observational concepts by defining them in terms of observationally specifiable operations. Theoretical terms not so reducible were seen as a conceptual extravagance, covering the operational base of science with an unwanted layer of metaphysics.

This is a false view of the scientific enterprise. In as much as the aim of science is to discover nature's ways of working, dilute operationalism is more of a hindrance than a help. Many of nature's ways of working are at first obscure and hidden from our view. An approach to science that does not let us think beyond that which can be currently observed prevents us from understanding these hidden ways. Commenting on this variety of operationalism, W.M. O'Neil says:

> It urges the scientist, in effect, not to take risks incurred in moving far from the facts. However, it may properly be asked whether science can be undertaken without taking the risks of skating on the possibly thin ice of supposition. The important thing is to know when one is on the more solid ground of observation and when one is on the ice. (1969, p. 154)

More seriously still, this variety of operationalism incurs a logical error. The events involved in an operation (or its outcome) are at most only causally related to those hidden workings that theoretical concepts are intended to elucidate. To define theoretical concepts in terms of such events is to violate the principle that cause and effect must be logically distinct occurrences (a principle attributed to Hume, 1888). For example, if the strength of hunger drive is defined in terms of hours of food deprivation then it cannot also be partly caused by it, or if spatial ability is defined by performance on some tests then it cannot be invoked to explain such performance. So, quite contrary to dilute operationalism, theoretical concepts *must not* be defined operationally.

Both Bridgman's classical operationalism and the psychologists' dilute operationalism involve a deliberate confusion between concepts and the means (operations) by which they are identified. This confusion is at its most general in

Bridgman's Berkeley-like belief that "it is meaningless to separate 'nature' from 'knowledge of nature' " (1927, p. 60). In the measurement context it takes the form of a confusion of "the act or process of measuring with the object of the act, namely the quantity in question" (Byerley, 1974, p. 376). The error here is simply that of confusing a relation with one of the entities involved in it. Knowing something, identifying it, or measuring it is a relation between the observer and the thing known, measured or identified. The measurement operation, on which Bridgman puts so much emphasis, is simply the specific way the relation of measuring occurs. The logical form of the situation is: person *A* measures (using operation *X*) variable *Y*. *Y* could only be defined in terms of *X* if it was constituted by it. However, relations cannot constitute the entities that they hold between, otherwise there would be no entities to stand in the relation. That is, if person *A* measures variable *Y* then *Y* must exist independently of measurement, otherwise there would be nothing to measure. The confusion of an entity with a relation that it enters, if carried far enough, denies the possibility of nature existing independently of the observer and makes science impossible. Operationalism is the thin end of subjectivism.

The fact that operationalism is false means that the operationalist theory of measurement must be rejected. Useful as it has been to psychologists over the last 50 years in sustaining the image of psychology as a quantitative science, its philosophical confusions mean that that image may be just an illusion. If operationalism is denied then the question of whether or not a given operation really measures a particular variable, or any variable at all, must be a genuine issue. So psychology, which possesses a wide range of number-generating procedures, may really possess no measurement procedures at all. This issue can only be judged relative to a sounder theory of measurement than operationalism.

## THE REPRESENTATIONAL THEORY OF MEASUREMENT

This theory is currently the orthodox theory of measurement within the philosophy of science. It is said (Adams 1979, Krantz, Luce, Suppes, & Tversky, 1971) to have had its origins in the work of the German mathematician, Holder (1901). In English, it found early articulation in Russell's *Principles of Mathematics*, when he wrote:

> Measurement of magnitudes is, in its most general sense, any method by which a unique and reciprocal correspondence is established between all or some of the magnitudes of a kind and all or some of the numbers, integral, rational or real, as the case may be. (Russell, 1903 p. 176)

Campbell's (1920) was its most influential formulation and there it is applied to physical measurement, at least as it stood early this century. It is his version or versions based on it that have since been presented in many introductory texts in the philosophy of science (e.g., Carnap, 1966, Cohen & Nagel, 1934, and Pap, 1962).

Stevens' liberalized version of Campbell's theory received a set-theoretical presentation in Suppes and Zinnes (1963). The set-theoretic approach became axiomatic in Krantz et al. (1971). This version (which I call "Suppes' theory") (cf. R.D. Luce, 1979) is the version presented in this chapter. The set-theoretical symbolism is largely dispensed with because it obscures matters for the non-mathematical student. A recent and relatively nontechnical resume of this theory is presented by Narens and Luce (1986). A much more complete, although highly technical presentation is Narens (1985).

## The Numerical Representation of Empirical Systems

According to the representational theory of measurement the role of numbers in measurement is to represent. Numbers are assigned to empirical entities in such a way that certain relations between the numbers assigned represent empirical relations between the entities. Representationalists make a distinction between empirical entities and numerical ones. Empirical entities are "identifiable entities, such as weights, persons, attitude statements, or sounds" (Suppes & Zinnes, 1963, p. 7). What is meant by "identifiable" here is not obvious, for if numbers are not also identifiable in some sense it is unclear how they could be used at all. Luce (1979) prefers to define empirical entities as "concrete objects or events" (p. 94), a construal that Adams (1979) further narrows down to "concrete observable things" (p. 208). Here, the adjective "concrete" is obviously intended to distinguish empirical entities from *abstract entities*. In recent American philosophical parlance, abstract entities are those not located in space or time. Although rarely made explicit by these authors, the distinction is only complete if numbers are then taken to be abstract entities. This view of numbers is the conventional wisdom of our time, however, if numbers are abstract in this special sense, then their apparent involvement in "concrete" empirical contexts such as measurement requires explanation. So although it is true that the representational theory does not logically *require* an "abstract" view of number, it does, as a matter of fact, include it. Indeed, as already indicated, it is precisely because this view of number is so widespread that the representational theory of measurement is so popular. Bring numbers back to earth (as is done in chapter 3) and the representational theory is no longer needed.

One of Suppes' central concepts is that of a *relational system*. A relational system is a class of entities together with one or more relations into which the entities enter. For example, suppose that the entities involved are rods of various lengths and that the relation concerned is that of *being at least as long as*. Then the rods standing in this relation to one another constitute a relational system.

Relational systems possess structure. The structure is constituted by the properties of the relations involved. For example, the relation of being at least as long as has the properties of being *transitive* and *strongly connected*. What these terms mean can be indicated more clearly if some symbols are used. Let . . ., "$x$", "$y$", "$z$", . . .stand for entities in the class under consideration. Let "$R$" stand for the relation involved and let expressions such as "$R(x,y)$" mean that $x$ stands in the relation $R$ to $y$. Then, a relation $R$ is transitive relative to a class if and only if, for all $x$, $y$ and $z$ in that class, if $R(x,y)$ and $R(y,z)$ then $R(x,z)$. A relation is strongly connected relative to a certain class if and only if, for all $x$ and $y$ in that class, either $R(x,y)$ or $R(y,x)$. (See Appendix 1 for other properties of binary relations.)

The properties that relations have cannot be taken for granted. They must be discovered by observation and experiment. To continue with the example of the rods, any two rods can be placed side by side in parallel so that the left-hand ends terminate together (as in Fig. 2.1). Then it can be observed that rod $x$ is at least as long as rod $y$, if $y$'s right-hand end does not terminate to the right of $x$'s. Then taking the rods pair by pair the properties of this relation can be discovered. That is, it can be seen that the relation is transitive and strongly connected.

According to the representational theory, measurement depends on finding a numerical relational system that exhibits a structure similar to that of the empirical relational system under consideration. A numerical relational system is one in which the entities involved are numbers and the relations are numerical relations. An example is the set of all positive integers less than 100, and the relation of being at least as great as (conventionally symbolized as "$\geqslant$"). Two relational systems are similar in structure when corresponding to each relation in the first system there is a relation in the second system that possesses the same properties. For example, $\geqslant$ is also transitive and strongly connected. If one relational system has a structure similar to a second relational system, then the first system may be

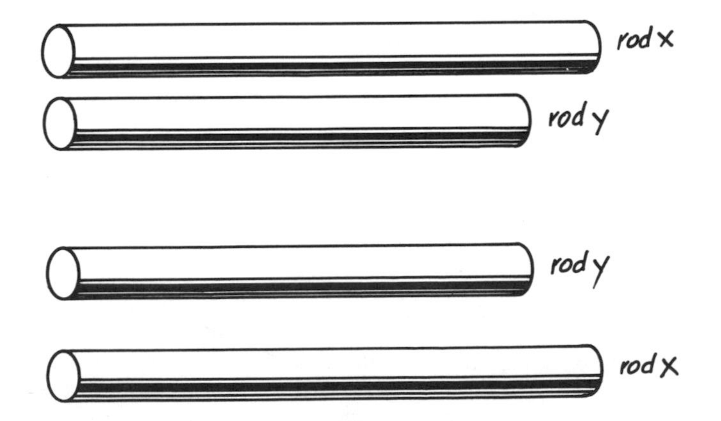


FIG. 2.1 If any two rods, $x$ and $y$, are side by side in parallel so that their left-hand ends terminate at the same perpendicular line then $x$ is at least as long as $y$ if and only if the right-hand end of $y$ does not terminate at a point to the right of $x$'s.

used to represent the second, providing, of course, that the first system possesses at least as many entities as the second. Thus the aforementioned numerical relational system may be used to represent the empirical relational system mentioned in the rods example.

The numerical representation would be achieved by matching numbers to objects so that the order of length of the objects is reflected in the order of magnitude of the numbers. That is, each rod would be assigned a single number. Let $n(x)$ be the number assigned to any rod, $x$. Then the numerical representation is achieved when the numbers are assigned according to the following rule: rod $x$ is at least as long as rod $y$ if and only if $n(x) \geqslant n(y)$. The rods are said to be *mapped into* the numbers.

A mapping of objects into numbers is *one to one* when each object is assigned a single number, that number being different from the number assigned to any other object. A mapping of objects into numbers is *many to one* when the second of these two conditions is relaxed and the same number may be assigned to more than one object. The representation of one relational system by another is called an *isomorphism* when the mapping is one to one, and it is called a *homomorphism* when the mapping is many to one. It is usually the case in measurement that more than one object is assigned the same number. Hence, measurement generally involves a homomorphism between an empirical relational system and a numerical relational system. Such a homomorphism (or, in the cases where it occurs, isomorphism) Suppes and Zinnes (1963) referred to as a *scale of measurement*.

In the rods example, the set of rods on which the observations are made must be a finite set. It is to this finite set that the numerical assignments are made according to the above rule. However, this finite empirical relational system is embedded within a much larger, indeed possibly infinite, one. This larger system consists of the set of all things having length and the relation of being at least as long as. Obviously, observations cannot be made on each pair of objects in this system. Despite that limitation, the available evidence confirms the hypothesis that this relation is also transitive and strongly connected on that set. So a homomorphism between this larger system and the positive real numbers ordered by $\geqslant$ may be hypothesized to exist. Thus the finite data structures observed are taken to be representative of the underlying infinite structures of which they are subsystems, in measurement as in all science. The scope of any established measurement scale is then taken to extend to all entities possessing the relevant attribute.

The above rods example is an instance of what Stevens (1946) called an *ordinal scale*. It is a very simple example of measurement according to the representational theory. A more complex example is measurement on what he called a *ratio scale*. Length may be measured on a ratio scale but to keep the examples distinct the measurement of weight is chosen to illustrate measurement of this kind.

The example will be kept simple by considering a set of objects (of various weights) small enough to fit into the balance pan of a beam balance like that illustrated in Fig. 2.2. This time two relations will be considered: that of one object being at least as heavy as another; and that of two objects taken together (concatenated) being at least as heavy as a third. For convenience the first relation will be symbolized as "$x \succcurlyeq y$" and the second as "$x \circ y \succcurlyeq z$" (following Krantz et al., 1971). The presence of these relations between the objects is detected using the beam balance as follows. $x \succcurlyeq y$ is taken to be true if, when just $x$ is placed in one pan and just $y$ in the other, the pan containing $y$ fails to descend. $x \circ y \succcurlyeq z$ is taken to be true if, when just both $x$ and $y$ are placed in one pan and just $z$ in the other, the pan containing, $z$ fails to descend. If neither pan descends in the first case it means that both $x \succcurlyeq y$ and $y \succcurlyeq x$ and this is abbreviated as $x \sim y$. The same result in the second case means that both $x \circ y \succcurlyeq z$ and $z \succcurlyeq x \circ y$ are true and this is abbreviated as $x \circ y \sim z$. Also, the fact that $x \succcurlyeq y$ and not ($y \succcurlyeq x$) is expressed as $x \succ y$. Similarly, $x \circ y \succcurlyeq z$ and not ($z \succcurlyeq x \circ y$) as $x \circ y \succ z$. If $x \sim y$ then $y$ is a replica of $x$ (for weight, that is) and $n$ concatenated replicas of $x$ (where $n$ is any positive whole number) are referred to as "$nx$." Finally, $x \circ (y \circ z)$ is the object obtained when $x$ is concatenated with the concatenation of $y$ and $z$.

Suppose that the behavior of the set of objects is observed on the beam balance and that the following facts are discovered about these two relations.

1. The relation $\succcurlyeq$ is found to be transitive and strongly connected.
2. For all $x$, $y$ and $z$ in the set, $x \circ (y \circ z) \sim (x \circ y) \circ z$.
3. For all $x$, $y$ and $z$ in the set, $x \succcurlyeq y$ if and only if $x \circ z \succcurlyeq y \circ z$ if and only if $z \circ x \succcurlyeq z \circ y$.
4. If for any $x$ and $y$ in the set $x \succ y$ then for any $w$ and z in the set there exists a positive whole number n such that $nx \circ w \succcurlyeq ny \circ z$.
5. For all $x$ and $y$ in the set, $x \circ y \succ x$.

Proposition 4 (which is sometimes referred to as an Archimedean condition) may seem obscure. It simply means that no matter how much heavier $z$ is than $w$ the weight difference between $x$ and $y$ multiplied by some $n$ can compensate for it.

FIG. 2.2 A schematic diagram of a beam balance.

That is, no weight difference is infinitely large relative to another weight difference. This condition might then seem to be partly numerical and thus violate the earlier stipulation that empirical relational systems be nonnumerical. The representationalist has an easy reply to this apparent objection. $nx$, it is asserted, is an empirical and not a numerical object. It is a collection of $n$ replicas of $x$. The set of all such collections itself forms an empirical relational system homomorphic to the positive whole numbers, and so numerical assignments can be made to such collections. The number one is assigned to collections like $x$ by itself, two to collections like $x \circ x$, three to collections like $x \circ (x \circ x)$, and so on. Hence, although, numerical expressions like "$nx$" are used, it is claimed that the objects or facts referred to remain nonnumerical. This interpretation is debatable and an alternative point of view is suggested in the following chapter.

Returning to the five propositions whose truth has been established by observations on the beam balance, Krantz et al. (1971, chapter 3) show that an empirical relational system of just that structure is homomorphic to a numerical relational system containing the relations $n_1 \geqslant n_2$ and $n_1 + n_2 \geqslant n_3$ (where, $n_1$, $n_2$, and $n_3$ are, of course, numbers). That is, numerical assignments may be made to the empirical objects such that for all $x$, $y$, and $z$ in the set:

(1) $x \geqslant y$ if and only if $n(x) \geqslant n(y)$, and
(2) $n(x \circ y) = n(x) + n(y)$.

So in this case the empirical operation of concatenation is represented by the numerical operation of addition.

It is interesting to note at this point the empirical concatenation operations of this kind may also be represented by the numerical operation of multiplication. An example mentioned by Suppes and Zinnes (1963) illustrates this. If to each entity $x$ the number $n_1(x) = e^{n(x)}$ (where $e$ is the base of the natural logarithms and $n(x)$ is an assignment made in accordance with the requirements 1, and 2 above) is assigned, then it is true that:

(3) $x \geqslant y$ if and only if $n_1(x) \geqslant n_1(y)$, and
(4) $n_1(x \circ y) = n_1(x) \times n_1(y)$
$= e^{n(x)} \times e^{n(y)}$
$= e^{n(x) + n(y)}$.

So following (3) and (4) would lead to a multiplicative representation of the same empirical relational system as is additively represented via (1) and (2). Ellis (1966) gives other examples of how an empirical concatenation operation of this kind can be numerically represented in other ways.

The representational theory of measurement must then explain why additive representations are preferred in measurement to any other possible kinds of numerical representations. Ellis' answer is that they are the simplest of possible representations. In the case of concatenation operations like the one just shown, this may be true. Alternative kinds of representations are also possible with other kinds of empirical relations. For example, because $\leqslant$ is also transitive and connected it could also be used to represent the empirical relation of being at least as long as mentioned in the rods example. Then longer rods would be assigned smaller numbers. Such a representation seems just as simple as the one conventionally chosen.

Empirical relational systems such as the one described in the weights example are called *extensive* or *additive* systems. N. R. Campbell's view was that extensive systems were the only ones capable of measurement. Russell's (1903) view differed. He considered measurement to be the numerical representation of *magnitude*, by which he effectively meant an empirical relational system involving an ordering relation (such as greater than or less than in some sense). This is also the opinion of both Ellis (1966) and Luce (1979). Stevens (1946) advocated an even wider concept. His famous definition includes *any* instance of the numerical representation of an empirical relational system as measurement, no matter what its structure is. In practice he drew the line with what he called *nominal scales*. These are the numerical representation of empirical systems of a purely classificatory kind. For example, if people are classified by gender with males assigned 1 and females 0, the result is a nominal scale of measurement in Stevens' scheme of things.

As we have seen, Stevens' liberalism enabled psychologists to regard their procedures as measurement even though Campbell's view denied them that status. Where then is the *correct* place to draw the line between measurement and nonmeasurement within the representational theory? Once the shift is made from the classical theory to the representational theory there can be no justification for denying any instance of numerical representation the status of measurement. To do so is to introduce an arbitrary limitation into the application of what is otherwise a clear principle: measurement is the numerical representation of empirical objects and relations. Stevens' thoroughgoing representationalism is the most defensible version.

Of course, not all representations will prove equally useful. But this observation simply reinforces the fact that representationalism is a version of instrumentalism: numbers are a tool of science and it is up to the scientist to use them to their greatest advantage. It is an ironic twist that the way psychologists use them is as a means of presenting their science as if it were a quantitative science, where "quantitative" is intended in the classical sense, not the representational.

Do all instances of measurement recognized by science conform to the representational pattern? Physics deals with over 100 measurable variables. All of them are functionally interrelated, and all of them are ratio scales in Stevens' sense. Although many like weight, length, angle, time, and electrical charge, are based on empirical relational systems involving a concatenation operation able to be represented by numerical addition, many obviously are not. Density is an example. Two objects of different densities, however they are combined, typically do not give an object whose density is the sum of their densities taken separately. How then can the representational theory explain the measurement of density?

In practice density is measured via its functional relationship to other variables, mass and volume, using the fact that, density = mass/volume. So the measurement of density is based on the prior measurement of mass and volume, and this kind of dependence characterizes what Campbell called *derived measurement*. He thought that derived measurement scales emerged through the discovery of constants in numerical relationships between extensive (or *fundamentally measurable*) variables.

Although this account may be historically plausible, it will not do as an explanation of the logic of derived measurement from the representational point of view. What needs to be exposed is the fact that the numbers assigned via derived measurement actually *represent* something empirical. For, if the representational theory is true then equations like the one above for density are, in the words of Krantz et al. (1971, p. 504), "only a shorthand summary of what is really a complex set of possible qualitative observations." By "qualitative" they mean nonnumerical.

So in cases of derived measurement one is actually dealing with an empirical relational system involving a number of quantitative variables. In the case of density this relational system involves not only density but also mass and volume. The "qualitative" relations between objects within this system must be such that they may be represented numerically by assigning to each object, $x$, three numbers, $d(x)$, $m(x)$, and $v(x)$ such that:

(1) $d(x) = m(x)/v(x)$, and

(2) $m(x)$ and $v(x)$ are proportional to measures of mass and volume obtained fundamentally.

The character of such an empirical relational system is too complex to delve into in this chapter. Suffice it to note at this stage that such a system would be observed if objects were classified according to density (which they would be if classified according to the kind of material they are composed of), ordered according to volume, and "qualitative" observations made on the associated masses. Something of the flavor of such a system is given in discussions of the theory of conjoint measurement (see chapter 4 below and Krantz et al., 1971). So the representational theory is able to give an account of the class of measurements Campbell calls derived.

## The Theory of Scale Types

There is always an arbitrariness in the numbers chosen to do the job of measurement, according to the representational theory. Having decided what numerical relations to use in representing the empirical relations, different sets of numbers may be assigned to the empirical entities to achieve the desired homomorphism.

Thus, different scales for the same variable may be obtained. Such scales will not differ in terms of how any given empirical relation is represented numerically, however they will differ in the numerical assignments involved. This point may be clarified by considering an example.

Consider again the rod example treated earlier in this chapter. There an ordinal scale was constructed on the basis of the relation of being at least as long as. Suppose that *a, b, c,* and *d* are four rods and the numerical assignments made in scale 1 (see Table 2.1) reflect their length order. Because the numbers assigned under scale 2 are in exactly the same order, they also reflect the same empirical order relationships. Thus, for these four objects, scales 1 and 2 represent the empirical relational system involved equally well. Of course, there are infinitely many other sets of numerical assignments that would also do. On the other hand, scale 3 does not represent length order by numerical magnitude, so it will not do.

Stevens posed the problem of how all ordinal scales for the same variable are related to each other. Suppes called this the *uniqueness problem* for ordinal scales. It is the problem of how unique the numerical assignments are in the case of an ordinal scale. Or, in other words, how may the numerical assignments on any ordinal scale be changed without changing the convention that empirical order is represented by numerical magnitude?

The answer, obviously, is that they can be changed to anything at all providing their order of magnitude is left intact. That is, if $n_i(x)$ is the number assigned to $x$ on scale $i$ and $n_j(x)$ is the number assigned to $x$ on scale $j$, then the transformation from scale $i$ to scale $j$ leaves the homomorphism intact if and only if, for all pairs of objects $x$ and $y$,

$$n_i(x) \geqslant n_i(y) \text{ if and only if } n_j(x) \geqslant n_j(y).$$

Such a scale transformation is called an *increasing monotonic* transformation. Stevens calls increasing monotonic transformations the class of admissible scale transformations for ordinal scales of measurement. Ordinal scales are said to be unique up to increasing monotonic transformations.

In contrast to ordinal scales, consider the example of weight measurement given earlier in the section on "The Numerical Representation of Empirical

TABLE 2.1
Hypothetical Ordinal Scale (Scales 1 and 2) and Nominal Scale (Scale 3) Measures of the Lengths of Four Rods, *a*, *b*, *c*, and *d*

| | Numerical Assignments | | |
|---|---|---|---|
| *Rods* | *Scale 1* | *Scale 2* | *Scale 3* |
| *a* | 4 | 10 | 4 |
| *b* | 3 | 9 | 10 |
| *c* | 2 | 3 | 8 |
| *d* | 1 | 2 | 9 |

Systems." Let *a, b, c,* and *d* be four objects whose weights are measured and suppose that $a \circ a \sim b$, $a \circ b \sim c$, and $a \circ c \sim d$. Table 2.2 lists four sets of numerical assignments that might be made to these four objects. Scales 1 and 2 represent these empirical relations in the manner described in the aforementioned section. That is, $n(a) + n(a) = n(b)$, $n(a) + n(b) = n(c)$, and $n(a) + n(c) = n(d)$. In scale 3 the concatenation relationships are not represented by numerical addition, but the weight order is represented by the order of magnitude of the numbers. In scale 4 not even this is the case, although each different object has been assigned a different number.

Because scale 3 is related to both scales 1 and 2 by an increasing monotonic transformation, and because scale 3 does not represent all of the available empirical information in the manner of a ratio scale, it follows that in ratio scale measurement the class of admissible scale transformations must be narrower than it is in the case of ordinal scales. In fact, as is obvious, scale 1 is simply scale 2 multiplied by 4. This illustrates the fact that if either scale is multiplied by a positive constant, then the transformed scale preserves the homomorphism. A ratio scale is defined by the fact that $x \circ y \sim z$ if and only if $n(x) + n(y) = n(z)$ and if each number is multiplied by a positive real number $k$ then this gives $k \cdot n(x) + k \cdot n(y) = k \cdot n(z)$, which is true whenever $n(x) + n(y) = n(z)$ is true and conversely. Such a transformation is called a *positive similarities* transformation and ratio scales are said to be unique up to such transformations.

Stevens distinguished what he thought were two other important scale types. The *nominal scale* is based on classification and assigns the same number to objects that are equivalent (in the required sense), and different number to objects that are not. For example, scale 4 in Table 2.2 is a nominal scale for weight. The class of admissible transformations for nominal scales is the class of *one to one* transformations. That is, if $n_i(x)$ is the number assigned to $x$ within nominal scale $i$ and $n_j(x)$ is the number assigned within nominal scale $j$ then the transformation from $i$ to $j$ is one to one if and only if $n_i(x) = n_i(y)$ if and only if $n_j(x) = n_j(y)$, for all pairs of objects $x$ and $y$.

The *interval scale* is one in which the class of admissible scale transformations

TABLE 2.2
Hypothetical Ratio Scale (Scales 1 and 2), Ordinal Scale (Scale 3), and Nominal Scale (Scale 4) Measures of the Weights of Four Objects, *a, b, c,* and *d*

| | *Numerical Assignments* | | | |
|---|---|---|---|---|
| *Objects* | *Scale 1* | *Scale 2* | *Scale 3* | *Scale 4* |
| *a* | 4 | 1 | 1 | 9 |
| *b* | 8 | 2 | 4 | 7 |
| *c* | 12 | 3 | 5 | 8 |
| *d* | 16 | 4 | 10 | 4 |

is the class of *positive linear* transformations. That is, two interval scales, $i$ and $j$, for the measurement of the same variable will be related by the following kind of equation: $n_j(x) = a \cdot n_i(x) + b$ (where $a$ is some positive number and $b$ is either a positive number or a negative one). For example, in temperature measurement the Farenheit (°$F$) and the Celsius (°$C$) scales are related by the following linear transformation: $C = (5/9) .F - 160/9$.

An interval scale involves the numerical representation of relations upon differences between entities with respect to some attribute. It requires an ordering upon such differences and a relation of composition upon them. That is, a relation equivalent to the following kind: difference $x$ is equal to difference $y$ plus difference $z$. In the case of temperature this relation is empirically determined through the hypothesis that temperature differences are directly related to volumes (such as the volume of mercury in a thermometer). Because volume is measured on a ratio scale, this makes temperature differences measurable on a ratio scale. This case illustrates very well the fact than an interval scale is really a ratio scale upon differences.

A staunch critic of Stevens' theory of scale types is W. W. Rozeboom (1966), who has described it as "complete nonsense" (p. 188). His criticism is quite subtle. In chapter 1 the point was made that a relation may be defined as a set of ordered $n$-tuples. Such a definition is called *extensional*. That is, it is alleged that relations may be defined by reference to the entities standing in the relation rather than by reference to the character of the relation itself. A binary relation then becomes a set of ordered pairs of entities; a ternary relation, a set of ordered triples; and so on. Allowing this point, consider any homomorphic assignment of numbers to a set of empirical entities. The numbers so assigned, simply because they are numbers, stand in a great many relationships to one another. Rozeboom's criticism of Stevens' theory is based on the premise that each such numerical relation represents an empirical relation, even though it may only be an extensionally definable one. For example, suppose that a set of people are classified according to eye-color: persons $a$, $b$, and c all have blue eyes; $e$, $f$, and $g$ all have brown eyes; and both $i$ and $j$ have green eyes. This classification is an empirical relational system, the relation involved being that of having the same colored eyes as (call it $R_1$). Let this empirical relational system be numerically represented as follows: assign the number 2 to $a$, $b$, and $c$; the number 3 to $e$, $f$, and $g$; and the number 5 to $i$ and $j$. This creates a nominal scale in which the relation of being equal to represents $R_1$. Now $2 + 3 = 5$ is a numerical relation holding between the numbers used in this nominal scale. Does this numerical relation represent any empirical relation holding between the eight people $a$, $b$, $c$, $e$, $f$, $g$, $i$, and $j$? Rozeboom thinks that it must. It represents the following extensionally defined relation: $R_2 = \{\langle a,e,i\rangle, \langle a,e,j\rangle, \langle a,f,i\rangle, \langle a,f,j\rangle, \langle a,g,i\rangle, \langle a,g,j\rangle, \langle b,e,i\rangle, \langle b,e,j\rangle, \langle b,f,i\rangle, \langle b,f,j\rangle, \langle b,g,i\rangle, \langle b,g,j\rangle, \langle c,e,i\rangle, \langle c,e,j\rangle, \langle c,f,i\rangle, \langle c,f,j\rangle, \langle c,g,i\rangle, \langle c,g,j\rangle\}$. It represents this relation because $R_2$ holds between any ordered set of three people, $x$, $y$, and $z$ (from the original set of eight), if and only if $n(x) + n(y) = n(z)$ (where $n(x)$, $n(y)$, and $n(z)$ are the numbers assigned to $x$, $y$, and $z$

respectively). So the empirical relation $R_2$ has been given an additive representation. Of course, this additive representation is only preserved by a positive similarities transformation of 2, 3, and 5. Hence, what began as a nominal scale has been shown to be a ratio scale as well. The distinction between Stevens' scale types have collapsed.

The argument here is correct up until the last step, providing the initial premise that relations are extensionally definable is granted. Any numerical assignment to empirical objects, be it initially a nominal or ordinal scale, will additively represent some extensionally defined empirical relation and so will also be a ratio scale (providing that the numbers assigned are additively related). But this argument does not entail the collapse of Stevens' theory.

One could save Stevens' theory by denying the principle that relations are extensionally definable or by arguing that relations like $R_2$ above are not of any scientific significance. Such moves, valid though they may be, are not necessary. Stevens' theory is saved by the fact that empirical relational systems are partly constituted by the relations involved in them, and even though two systems may involve precisely the same objects they are different if they contain different relations. So the eight people together with $R_1$ is *one* empirical relational system, and the same people together with $R_2$ constitutes a *different* empirical relational system. The first system, when represented by 2, 3, and 5 together with numerical equivalence (=), produces a nominal scale. If the numbers assigned are transformed by anything other than a one-to-one numerical transformation then = no longer represents $R_1$. The second empirical relational system, when represented by 2, 3, and 5 together with the relation of numerical addition ($N_+$), produces a ratio scale. If the numbers assigned are transformed by anything other than a positive similarities transformation then $R_2$ is no longer represented by $N_+$. So the two different empirical relational systems produce two different scales. What they have in common are the empirical objects measured and the numerical values assigned, however the scales involved are no more the same than they would be if the hardness values assigned to a set of minerals on Mohs' scale of hardness fortuitously equalled their weight in grams.

What follows from Rozeboom's argument is not the collapse of Stevens' theory but the following quite different conclusion. Given a scale of any type on a set of empirical objects there also exists a scale of any other type involving exactly the same numerical assignments. In particular, it follows that for each nominal scale on a set of empirical objects, there exists a ratio scale involving exactly the same numerical assignments as the nominal scale, and representing some extensionally defined empirical relation not included in the nominal scale's empirical relational system.

This conclusion raises an interesting question. Other things being equal, ratio scales are always preferred to nominal scales, involving as they do the representation of more empirical information. Why then would anyone ever prefer a nominal scale to the ratio scale it carries along with it? There is no universal valid reason. If a researcher establishes a nominal scale representation and then extensionally defines the empirical relation additively represented by the numbers employed, he may find this relation to be of enormous scientific interest. He would then be quite justified in preferring this ratio scale to his previously established nominal scale. The matter is purely one of scientific interest. However, let the reader be warned. This is not a recommended method for finding scientifically interesting empirical relationships. The empirical relation extensionally identified by such a process is identified only as an artifact of the numbers used in the nominal scale. To expect such a relation to be of any scientific interest displays a touching faith in serendipity. The a priori probability that such a fortunate event will occur must be close to zero.

Rozeboom's criticism is based on a true observation but it fails to take account of the instrumentalist character of the definition of the concept of a measurement scale used within the representational theory of measurement. Any homomorphic assignment of numbers to empirical objects will always represent a large class of, perhaps only extensionally definable, empirical relations. Within this large class the scientist focuses on the small set of empirical relations of interest to him. It is how these relations and these alone are numerically represented that characterizes a scale according to the representational theory of measurement. That other empirical relations are also represented is ignored, and rightly so, given that the numbers are only to be used as an instrument. Stevens' theory of scale types describes how the numbers used may be changed without changing which numerical relations represent the empirical relations of interest. It specifies the degrees of freedom available in the choice of numbers relative to the empirical relations of interest, and the numerical relations chosen to represent them. The fact that, no matter what numbers are chosen within these degrees of freedom, they always represent other (perhaps, only extensionally definable) empirical relations must not be denied, but it is of no relevance to the theory of scale types. However, it is of relevance to another problem encountered by the representational theory of measurement and that is the so-called problem of permissible statistics.

## THE PROBLEM OF PERMISSIBLE STATISTICS

Stevens' classification of scale types was no trivial matter. What differentiates scale types is the character of the relations within the empirical and numerical relational systems involved in a measurement scale. He recognized that the purpose of measurement was the inference of empirical conclusions from the numerical assignments made. He further recognized that the character of valid inferences from measurements must be relative to scale type, simply because such inferences depend on the character of the empirical information represented. According to the representational theory a measurement scale is an instrument of deduction. As such it contributes no content to any conclusions obtained: it simply lubricates the inference process.

Suppose that the eight objects listed in Table 2.3 are measured for weight on a ratio scale (e.g., the metric grams scale) and that the measurements are as listed. The objects belong to either set 1 or set 2. The mean of the weight measurements for objects in set 1 is 8. The mean for objects in set 2 is 10. Since 10 is greater than 8 it immediately follows that the mean weight in grams of objects in set 2 is greater than the mean weight in grams of objects in set 1. This conclusion is a proposition about the weight measurements and hence about the numbers. It is tempting to move from this purely *numerical* conclusion to the nonnumerical, *empirical* conclusion that the mean weight of objects in set 2 is greater than the mean weight of objects in set 1. This conclusion is a proposition about the weights (rather than the weight measurements) and so about some of the objects within the empirical relational system. Does this second conclusion follow validly from the first? It does, but this kind of inference is not valid with just any kind of measurement scale whatsoever.

Suppose that the same objects are measured on an ordinal scale of hardness. Such a scale is based upon a single empirical relation. This is the relation of being harder than which is assessed by rubbing two objects together to see which one scratches which. If $x$ scratches $y$ then $n(x) > n(y)$. The hardness measures for these objects on a hypothetical scale $A$ are shown in Table 2.4. The mean of the scale $A$ measures for set 1 is 5.5 and the mean for the objects in set 2. is 4.5. Since 5.5 is greater than 4.5 it immediately follows that the mean of the scale $A$ measures for objects in set 1 is greater than the mean of the scale $A$ measures for objects in set 2. Does it follow validly from this merely numerical conclusion that the mean hardness of objects in set 1 is greater than the mean hardness of objects in set 2? It cannot!

Consider hardness measures of these eight objects on a different hypothetical ordinal scale, scale $B$ (see Table 2.5). Scales $A$ and $B$ are related by an increasing monotonic transformation (i.e., the numbers are in the same order of magnitude). Hence, these two scales do an equally satisfactory job of representing the empirical *harder than* relation. A choice between them would be quite arbitrary.

TABLE 2.3.
Hypothetical Ratio Scale Measure of Weight of the Eight Objects, *a* to *h*

| *Objects* | | *Scale Values* |
|---|---|---|
| Set 1 | *a* | 2 |
| | *b* | 6 |
| | *c* | 10 |
| | *d* | 14 |
| Set 2 | *e* | 4 |
| | *f* | 8 |
| | *g* | 12 |
| | *h* | 16 |

TABLE 2.4.
Hypothetical Ordinal Scale (Scale *A*) Measures of the Hardness of the Eight Objects, *a* to *h*

| *Objects* | | *Scale A Values* |
|---|---|---|
| Set 1 | *a* | 1 |
| | *b* | 6 |
| | *c* | 7 |
| | *d* | 8 |
| Set 2 | *e* | 2 |
| | *f* | 3 |
| | *g* | 4 |
| | *h* | 9 |

However, the mean of the scale *B* hardness measures for objects in set 2 (7.25) is greater than the mean of the scale *B* hardness measures for objects in set 1 (7). So if it is valid to infer from the scale *A* measures that the mean hardness of objects in set 1 is greater than the mean hardness of objects in set 2, then it is also valid to infer the contradictory conclusion from scale *B* measures. This is because in both cases the form of the argument is the same.

In both cases the empirical information forming the premises of the argument (i.e., the set of hardness relationships between the eight objects) is the same and itself noncontradictory. Although different numbers are used to represent this information, the same representation rule is used (i.e., $x$ is harder than $y$ if and only if $n(x) > n(y)$) and this rule is internally consistent. The arithmetical argument from the measures themselves to the relationship between the means of the measures is of the same valid form in both cases. Therefore, up to this point in the two arguments it is not possible that mutually contradictory conclusions could be entailed. Only when the empirical conclusions about the mean hardnesses are inferred does the contradiction arise. Hence, that last step must be invalid, for the

TABLE 2.5.
Hypothetical Ordinal Scale (Scale *B*) Measures of the Hardness of the Eight Objects, *a* to *h*

| *Objects* | | *Scale B Values* |
|---|---|---|
| Set 1 | *a* | 1 |
| | *b* | 8 |
| | *c* | 9 |
| | *d* | 10 |
| Set 2 | *e* | 5 |
| | *f* | 6 |
| | *g* | 7 |
| | *h* | 11 |

same set of noncontradictory premises cannot entail contradictory conclusions. So this form of argument is not valid given ordinal scale measurements.

Why then is this form valid given ratio scale measurements? Simply because the argument is to a conclusion that is already entailed by the empirical premises. To see this, the empirical analogue of the otherwise numerical notion of a mean must be specified. For the case of weight this is as follows. If $n$ objects (not necessarily all of the same weight) perfectly balance (i.e., weigh the same as) another $n$ objects (this time all objects of the same weight), then each of the objects in the second group equals the mean weight of the first group of objects. Therefore, it follows by inspection of Table 2.3 that the four objects in set 2 will outweigh the four objects in set 1 and, will have a greater mean weight. This conclusion follows validly from the empirical information alone, the arithmetic used earlier being merely a deductive convenience.

Even though it is obvious from his writings that Stevens recognized the above facts he failed to set the argument out in this fashion. Furthermore, he misrepresented the issue by laying down prescriptions about what statistics ought not to be computed given measurement scales of the various types. For example, of ordinal scales he said, "In the strictest propriety the ordinary statistics involving means and standard deviations ought not to be used with these scales, for these statistics imply a knowledge of something more than the relative rank-order of the data" (Stevens, 1946; p. 679). However, the matter is not one of what ought or ought not to be done. It is simply a matter of fact: of what kinds of conclusions validly follow from what kinds of premises. Stevens further obscured the issue by attempting to justify his prescriptions on the basis of the invariance of the statistics computed under admissible scale transformations. Although this line is not without merit, Adams, Fagot, and Robinson (1965) show that the sense of invariance intended by Stevens is not clear.

Many psychologists, confident that their freedom to compute was as inalienable as their freedom to speak, took up arms in the cause of computational libertarianism (see for example Burke, 1953; Lord, 1953) and so began the "permissible statistics" controversy. From the start it was misdirected. All computations are permissible, it is just that some are not helpful in the derivation of valid empirical conclusions from measurement data.

That the issue was not one of *permissible* statistics was recognized by Suppes (1959). However, viewing the matter through neopositivist lenses, he also misperceived it, supposing it to be one of the empirical meaningfulness of measurement statements. This view has largely become the accepted wisdom (see for example, Adams, Fagot, and Robinson, 1965; Luce, 1979; and Roberts, 1976, 1979), though Suppes (1979) has recently expressed second thoughts.

As a solution to the problem, Suppes and Zinnes proposed the following criterion of empirical meaningfulness: "A numerical statement is *meaningful* if and only if its truth (or falsity) is constant under admissible scale transformations of any of its numerical assignments, that is, any of its numerical functions expressing the results of measurements" (1963, p. 66).

This criterion means that statements like the following are not empirically meaningful.

1. The mean of the scale *A* hardness measures for objects in set 1 is greater than the mean of the scale *A* hardness measures for objects in set 2.

If an admissible scale transformation (i.e., an increasing monotonic transformation) is applied to the numerical assignments on which it is based, and the scale *B* values result, then statement 1 goes from being true to being false. Hence, its truth is not constant under admissible scale transformations of its numerical assignments, so it must be classed as empirically meaningless.

On any ordinary understanding of the word "meaningful", statement 1 is meaningful. If it were not it could be neither true nor false. However, the adjective "empirical" is intended to specify a narrower sense of meaningful than that used in ordinary discourse, and Adams, Fagot, and Robinson (1965) have attempted to explain this narrower sense (actually, they preferred the term "scientific significance" to that of "empirical meaningfulness"). A paraphrase of their view is that: A numerical statement is not empirically meaningful if it contains expressions denoting numerical relations, having no empirical analogue within the empirical relational system involved in the scale under discussion. Thus, statement 1 is not empirically meaningful, because the empirical relational system involved in any ordinal scale does not contain an analogue of the numerical relation of *being the mean of*. In contrast to this, the empirical relational systems involved in ratio scales do. So, to put the matter as simply as possible, Adams, Fagot, and Robinson are suggesting that statements like 1 above are not empirically meaningful because they have no empirical interpretation in the relevant empirical relational system.

Is this a good enough account of what could be meant by being empirically meaningless in this context? The answer is no, and for two reasons. In the first place, it concedes far too much to verificationist theories of meaning. Just because a variable (such as hardness) is so far only known to be ordinal, it does not follow that it is empirically meaningless to hypothesize that its structure is really additive (like that of weight or length). Given such a hypothesis, the notion of mean hardness is empirically meaningful, (though speculative and, therefore, evil in the eyes of operationalists and positivists) even though it is not definable in terms of any hardness relations yet known. Of course, nothing about such hypothesized mean hardness follows from statement 1, but that is not relevant to the issue of empirical meaningfulness.

Second, Rozeboom's (1966) observation that any numerical relation between numerical assignments must represent some (perhaps extensionally defined) empirical relation implies that the mean of a set of ordinal hardness measures *does* correspond to *some* empirical relation between the objects measured. Even though this relation will not be involved in the empirical relational system underlying the ordinal scale, it does constitute an empirical interpretation of the mean. Thus, no well-defined numerical relation upon measurements is ever devoid of an empirical interpretation and so must always be empirically meaningful.

However, even if Adams', Fagot's, and Robinson's sense of empirical meaningfulness had been acceptable it turns out not to be consistent with Suppes' and Zinnes' criterion. If the objects in sets 1 and 2 are rearranged so that all objects in set 1 are harder than all objects in set 2 then the truth of statement 1 remains constant under all admissible scale transformations. Thus according to Suppes' and Zinnes' criterion, it would be empirically meaningful under such circumstances, even though the sole empirical relation involved in the relevant empirical relational system remains unchanged, and incapable of defining an empirical analogue of the mean. So Suppes and Zinnes may well have meant something quite different by "empirically meaningful" from the suggestion made by Adams, Fagot, and Robinson. Whatever Suppes and Zinnes may have meant, it must have been very subtle: simply by rearranging the memberships of sets 1 and 2, statement 1 is transformed from being "empirically meaningless" to being "empirically meaningful."

The problem has never been anything other than simply one of the valid inference (Michell, 1986). Because the role of numbers in measurement, according to the representational theory, is simply to represent empirical facts and through representing them facilitate the deduction of empirical conclusions, the numbers themselves cannot contribute any content to the conclusions arrived at. Campbell was in no doubt that the whole point of applying numbers to reality was, "to enable the powerful weapon of mathematical analysis to be applied to the subject matter of science" (1920, pp. 267–268).

And as Field observed, "the conclusions we arrive at by these means are not genuinely new, they are already derivable in a more long-winded fashion from the premises without recourse to mathematical entities" (1980, pp. 10–11). This, in a nutshell, is the solution to Stevens' problem of permissible statistics within the framework of the representational theory of measurement. Measurement can only validly lead to those empirical conclusions already entailed by the empirical premises. These premises will be propositions about the empirical entities and the empirical relations that they enter into. The empirical relations concerned are those involved in the empirical relational system on which the scale is based. The relations within the numerical relational system will have been chosen because they possess the same formal properties as these empirical relations. Thus for each valid empirical argument there will be a correspondingly valid numerical argument involving just those numerical relations and no others. Thus, if all numerical inferences from measurements are restricted to valid argument forms involving just those numerical relations representing the relevant empirical relations and to no others, then all inferences to the appropriate empirical interpretations of the numerical conclusions obtained will be valid, and no valid inferences of that kind will be excluded. The use of argument forms involving any other numerical relations will then be unnecessary to those whose interest is validity, for the use of such numerical relations is liable to lead to invalidity.

Applying this solution to the above example, it can be seen that the calculation of means of ordinal scale measurements is generally not helpful in scientific research. There is nothing to stop one from doing it and any conclusions arrived at, will be just as empirically meaningful as any other conclusions one arrives at in scientific investigation. It is just that considering only the empirical data on which the ordinal scale is based, no empirical conclusions about means validly follow. To compute the mean is to go beyond the data given, and to infer empirical conclusions about it, is to infer what cannot validly follow from that data. Rozeboom's point implies that there always will be a set of empirical propositions, (about extensionally defined relations) that do entail empirical interpretations of whatever conclusions about means follow from the numbers assigned. However, these propositions are not the premises that the scientist employing the ordinal scale is using. Of course, he always has the option of using them, but if he does he is no longer working with an ordinal scale and it is then encumbent on him to explicate the empirical relational system with which he is working.

So Stevens' prohibition against calculating means of ordinal data does have something to recommend it: ordinal data alone entails nothing about means, so following his prescription excludes no valid consequences of one's data. Likewise, his prescriptions on the permissibility of other statistics relative to types of measurement scales have similar support: they do not exclude the inferences of any valid conclusions from one's data.

## A CRITIQUE OF REPRESENTATIONALISM

The literature on measurement theory contains few critiques of the representational theory. This is because in one guise or another it is almost universally accepted amongst measurement theorists. Since 1966, E. W. Adams has been almost its lone critic, and in two papers (1966 & 1979) has expressed his doubts about it. I am not convinced that any of his criticisms is fatal to the theory and, ironically, the greatest problem for the theory is a feature that Adams apparently regards as no disadvantage at all. This is the problem of the meaning of measurement statements.

While discussing the alleged distinction between theoretical and observational statements Adams makes the following remark about the representational theory (which he calls F.M., i.e., fundamental measurement, theory): "And here F.M. Theory, crude as it may be at present, has an important insight to contribute which is too frequently overlooked. This is that numerical measurements are *not* direct observational 'data' and that challenges to the empirical character of science which presupposes this are simply mistaken" (1979, p. 220).

Adams is correct: the view that measurements are not direct observational data does follow from the representational theory of measurement and it is a view that is frequently overlooked. It is frequently overlooked because many scientists and philosophers adopt the opposite view, namely, that at least some statements expressing the results of measurements are directly observational. Statements such as,

1. The length of *x* is 2.5 meters, or
2. The weight of *y* is 3.12 kilograms.

These are commonly taken to be reports of direct observations and free of any nonobservational concepts. That is, the metrical predicates, *2.5 meters* and *3.12 kilograms*, are like many other metrical predicates, interpreted empirically and realistically. They are taken to refer to particular values of the length and weight variables, values which may be directly observed. For example, 2.5 meters is taken to be a length which is two and a half times that of the standard meter rod in France. This realistic interpretation of metrical predicates depends on the realistic interpretation of numerical terms like "two and a half." However, that is how numerical terms are ordinarily understood. It is this kind of realistic interpretation of metrical predicates that is disallowed by the representational theory, and it is why this theory implies that measurement statements are not observational.

According to the representational theory, statements like 1 and 2 do not describe the empirical objects that they refer to (i.e., objects *x* and *y*), neither do they describe relationships between such objects. According to this theory, the meanings of 1 and 2 may be paraphrased as follows:

3. The number assigned to *x* on the meter length scale is 2.5.
4. The number assigned to *y* on the kilograms weight scale is 3.12.

These statements merely relate the empirical entities *x* and *y* to numbers. Because numbers are held to be external to the empirical situation under study (i.e., *x* and *y* and their length and weight relations to other empirical objects) statements 3 and 4 cannot be describing that situation.

This difference between the representational theory and the ordinary realistic interpretation of measurement statements extends to the inferences made from such statements. Ordinarily, statements 1 and 5 would be taken to imply statement 6.

5. The length of *y* is 5 meters.
6. The length of *y* is twice the length of *x*.

However, according to the representational theory, 6 does not follow from 1 and 5. Statement 5 must be paraphrased as:

7. The number assigned to *y* on the meters length scale is 5.

Obviously, 3 and 7 do not entail 6 and so, according to the representational theory, neither do 1 and 5. What 3 and 7 do entail is:

8. The number assigned to *y* on the meters length scale is twice the number assigned to *x* on the meters length scale.

Statement 8 only leads to 6 given certain facts about the meters length scale or, equivalently, given certain facts about the empirical relational system on which it is based. The representationalist must argue that the ordinary habit of inferring statements like 6 from 1 and 5 presumes these facts. This would be news to most people with a practical interest in measurement, including both scientists and tradesmen.

The difference, however, bites more deeply. According to the representational theory, statements like 6 are semantically ill-formed because they mix numerical and empirical modes of discourse. One things' being twice another is a relationship of a numerical kind. The lengths of *x* and *y* are nonnumerical properties. Because representationalism is premised upon the assumption that numbers (and their relations) are external to the empirical relational system involved in measurement, statement 6 cannot be taken literally. On the ordinary realistic view numerical relations are taken to hold between nonnumerical things and the meaning of 6 is obvious. On the representational view statement 6 must be understood metaphorically as meaning something like,

9. The lengthwise concatenation of *x* with an object of the same length produces an object of the same length as *y*.

The matter of importance here is not the difference in meaning (or lack of it) between statements 6 and 9 on a realistic interpretation, but the fact that statements like 6 have no literal meaning on the representational view. For statements like 6 (i.e., those asserting numerical relations between empirical entities) are the bread and butter of quantitative science.

The problem is exacerbated by the fact that such "mixed–mode" statements achieve considerable complexity in much of scientific discourse. While it requires little effort to see through a statement like 6 to something like 9 behind it, more complex mixed–mode statements are less transparent. What, according to representationalism, is the literal meaning of such "metaphorical" statements as 10?

10. The product moment correlation coefficient between height and weight amongst school children in Sydney is .65.

A product moment correlation is a numerical relationship and its coefficient is a real number. Yet what is held to stand in this numerical relationship is height and weight, both of which are empirical (nonnumerical) properties. It may be tempting for a representationalist to suggest that 10 is really a statement about numbers (i.e., the measurements of height and weight), but it is not. Statement 10 may be based on measurements, but it asserts the existence of a relationship between the attributes measured. That some relationship exists between the children's height and weight in the empirical domain, given that 10 is true, cannot be denied. And it will be in virtue of this relationship's existence that 10 is true. Yet, it is a relationship that is remarkably difficult to describe without recourse to numerical terms such as "mean," "variance," "covariance," and "ratio," also it is one that scientists never refer to in anything other than numerical terms.

However, the solution given to Stevens' problem of permissible statistics, required that any valid inferences from measurements to empirical facts must be implications already entailed by the empirical data itself. It now appears that even in cases of moderate complexity we know of no way to make the inference other than via the use of numbers, because our nonnumerical empirical language is too poor. As far as most scientific results and generalizations of a quantitative kind are concerned, the language used to describe them does not penetrate the representation to the reality represented. The representationalist is forced to believe in the existence of relationships that he is in practice unable to describe other than indirectly or metaphorically, through the medium of the language of mathematics. Because this is held to be the language of "abstract" (i.e., nonspatio–temporal) entities, the curious picture that the representationalist paints of the quantitative scientist is of one made to use the language of the nonempirical in order to discourse on the empirical.

The representationalist is led to this puzzling destination through his conviction that numbers are external to the empirical facts involved in measurement. How has such a conviction gained currency in the face of scientific practice, which treats numbers otherwise? The answer is that those who have developed this theory stand within a philosophical tradition that takes it for granted that numbers are not empirical kinds of things. From such a point of view the application of mathematics to reality is a deep problem in need of explanation, and the representational theory was devised to serve that purpose. On the other hand, if numbers are accepted in the same way as quantitative scientists implicitly treat them (i.e., as empirical) then the fact of their use is hardly a problem at all. Then the representational theory becomes a liability, for it prises apart the numerical concepts used in science from the empirical reality studied. There is nothing logically incoherent about the representational theory, however if the empirical realist theory of measurement described in the next chapter is true, then representationalism is empirically false.

# Chapter 3

# What Quantity And Measurement Really Are

## QUANTITY

What are the marks of quantity? What distinguishes a quantitative from a nonquantitative variable? The marks of quantity are order and additivity: the values of a quantitative variable are ordered and possess additive structure. It is the aim of this chapter to make explicit the meaning of these claims.

There is, however, a preliminary point to clarify. What is a variable? Very generally, it is anything relative to which objects may vary. Length is a variable, different objects may have different lengths. Color is a variable, for different objects may be of different colors. Sex is a variable, some things being female and some male. Consider length in more detail. The variable of length is simply the class of all lengths. Each particular length is a property that some things might possess. So a variable may be a class of properties. Not just *any* class of properties constitutes a variable. The properties of being 5-feet long, of being pink, of being female, and of being highly intelligent taken together do not form a variable because some object may possess more than one of these properties simultaneously. Properties only form a variable if they are mutually exclusive, that is, if nothing can possess more than one of them simultaneously. The class of all lengths is a variable for any object can only be one length at a time.

It is not only classes of mutually exclusive *properties* that form variables. Classes of mutually exclusive *relations* do so as well. The distinction between properties and relations is an important one. Things possess properties singly. The fact that my pen is ten centimeters long is a fact about it and nothing else. On the other hand, relations involve pluralities of things. If the pen is on the desk then this situation involves both the pen and the desk. Binary relations involve two things, ternary relations three things, and so on. Of course, everything has many properties and stands in many relations to other things.

Another example of a relation is velocity. It is a binary relation. The velocity of $A$ relative to $B$ is a matter involving only $A$ and $B$. Of course, the velocity of $A$ relative to $B$ may vary and it can only be one value at a time. Hence, it is a variable. It is true that the velocity of $A$ relative to $B$ and the velocity of $A$ relative to $C$ may differ at any point in time, but this does not mean that $A$ has more than one velocity at a time. $A$, by itself, does not have a velocity. It is pairs of things, *A and B*, and *A and C*, and so on, which have velocities.

Another class of relations forming a variable is the following: being the father of, being the mother of, being the sister of, being the brother of, and being the child of. Cannot certain pairs of people stand in more than one of these relations to each other? If $A$ is the father of $B$, then $B$ is the child of $A$, and so $A$ and $B$ are involved in both relations at once. However, a binary relation holds not simply between a pair of things but between an *ordered pair*. Hence, a class of binary relations forms a variable only if no more than one of the relations within it ever holds between a particular ordered pair of entities at any one time. A similar point applies to ternary relations and ordered triples, quarternary relations and ordered quadruples, and so on.

Within this book, the particular properties or relations constituting a variable will be referred to as *values of that variable*. For example, being 6-meters long is a value of the length variable; being female is a value of the sex variable; and traveling at 100 meters per second relative to something is a value of the velocity variable. When it is said that a quantitative variable is ordered and additive, it is meant that there are ordinal and additive relations between the values of the variable.

The first fact to note about a quantitative variable is that its values are ordered. For example, lengths are ordered according to their magnitude, six meters is greater than 2 meters, and so on. Similarly, the values of other quantitative variables are ordered according to their magnitudes. The familiar symbols, "$\geqslant$" and "$>$" will be used to denote this relation of magnitude, "$\geqslant$" meaning "at least as great as," and "$>$" meaning "greater than." Also, the symbol "$=$" will be used to signify identity of value. (For more information on the concept of order the reader is referred to Appendix 1).

Let $X$, $Y$, and $Z$ be any three values of a variable, $Q$. Then $Q$ is *ordinal* if and only if

(1) if $X \geqslant Y$ and $Y \geqslant Z$ then $X \geqslant Z$ (transitivity);

(2) if $X \geqslant Y$ and $Y \geqslant X$ then $X = Y$ (antisymmetry); and

(3) either $X \geqslant Y$ or $Y \geqslant X$ (strong connexity).

A relation possessing these three properties is called a *simple order*, so $Q$ is ordinal if and only if $\geqslant$ is a simple order on its values. All quantitative variables are simply ordered by $\geqslant$, but not every ordinal variable is quantitative, for quantity involves more than order. It involves additivity.

Additivity is a ternary relation, symbolized as "$X + Y = Z$". Let $Q$ be any ordinal variable such that for any of its values $X$, $Y$ and $Z$

(4) $X + (Y + Z) = (X + Y) + Z$ (associativity);
(5) $X + Y = Y + X$ (commutativity);
(6) $X \geqslant Y$ if and only if $X + Z \geqslant Y + Z$ (monotonicity);
(7) if $X > Y$ then there exists a value $Z$ such that $X = Y + Z$ (solvability);
(8) $X + Y > X$ (positivity); and
(9) there exists a natural number $n$ such that $nX \geqslant Y$ (where $1X = X$ and $(n + 1)X = nX + X$) (Archimedean condition).

In such a case the ternary relation involved is *additive* and $Q$ is a *quantitative variable*.

These nine conditions (the ordinal and the additive) are *uniformities of coexistence* (J. S. Mill, 1848). What is meant by calling them this is that these conditions do nothing more than describe the structure of the variable. They do not, of themselves, describe the behavior of any objects possessing values of the variable. To presume that they do is to make Campbell's mistake. How the additive structure of a quantitative variable is reflected in the behavior of relevant objects is a matter that depends also on the kinds of objects they are (i.e., upon the laws of nature relating to them in virtue of their other properties, and the other relations into which they enter). The issue of how quantitative structure may be detected is discussed in the next chapter. Here our focus is the concept of quantity itself.

The fact that these conditions are uniformities of coexistence affects the interpretation of the additive relation. $X + Y = Z$ does not mean that $X$ *added to* $Y$ is the same as $Z$. That is far too operational an interpretation. Rather, $X + Y = Z$ is a relation between $X$, $Y$, and $Z$. It is the relation of $Z$ being entirely composed of discrete parts $X$ and $Y$.

Hence, condition (4) may be interpreted this way: the value entirely composed of discrete parts $X$ and $(Y + Z)$ (where $Y + Z$ is the value entirely composed of discrete parts $Y$ and $Z$) is the same as the value entirely composed of discrete parts $(X + Y)$ and $Z$ (where $X + Y$) is the value entirely composed of discrete parts $X$ and $Y$).

Condition (5) means that the value entirely composed of discrete parts $X$ and $Y$ is the same as the value entirely composed of discrete parts $Y$ and $X$. So (4) and (5) together imply that the order of the parts constituting any value of a quantitative variable is irrelevant.

In the same vein, (6) means that if $X \geqslant Y$ then a value entirely composed of discrete parts $X$ and $Z$ is at least as great as a value entirely composed of discrete parts $Y$ and $Z$.

Condition (7) requires that the variable be additively complete. If $X > Y$ then

$X$ will be entirely composed of discrete parts $Y$ and some other value of $Q$, $Z$. (7) requires that $Z$ exist.

Condition (8) states that the value entirely composed of discrete parts $X$ and $Y$ is greater than $X$ itself. This is what it means to say that all values of the variable are *positive*. In this book our interest is only in such variables. Krantz et al. (1971) indicate how quantities with nonpositive values may be described.

Condition (9) ensures that no value, $Y$, of the variable is infinitely greater than any other value, $X$. It is called the *Archimedean* condition after the ancient Greek mathematician, Archimedes of Syracuse, who is said to have been the first to state it explicitly. However, it may well have been known earlier than Archimedes for it is implicit in Definition 4 of Book V of Euclid's *Elements*. Within condition (9), the meaning of the expression "$nX$" may seem obscure. As mentioned, $n$ is a natural number, that is, one of the infinite series 1, 2, 3, . . . . The expression "$nX$", therefore, refers to the value of the variable which is entirely composed of the discrete parts $X$ and $X$ and . . . etc. (until $n$ of them are listed). However, because there is only one value $X$ how can $n$ discrete $X$s be referred to? To understand this requires understanding the concept of composition in terms of identical parts. This is a familiar enough concept. Consider a liter of water which is composed of a large number of water molecules, all identical to one another.

However, an obscurity remains due to the fact that such molecules are physical objects, while the value, $X$ of some quantitative variable is a property or a relation. It may help then to consider length, the paradigm of quantity. Let the objects involved be a set of straight, rigid rods of various lengths. Then $X + Y = Z$ means that if any rod, $a$, is of length $Z$, then $a$ is entirely composed of two parts, $c$ and $d$, such that $c$ is of length $X$, and $d$ is of length $Y$. Of course, here the sense in which $a$ is entirely composed of $c$ and $d$ is quite obvious: there will be a point along the extent of $a$ such that everything from one end up to that point is $c$ and everything beyond it to the other end is $d$. This is illustrated in Figure 3.1. Thus, in this case, the expression "$nX$" refers to the length of a rod, $b$, which is entirely composed of $n$ discrete parts

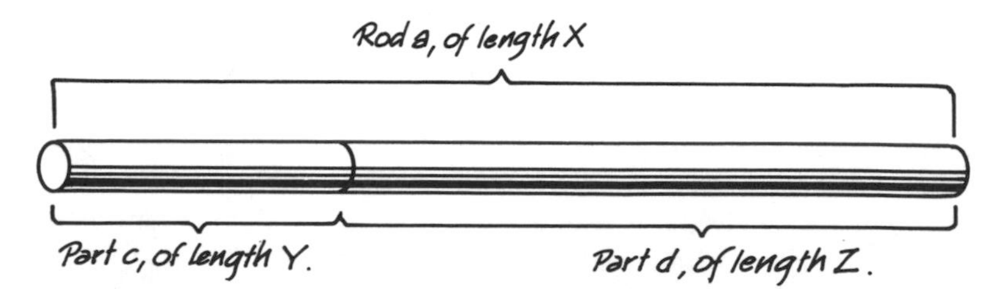


FIG. 3.1 The meaning of the additivity relation, $X = Y + Z$, is illustrated with respect to length by rod $a$, of length $X$. Rod $a$ is entirely composed of the discrete parts $c$ and $d$, where $c$ is of length $y$ and $d$ is of length $Z$.

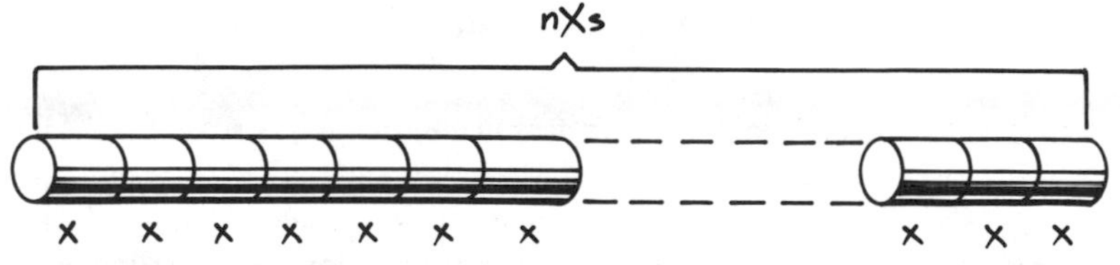


FIG. 3.2 For the case of length, the meaning of the expression "$nX$" is given by the length of a rod $b$ which is entirely composed of $n$ discrete parts each of length $x$.

each of length $X$ (cf. Fig. 3.2). So the Archimedean condition asserts that no matter how small length $X$ is and no matter how large length $Y$ is, there is an $n$ such that $nX \geqslant Y$.

The example of length here may give the false impression that if $X + Y = Z$ and object $a$ possesses value $Z$, then $a$ can be decomposed into parts $c$ and $d$, where $c$ possesses $X$ and $d$, $Y$. However this is not necessary, for our ability to so decompose object $a$ depends on the kind of thing $a$ is (apart from being $Z$, that is), and on our technological capacities. Another example will clarify this point. Suppose that $X$, $Y$, and $Z$ are densities and $a$ is an iron cube of uniform density. Now if $X + Y = Z$ and $a$ is $Z$ then $a$ will be entirely composed of parts $c$ and $d$, such that $c$ is $X$, and $d$ is $Y$, but these will not be parts into which we can decompose $a$. The reason, of course, is that $a$, $c$, and $d$ must all be of the same volume, though they must differ in mass. Hence, $c$ and $d$ will be "ghosts" of $a$, identical to it in external size and shape, but differing in inner constitution, in that some of the matter composing $a$ constitutes $c$ (say, every second or third molecule of iron in $a$) and the rest constitutes $d$. These parts of $a$ exist, however there is no way that it can be decomposed into them.

It is in this sense that these nine laws of quantity are uniformities of coexistence, rather than realizable operations. All quantities share a similar structure, but not all objects possessing quantitative attributes or entering into quantitative relations manifest that quantitative structure in the same manner.

Within this book, these nine conditions will be taken to be the paradigm of quantity. It is recognized that there are exceptions (e.g., some quantities admit negative values, some are periodic, and some possess maximal values). The interested reader is referred to Krantz et al. (1971) for a definition of such variables. In all these cases some modification of one or more of these nine conditions is necessary. However, these nine conditions are regarded as defining the paradigm of quantity because they describe the common structure of the two basic quantities that, historically, have shaped attempts at quantification. These are aggregate magnitude and length. These conditions describe what is common to these two quantities, and any nonnumerical variable that shares these common features is capable of measurement. In what follows, unless otherwise stated, a quantitative variable will be taken to be one that satisfies these nine conditions.

## CONTINUOUS QUANTITY

Aristotle divided quantity in two, discrete and continuous. An example of discrete quantity is aggregate magnitude (ie., what is common to all classes or aggregates of the same size). That which is common to all aggregates of some specific size is the property of being an *n* membered aggregate, (for some particular natural number, *n*) and the class of all such properties constitutes a quantity. Any value of this quantity may be assessed by considering its numerical relation to that of the unit value, (the property of being a single membered aggregate) and this is what is discovered by counting. However, the values of a continuous quantity cannot be assessed by counting relative to a common unit. Instead, they must be measured. Measurement is the identification of some value of a continuous quantity relative to an arbitrarily chosen unit, via their numerical relation. In order to understand this statement the relationship between continuous quantity and number must be explicated. That in turn requires defining the concept of a continuous quantity.

The quantitative variables treated within the physical sciences are, for the most part, accepted as being continuous. In short, this means that there are no *gaps* between any pairs of values within these variables. In physical theories, for example, space and time are thought of as continuous rather than as fundamentally granulated.

At first sight it might be thought that if a quantitative variable also satisfies condition (10) then it must be continuous.

(10) If $X$ and $Y$ are any values of $Q$ such that $X > Y$ then there exists $Z$ in $Q$ such that $X > Z > Y$ (density).

This condition means that between any two different values of a quantitative variable there lies a third. Such a variable is infinitely divisible (in principle) and so it might be thought to be continuous. However, it is not. The rational numbers are dense but they are not continuous.

Obviously, the natural numbers are not dense. Between any two consecutive natural numbers, $n$ and $n+1$, there is no third value. However, the *rational* numbers are dense. The (positive) rational numbers are all the numbers $n/m$, where $n$ and $m$ are any natural numbers. They are, in short, the whole numbers together with all of their fractional parts. Given any two rational numbers, $n/m$ and $p/q$, there will be the rational number $1/2(n/m + p/q) = (nq + mp)/2mq$ falling between them. Hence, they are dense.

If condition (10) captured the meaning of continuity then all lengths (which are presumed to be continuous) would be measurable by rational numbers. However, it is well known that they are not. If the length of the side of a square is one unit then the length of the diagonal is $+\sqrt{2}$ units, and $+\sqrt{2}$ is not a rational number (i.e., there are no natural numbers, $n$ and $m$, such that $+\sqrt{2} = n/m$). So relative to any unit length, $X$, there will be gaps between the lengths measurable by rational numbers.

If not in density, then wherein does continuity reside? Consider the lengths measurable by all rational numbers (relative to some unit). They will fall into two classes: those whose measure is less than $+\sqrt{2}$, and those whose measure is greater than $+\sqrt{2}$. The former class has no greatest member, for there is no greatest rational number less than $+\sqrt{2}$. As they increase in value the lengths within this class get closer and closer to being $+\sqrt{2}$ units but never reach it. Similarly, the latter class has no smallest member, for there is no smallest rational number greater than $+\sqrt{2}$. As they decrease in value the lengths within this class also get closer and closer to being $+\sqrt{2}$ units but never reach it. Between these two classes is the length of the diagonal of the unit square (the square whose sides are one unit long). This length is the smallest length greater than any in the first class, and the largest length smaller than any in the second class. It therefore fills the gap between these two classes. What is needed is some general way of specifying such gap–fillers. Of course, $+\sqrt{2}$ is not the only one.

These gap–fillers may be specified along the following lines. The class of all lengths whose measure is less than $+\sqrt{2}$ is *bounded above* by the length of the diagonal of the unit square. That is, all members of this class are less than that length. Furthermore, it is the *least upper bound* of that class because it is the smallest length greater than any in that class. It is through generalizing this concept of a least upper bound that the concept of continuity may be captured.

Let $\alpha$ be any nonempty set of lengths, then $\alpha$ is *bounded above* if there exists a length, $Y$, such that for all $Z$ in $\alpha$, $Z \leqslant Y$. $Y$ is then an *upper bound of* $\alpha$. A length, $X$, which is an upper bound of $\alpha$ is a *least upper bound* of $\alpha$ if it is such that for every upper bound of $\alpha$, $Y$, $X \leqslant Y$. Then the length variable is continuous if and only if every nonempty set of lengths which has an upper bound has a least upper bound. If this condition is satisfied then there will be no gaps in the length variable like that into which the length of the diagonal of the unit square falls. Thus, a quantitative variable, $Q$, which is dense is also *continuous* if and only if,

(11) Every non-empty set of values of $Q$ which has an upper bound has a least upper bound.

## CONTINUOUS QUANTITIES AND REAL NUMBERS

The view stemming from Campbell (1920) and formalized by Krantz et al. (1971), is that quantities are measurable because they are *isomorphic to a subsystem of the real numbers*. That is, they have a structure similar to that of a portion of the real number system. Krantz et al. prove that a variable satisfying conditions (1) – (9) has this relation to the real numbers. As they then go on to show, in the spirit of Campbell's theory, this fact enables numerical assignments to be made to the values of the variable, and such assignments are similar to those used in measurement. True as these observations are, it is a mistake to think that they reveal the nature of measurement. For the connection between continuous quantities and real numbers is much more intimate than the representationalists suggest. Bostock (1979) shows that *ratios* of values of a continuous quantity are identical in structure to the real number system. Hence, he boldly argues, such ratios are the real numbers. If true, this means that in measurement numbers are not assigned to values of a quantitative variable, rather ratios of these values *are* numbers, and it is because of this fact that we find numbers in measurement. Measurement is seen to be the discovery of numerical relationships between the values of a quantitative variable. This position has the attractive advantage of showing that the numerical statements reporting measurements are thoroughly empirical, observational reports. This is in sharp contrast to the representational theory which implies that measurement statements, because they are in part numerical, are not direct reports of observations (cf. Adams, 1979). This position also links measurement exclusively to quantity and, so, outlaws the quite promiscuous concept of measurement hitherto encouraged within psychology.

It is convenient to begin with some brief comments about numbers themselves. There is a traditional, though no longer widely held, view according to which numbers are ratios of quantities (e.g., "the abstracted ratio of any quantity to another quantity of the same kind, which we take for unity" (Newton, 1728/1967 p. 2)). On this view, the natural, integral, and rational numbers all emerge as ratios of the quantity, aggregate magnitude. Any natural number, $n$, is the magnitude of an $n$-membered aggregate relative to that of a single-membered aggregate; any integer, $+$ or $-$ $n$, is the magnitude of a positive or negative difference of $n$ members between aggregates relative to that of a single-membered aggregate; and any rational number, $n/m$, is the magnitude of an $n$-membered aggregate to that of an $m$-membered aggregate. The two great strengths of this view are that it makes the numbers empirical relations, and makes them all the same kind of relations, (ratios) (see Forrest & Armstrong, 1987, for a more philosophical treatment of this view). As will be shown the same kind of view can be held about the real numbers.

Modern set-theoretical accounts of the number systems have departed from this simplicity. Typically, the natural numbers are thought of as sets constructed upon the empty set, $\varnothing$ (i.e., $0 = \varnothing$ and $n = \{n-1\}$); the integers as sets of ordered pairs of natural numbers; and the rationals as sets of ordered pairs of integers. Of interest here is the way in which the work of the German mathematician, R. Dedekind, enabled the real numbers to be constructed as infinite sets of rational numbers, for this work also shows that they may also be taken to be ratios of quantities.

Dedekind noted that each real number cuts the rational numbers into two classes. For example, $+\sqrt{2}$ cuts the positive rational numbers into those whose square is less than two and those whose square is greater than two. Thus, he suggested, $+\sqrt{2}$ is just the cut between these two classes of rational numbers (see Dedekind, 1909). Because the location of this cut is uniquely determined by just one of these classes (say, those whose square is less than two) $+\sqrt{2}$ may be identified with that class. More generally, all real numbers, both rational and irrational alike, may be thought of as cuts between classes of rational numbers, and may be identified with infinite classes of rational numbers.

Such cuts became known as "Dedekind cuts" and Bostock (1979) gave the following general definition of them:

> A cut is in effect a set which contains *all* rational numbers less than some real number which is their least upper bound, and it may be defined (without mentioning real numbers) as a non-empty set of rationals such that (i) there are some rationals not in the set, (ii) if any rational is in the set then all rationals less than it are in the set, and (iii) if any rational is in the set then some rational greater than it is in the set. (p. 200)

Modern set-theoretical accounts of the real numbers identify them with Dedekind cuts. At first sight this definition of the real numbers seems far removed from the numbers we know through measurement. In fact, as will become evident, the connection is intimate.

Algebraically, the real number system is described as a *complete ordered field* (see, for example, Birkhoff & MacLane, 1965). Such a structure is characterized by the following 13 conditions. Let $a$, $b$, $c$, and $d$ be any real numbers, then

1*. If $a = b$ and $c = d$ then $a + c = b + d$ and $a \cdot c = b \cdot d$;
2*. $a + b = b + a$ and $a \cdot b = b \cdot a$;
3*. $(a + b) + c = a + (b + c)$ and $(a \cdot b) \cdot c = a \cdot (b \cdot c)$;
4*. $a \cdot (b + c) = a \cdot b + a \cdot c$;
5*. $a + 0 = 0 + a = a$;
6*. $a \cdot 1 = 1 \cdot a = a$;
7*. $a + (-a) = (-a) + a = 0$;
8*. $a \cdot (1/a) = (1/a) \cdot a = 1$;
9*. One and only one of the following is true: $a = b$ or $a > b$ or $b > a$;
10*. If $a > b$ and $b > c$ then $a > c$;
11*. If $a > b$ then $a + c > b + c$;
12*. If $a > b$ and $0 < c$ then $a \cdot c > b \cdot c$; and
13*. Every nonempty set of real numbers that has an upper bound has a least upper board.

(Note that in these conditions $a + b$, $a \cdot b$, $-a$, $1/a$, 1, and 0 are also real numbers, $1 \neq 0$ and $=$ is taken to be reflexive, symmetric, and transitive).

This then is a brief sketch of the now widely accepted picture of the real numbers. As Bostock (1979) has argued it can be shown that ratios of values of continuous quantitative variables possess all the properties the real numbers are said to have. That is, these ratios also form a complete ordered field.

To begin with, what is such a ratio? The answer may be illustrated by taking length as the example again. The concept may be explained by working from simple cases to the difficult ones. Let $X$ and $Y$ be any two lengths. What does it mean to say that the ratio of $X$ to $Y$ is $n$ (i.e., that $X/Y = n$), where $n$ is some natural number? Suppose that $X$ is the length, six meters, and that $Y$ is the length, three meters. What does $X/Y=2$ mean? The fact that $X/Y = 2$ may be expressed as $X = 2Y$ (i.e., $X$ is twice $Y$), which means that in this case the ratio of $X$ to $Y$ is just the fact that $X$ is $2Y$. More generally, if $X/Y = n$ then this is the fact that $X = nY$ and because the concept of being $nY$ has already been unfolded (see section on "Quantity," earlier in this chapter) this account is quite explicit. The relation in which $X$ stands to $Y$ here is that of one thing equalling n of another.

Very many ratios do not equal natural numbers. If $X$ is the length, 6 meters, and $Y$, the length 9 meters, then $X/Y = 2/3$. What then does it mean to say that $X/Y = n/m$ (where $n/m$ is some rational number)? The answer is, it simply means that $mX = nY$. In this case the relation in which $X$ stands to $Y$ is that of m of one thing equalling n of another.

These cases are simple compared with the next. What does $X/Y$ mean when its value is irrational? Let $X$ be the length of the diagonal of a square and $Y$ the length of each of the sides. Then, $X/Y = +\sqrt{2}$. What does this mean? Let $R(<X/Y)$ be the class of all positive rational numbers less than $X/Y$. That is, $R(<X/Y)$ is the class of all positive $n/m$ such that $n/m < X/Y$ (i.e., $nY < mX$). Of course, it is quickly recognized that $R(<X/Y)$ is just the Dedekind cut which $+\sqrt{2}$ is conventionally taken to be. Corresponding to each $n/m$ in $R(<X/Y)$ is a true inequality, $nY < mX$. The meaning of $X/Y = +\sqrt{2}$ is just this infinite class of inequalities. That is, $X/Y = +\sqrt{2}$ means

$$Y < X$$

$$14Y < 10X$$

$$141Y < 100X$$

$$1414Y < 1000X$$

$$14142Y < 10000X$$

$$\cdot$$

$$\cdot$$

$$\cdot$$

$$nY < mX \text{ (where } + (n/m)^2 < 2).$$

Thus, the relation between $X$ and $Y$ in this case, which is their ratio, is an infinite class of relations of the kind, m of one thing being greater than n of another. This reveals the intimate connection between Dedekind cuts and ratios of values of continuous quantities. To state the matter in its most general form, let $R(>X/Y)$ be the class of all positive rational numbers greater than $X/Y$, and $R(=X/Y)$ be the class of all positive rational numbers equal to $X/Y$. Of course, $R(=X/Y)$ is empty if $X/Y$ is irrational. As was recognized by Euclid, any two ratios of values of a quantitative variable, $X/Y$ and $W/Z$, are identical (i.e., the same ratio) if and only if,

$$\begin{aligned} R(<X/Y) &= R(<W/Z), \\ R(=X/Y) &= R(=W/Z) \text{ and} \\ R(>X/Y) &- R(>W/Z). \end{aligned}$$

Then the ratio of $X$ to $Y$ is the infinite class of true relationships between $X$ and $Y$ of the following three kinds:

(i) $mX < nY$;
(ii) $mX = nY$; and
(iii) $mX > nY$

(for all natural numbers $n$ and $m$). In cases where $X/Y$ is irrational there will be no relations of kind (ii). But, if $X/Y$ is not irrational then relations of kind (ii) will exist. Any one such relation entails all of the others, not only those of kind (ii), but those of kinds (i) and (iii) as well. In such cases $X/Y$ may be identified with any relation of kind (ii) which is true of it. In all other cases (i.e., the irrational cases), $X/Y$ means nothing more nor less than the two infinite classes of relations of kinds (i) and (iii) which are true of it. For convenience it may be identified with just one of these classes.

It will now be obvious from the previous discussion, that corresponding to each ratio of values of a continuous variable there is a Dedekind cut, $R(<X/Y)$. If the continuous variable is unbounded in at least one of two senses then corresponding to each Dedekind cut there is a ratio of values of that variable. These two senses are as follows:

(12a) Let $Q$ be a continuous quantitative variable, then $Q$ is *unbounded above* if for every $X$ in $Q$ and every natural number, $n$, $nX$ exists.

(12b) Let $Q$ be a continuous quantitative variable, then $Q$ is *unbounded below* if for every $X$ in $Q$ and natural number, $n$, $Y$ exists such that $nY = X$.

Further insight into the connection between these two systems (the ratios of values of any unbounded continuous quantity, $Q$, and the real numbers) can be gained by seeing how each of the basic concepts within the real number system,

(i) unity or 1;
(ii) zero or 0;
(iii) the addition relation: $a + b = c$;

(iv) the multiplication relation: $a \cdot b = c$;
(v) the additive inverse: $-a$; and
(vi) the multiplicative inverse: $1/a$;

has a simple analogue within the system of ratios.

(i) *Unity:* for any value $X$ of $Q$, $X/X = 1$.

Specification of the zero element requires the concept of a *difference* between two values of $Q$. The difference between any two values $X$ and $Y$ of $Q$ is the value, $Z$, such that either $X = Y + Z$ or $Y = X + Z$. If $X = Y + Z$ then the difference between $X$ and $Y$ is called "$+Z$"; if $Y = X + Z$ then the difference between $X$ and $Y$ is called "$-Z$". Relative to the difference between $X$ and $Y$ the "+" or "−" preceding "$Z$" simply indicates whether it is the composition of $Z$ with the second term ($Y$) or the first term ($X$) which equals the other term. If $X = Y$ then there is no such $Z$ (i.e., there is no difference between them) and this is written as "0". That is,

(a) $X - Y = +Z$ if and only if $X = Y + Z$;
(b) $X - Y = -Z$ if and only if $Y - Z = +X$; and
(c) $X - Y = 0$ if and only if $X = Y$.

Then the ratio of any difference, $X - Y$, to any other value, $W$, is as follows:

(d) $(X - Y)/W = +(Z/W)$ if and only if $X - Y = +Z$;
(e) $(X - Y)/W = -(Z/W)$ if and only if $X - Y = -Z$; and
(f) $(X - Y)/W = 0$ if and only if $X - Y = 0$.

Then,

(ii) *Zero:* for any values, $X$ and $Y$, of $Q$, $(X - X)/Y = 0$.
(iii) *Addition:* for any values, $U$, $V$, $W$, $X$, $Y$, and $Z$, of $Q$ $U/V + W/X = Y/Z$ if and only if for some value, $T$, of $Q$, $W/X = T/V$ and $Y/Z = (U + T)/V$. (For then, of course, $U/V + W/X = U/V + T/V = (U + T)/V = Y/Z$).
(iv) *Multiplication:* for any values, $U$, $V$, $W$, $X$, $Y$, and $Z$, of $Q$ $(U/V).(W/X) = Y/Z$ if and only if for some value $T$, of $Q$, $W/X = V/T$ and $Y/Z = U/T$. (For then, of course, $(U/V).(W/X) = (U/V).(V/T) = U/T = Y/Z$).
(v) *Additive Inverse:* as implied by (b) and (e) above, for any values $X$ and $Y$ of $Q$, $-(X/Y) = -X/Y$.
(vi) *Multiplicative Inverse:* for all values, $X$ and $Y$, of $Q$ $1/(X/Y) = Y/X$.

Given these correspondences it is a simple matter to prove that for any unbounded continuous quantity, the system of ratios of its values possesses precisely the structure of the real number system (for more details of this argument see Bostock, 1979). That is, this system of ratios is also a complete ordered field.

Although this does not prove that this system of ratios is the real number system, it means that there is no formal impediment in the way of such an identification. All one then needs are positive arguments for making it. Bostock (1979) argues that this identification makes it easy to explain why real numbers are applicable to such ratios. It also helps to explain why the theory of real numbers developed in such close association with the theory of continuous quantities as it emerged in physics (for an account of this history see Kitcher, 1983).

It is widely believed by modern philosophers that numbers belong not to the spatio–temporal realm that we inhabit, but that they are "abstract entities", existing in some mysterious way outside of space and time. To an empiricist this is not a plausible view. Arithmetic is not simply a branch of pure mathematics. It is a theory whose application is more extensive and more successful than virtually any other theory. How would these truths of arithmetic be known or applied, if they were not truths about the same empirical realm that we inhabit and apply them to? As psychologists we believe that knowing requires a causal process between the fact known and the knower. Causal relations outside of space and time cannot be conceived of, for causal relations are partly spatio–temporal relations. Hence, from the fact that we know the truths of arithmetic, it follows that they are truths about empirical things.

What empirical things could they be truths about? If some truth, like a law of nature for example, is successfully applied to some situation, then it must be a truth about that situation. That is, it must be about some of the properties and relations found in that situation. Truths about real numbers are applied to situations where continuous quantities are believed to exist. Thus they may well be truths about such quantities. The fact that ratios of values of continuous quantities have the same structure as the real numbers, leaves them as the most compelling candidate for what the real numbers are. Such ratios it is concluded, instantiate real numbers, and the theory of real numbers is just the theory of such ratios at a level of abstraction that ignores other features of them (such as the fact that one of these continuous quantities is length, another mass, and so on).

It follows from this identification that claims about, say, the ratio of length $X$ to length $Y$ being some real number, $r$, are empirical claims and, if true, literally true. That is, reference to numbers in quantitative science is literal and not merely metaphorical, as the representational theory of measurement would have it.

## MEASUREMENT

Having clarified these preliminary issues the meaning of measurement becomes obvious. Quite simply, measurement is a procedure for identifying values of quantitative variables through their numerical relationships to other values. Take a simple example. We wish to know the length of a timber beam. This may be done by relating its length to that called a meter. It is found to be $r$ meters long (where $r$ is some real number). Here $r$ is the ratio of the length of the beam to that of a meter and this *fact* enables the length of the beam to be characterized.

More generally, in measurement some (unknown) value of a quantitative variable is identified as being $r$ units. A *unit of measurement* is simply a particular value of the relevant variable. It is singled out as that value relative to which all others are to be compared. Let the unit be $Y$ and let the value to be measured be $X$. Then a measurement has the form $X = rY$. This, of course, is equivalent to $X/Y = r$. As has already been argued, statements of this form are empirical claims, each ratio of values of a continuous quantity being a real number. Measurement, then, is just the recognition of such facts.

If the value of $Y$ is already known and the aim is to identify $X$, then this is achieved by noting that $X = rY$, for this fact characterizes $X$ in terms of $Y$. Of course, $Y$ itself must be known independently of measurement (otherwise an infinite regress ensues) and so, generally, $Y$ is known by ostension. That is, the unit of measurement is instantiated in some object (called the *standard of measurement*) where it may be known by direct observation. If unknown values are then characterized by their numerical relations to a common unit, numerical relations between them may be inferred. For example if $X = rY$, and $Z = sY$, then $X/Z = r/s$. Measures relative to the same unit form a *scale of measurement*, and measurements on the same scale allow for further numerical relations to be deduced.

If $r$ is an irrational number then its precise numerical specification requires an infinite number of terms (inequalities). Because this is not possible, measurement utilizes not the irrational real numbers themselves, but rational approximations to them. Every real number can be approximated to any level of accuracy (at least in principle) by some rational number. That is, if $r$ is any real number and $e > 0$ the level of accuracy required, then there exists a rational number, $n/m$, such that $r + e/2 \geqslant n/m \geqslant r - e/2$. In measurement such rational approximation must be settled for: absolute accuracy is a myth.

This is a limitation forced on measurement simply because of its finite nature. The value of $e$ is determined by the limitations of our procedures. All measurement procedures have finite resolution: there is a level of accuracy beyond which they cannot take us. One of the ways that science advances however, is by improving the accuracy of its measurements through the development of new techniques.

Measurement requires the development of procedures whereby values $X$ and $Y$ may be brought into comparison and their ratio assessed. Such procedures are the methods of measurement. The development of such methods is called *quantification*. Logically prior to quantification, though in practice the two steps may be combined, is the process of showing that the variable involved is quantitative. Unless this step is completed any measurement methods proposed for a particular variable cannot be accepted. The claim that such procedures measure this variable remains speculative. This is because the measurement of any variable presupposes that it is a quantitative variable, and in the absence of confirming evidence this presupposition is at best speculation. This point is of particular importance when considering attempts at psychological measurement.

One does not need to show that all of conditions (1)—(13) are true. Confirmation of conditions (1)—(9) is sufficient. If a variable satisfies (1)—(9) but not (10)—(13) then ratios of its values may not constitute the full set of real numbers. However, ratios of its values will constitute a subset of the real numbers and hence its values will be measurable. Thus, the first step in attempts at psychological measurement is to test the hypothesis that the relevant variable (or variables) satisfy conditions (1)—(9).

It is surrounding this issue that much debate and confusion has developed within psychology over the past 50 years. It is not necessary to complete this step via the Campbellian process of fundamental measurement. To think so is to confuse the character of a quantity with the behavior of the objects manifesting its values. As will be shown in the next chapter, there is more than one way to confirm the existence of quantity.

This chapter has shown that to believe that a variable is quantitative is to believe that its values possess a definite kind of structure, that they are ordered and additive. Furthermore, it has been argued that if a quantitative variable is also both continuous and unbounded (either above or below) then ratios of its values constitute the system of real numbers. Hence, pairs of its values stand in numerical relations and this fact is what makes measurement possible and gives it its meaning. Therefore, the path to measurement must begin with the search for quantity.

# Chapter 4

# Searching For Quantity

To hypothesize that a particular variable is quantitative is one thing. To produce evidence supporting that hypothesis is another. The last chapter makes plain exactly what kind of structure one is hypothesizing when one takes a variable to be quantitative. The aim in this chapter is to examine some of the ways in which evidence corroborating that hypothesis may be obtained. Two very general ways are considered: extensive measurement and conjoint measurement.

Extensive measurement is the classical path to quantification. It was this path that led to the earliest known attempts at quantification. Roughly, it involves finding a way of combining objects that directly reflects the additive structure of the variable; for example, combining rods end to end in the same direction (for length), or combining marbles on a balance pan (for weight). So transparent is the evidence for quantity in this case that many have been tempted to identify this path to quantification with the desired end itself. This was Campbell's fallacy, though he was not the first nor the last to commit it. Attempts to apply the theory of extensive measurement to psychology have proved singularly unsuccessful.

Conjoint measurement involves a situation in which two variables ($A$ and $X$) are noninteractively related to a third ($P$). It is not required that any of the variables be already quantified, although it is necessary that the values of $P$ be orderable, and that values of $A$ and $X$ be independently identifiable (at least at a classificatory level). Then, via the order on $P$, ordinal and additive relations on $A$, $X$, and $P$ may be derived. This path to quantification was first described within the psychological literature by Luce and Tukey (1964) and since then has been applied to a number of psychological variables. However, these applications have been relatively sparse and their success modest. It appears that the majority of psychologists do not realize the significance of this development. It is the aim of this chapter to describe it in some detail and recommendations are made for a more rigorous application of conjoint measurement theory. Following this chapter, the remainder of the book is devoted to illustrating some uses of this theory within psychology.

## EXTENSIVE MEASUREMENT

Extensive measurement depends on the discovery of ordering and concatenation relations on the objects that directly reflect the quantitative structure of the variable involved. A simple example of extensive measurement has already been described in chapter 2 in connection with weight measurement using a beam balance. There, indeed, the five propositions describing the behavior of a set of objects directly mirror conditions (1)−(9) given in chapter 3.

In this case, placing two objects $a$ and $b$ together on the same balance pan constitutes addition of their weights. That is, if the weight of $a$ is $X$ and $b$ is $Y$ then the weight of the concatenated objects, $a \circ b$, is taken to be $X + Y$. Hence, the additive properties of the weight variable (conditions (4)−(9) of chapter 3) may be tested more or less directly. Conditions (7) and (9), because of their existential nature, may only be tested indirectly.

It is this approach to measurement that forms the basis of many of the measurement scales used in the physical sciences. As well as length and weight, it is applicable to the measurement of such variables as area, volume, duration (time), electrical resistance, plane angle, and many others. However, despite its importance in the physical sciences, it has proved to be of little use in psychology. One of the few attempts to apply it is that of Pollatsek and Tversky (1970) in their speculations surrounding the measurement of risk. In general, within psychology, the search for operations directly reflecting quantitative additivity has been in vain. Hence, no more will be said on this subject here. The reader is referred to Campbell (1920) and Ellis (1966) for more details on extensive measurement. Later in this chapter it is shown that extensive measurement is simply a special case of conjoint measurement.

## CONJOINT MEASUREMENT

Luce and Tukey (1964) proposed the theory of conjoint measurement specifically for quantification within the social sciences. As will be explained, it provides a way for the identification of quantitative structure other than via operations of concatenation (or physical addition). In fact it enables quantitative structure to be detected via ordinal relations upon a variable. Although psychology lacks concatenation operations, it possesses ordinal relations aplenty.

The theory is about the kind of situation where a quantitative variable, $P$, is a noninteractive function of two other variables, $A$ and $X$. For the moment "noninteractive" may be understood to mean "additive" or "multiplicative," although it is actually more general than this and a more accurate definition is given later. That is, conjoint measurement theory relates to situations of the kind $P = A + X$, or $P = A \times X$. Its application is specifically for those instances where none of $P$, $A$ or $X$ is already quantified. It requires that:

(i) variable $P$ possesses an infinite number of values;
(ii) $P=f(A,X)$ (where $f$ is some mathematical function);
(iii) there is a simple order, $\geqslant$, upon the values of $P$; and
(iv) values of $A$ and $X$ can be identified (i.e., that objects may be classified according to the value of $A$ and $X$ they possess).

Let us call a system satisfying (i)-(iv) *a conjoint system*. Then, if $\geqslant$ on $P$ satisfies *three special conditions* it follows that:

(v) $P$, $A$ and $X$ are quantitative; and
(vi) $f$ is a noninteractive function.

The three special conditions are:

(1) *Double Cancellation;*
(2) *Solvability; and*
(3) *the Archimedean condition;*

and these are described in detail below.

Before describing these conditions it may help to consider some examples of situations where (i)-(iv) are satisfied (or, believed to be so). Take a physical example, first. Let $P$ be mass, $A$, density, and $X$, volume. Values of $P$ may be ordered using, for example, a simple beam balance. Volumes, of course, could be classified by considering water displacement in some standard jar. And classifying objects according to the kind of material they are composed of classifies them according to density.

Or, to take a psychological example, suppose that $P$ is performance on some task (say, the time it takes to run a maze), $A$ is motivation and $X$ is amount of prior practice. Of course, it would be a simple matter to order the performances and classify subjects according to motivation (e.g., duration of food or water deprivation) and number of previous practice trials.

Such conjoint systems are easily contemplated visually if they are thought of as constituting a matrix where the rows are values of $A$, the columns, values of $X$, and the cells, values of $P$. Let $a, b, c, \ldots$ etc. be values of $A$, $x, y, z, \ldots$ etc. be values of $X$ and, since $P = f(A,X)$, the pairs, $ax, ay, \ldots, cy, cz, \ldots$ denote (possibly identical) values of $P$. Such a matrix is schematically represented

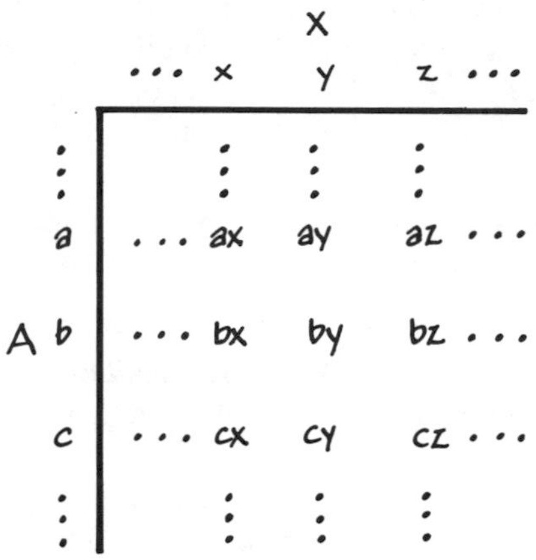

| | | X | | | | |
|---|---|---|---|---|---|---|
| | | ... | x | y | z | ... |
| | ⋮ | | ⋮ | ⋮ | ⋮ | |
| | a | ... | ax | ay | az | ... |
| A | b | ... | bx | by | bz | ... |
| | c | ... | cx | cy | cz | ... |
| | ⋮ | | ⋮ | ⋮ | ⋮ | |

FIG. 4.1 A schematic representation of a conjoint measurement matrix: . . . *a, b, c* . . . are values of variable *A*, . . . *x, y, z* . . . are values of variable *X* and . . . *ax, ay*, . . . , *cy, cz* . . . are values of variable *P* (*ax* being simply that value of *P* produced by the conjunction of *a* and*x*, etc.).

in Fig. 4.1. Such a visual representation helps in understanding the conditions (1)–(3).

## DOUBLE CANCELLATION

The condition of double cancellation states that if certain pairs of values of *P* are ordered by $\geqslant$ then other particular pairs of values will also be ordered. In this respect it is like the condition of transitivity that $\geqslant$ must satisfy (being a simple order). Indeed, in the context of conjoint measurement, the transitivity of $\geqslant$ on *P* is a special case of double cancellation.

As stated in most sources (cf. Krantz et al., 1971) double cancellation takes the following form. Let *a, b,* and *c* be any values of *A* and *x, y,* and *z* be any values of *X*, then $\geqslant$ on *P* satisfies *double cancellation* if and only if

$$\text{if } ay \geqslant bx$$

$$\text{and } bz \geqslant cy$$

$$\text{then } az \geqslant cx.$$

Thus stated the condition seems obscure, but some light is shed if double cancellation is seen as a consequence of that special case of a noninteractive relationship between *P, A,* and *X*,

$$P = A + X.$$

Given this relationship,

$$ay \geqslant bx \text{ if and only if } a + y \geqslant b + x$$

$$\text{and } bz \geqslant cy \text{ if and only if } b + z \geqslant c + y.$$

Summing the two right-hand inequalities gives

$$a + y + b + z \geqslant b + x + c + y$$

and because $b$ and $y$ are common to both sides of the inequality, they may be cancelled leaving

$$a + z \geqslant c + x$$

which, of course, is true if and only if

$$az \geqslant cx.$$

Hence, the connection between double cancellation and the relationship $P = A + X$ is easily seen. It is similarly connected to $P = f(A,X)$ (where $f$ is any non-interactive function).

Despite its simplicity double cancellation is a condition possessing considerable power. It tightly constrains the order on $P$. This may be illustrated in a $3 \times 3$ matrix. Let $a_1$, $a_2$, and $a_3$ be three values of $A$ and $x_1$, $x_2$, and $x_3$ be three values of $X$. The resulting conjoint matrix is that illustrated in Fig. 4.2.

Now because $a$, $b$, and $c$ in the double cancellation condition are *any* values of $A$, $a_1$, $a_2$, and $a_3$ may be substituted for them in any of 3! (=6) different possible ways. Similarly, $x_1$, $x_2$, and $x_3$ may be substituted for $x$, $y$, and $z$ in 6 different ways. This produces $6 \times 6$ (=36) different substitution instances of the double cancellation condition in the $3 \times 3$ matrix shown in Fig. 4.2 (or in any $3 \times 3$ conjoint matrix for that matter). These 36 different substitution instances are shown in Fig. 4.3.

They are not all logically independent of one another. In Fig. 4.3 they are in six different sets, each of six. Within each set the relevant order relations are between the same three values of P (or cells of the matrix). Arrows have been used to indicate these relations (i.e., $ax \geqslant by$ is represented by $ax \rightarrow by$, the

| | | X | | |
|---|---|---|---|---|
| | | $x_1$ | $x_2$ | $x_3$ |
| | $a_1$ | $a_1x_1$ | $a_1x_2$ | $a_1x_3$ |
| A | $a_2$ | $a_2x_1$ | $a_2x_2$ | $a_2x_3$ |
| | $a_3$ | $a_3x_1$ | $a_3x_2$ | $a_3x_3$ |

FIG. 4.2 A $3 \times 3$ conjoint matrix.

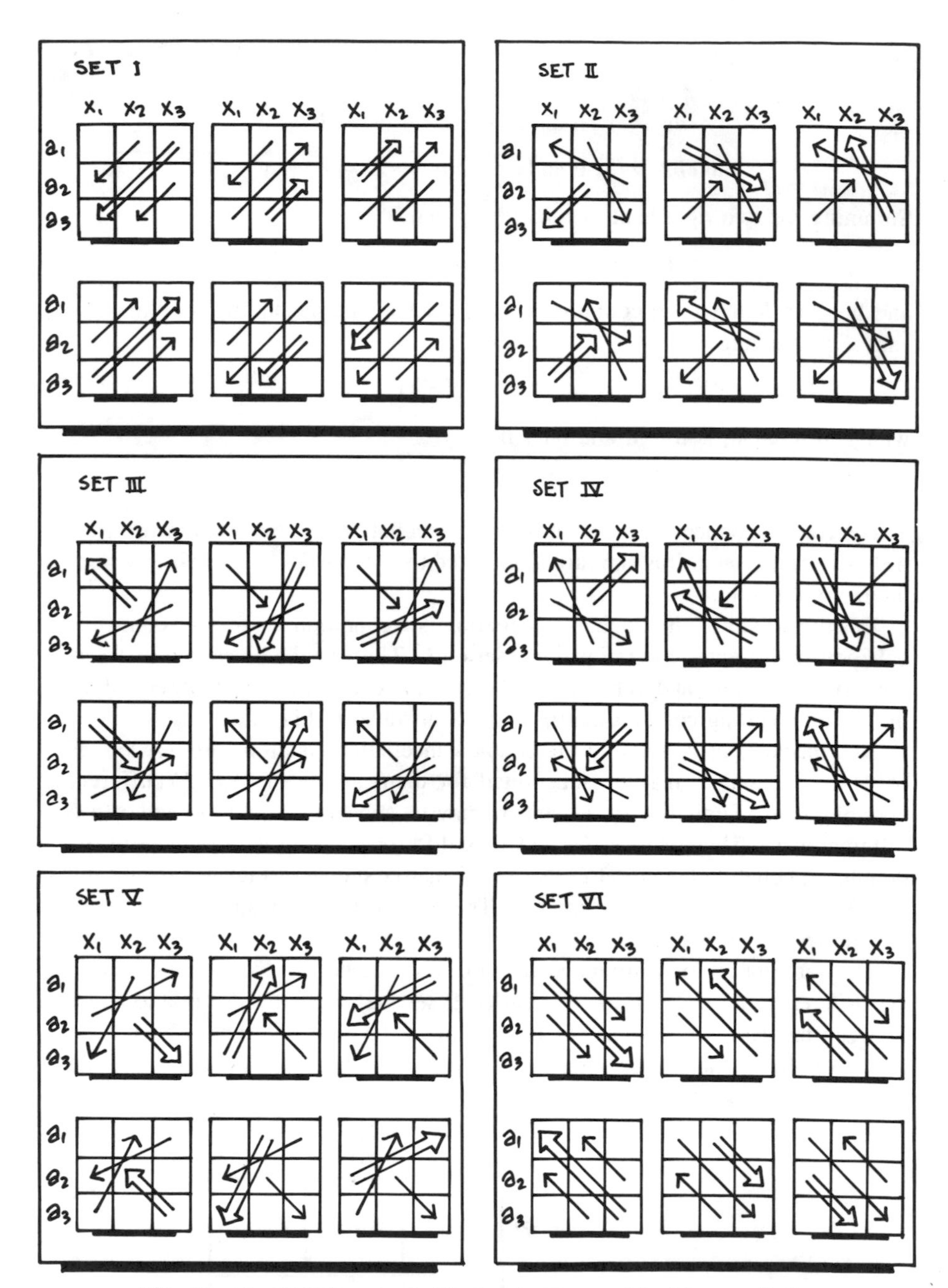


FIG. 4.3 The 36 different subsititution instances of double cancellation in a 3 × 3 matrix. Single line arrows between cells represent the antecedent order relations (⩾) and double line arrows the consequent order relations. Double cancellation means that if the orders indicated by the single line arrows hold then so must those indicated by the double line arrows.

single line arrows representing the antecedent orders, and the double line arrow the consequent order). Within each set of six, if one of the instances of double cancellation is true, all of them are. However, between sets the instances of double cancellation are logically independent of one another. Thus, within any $3 \times 3$ matrix there are six independent tests of the double cancellation condition, this condition being false if in any of the diagrams shown in Fig. 4.3, the antecedent order relations hold while the consequent one does not; otherwise it is satisfied. Obviously, satisfaction of double cancellation (in a conjoint matrix, even a $3 \times 3$ one) is no trivial matter.

As will be shown later, there is an even more general notion of double cancellation imposing even stronger constraints on the order within a conjoint matrix. However, double cancellation, as stated here is sufficient for the present purpose.

## SOLVABILITY

The solvability condition requires that the variables $A$ and $X$ be complex enough to produce any required value of $P$. It is formally stated as follows (cf. Krantz et al., 1971).

The order $\geqslant$ on $P$ satisfies *solvability* if and only if (i) for any $a$ and $b$ in $A$ and $x$ in $X$, a value of $X$ exists (call it $y$) such that $ax = by$ (i.e., both $ax \geqslant by$ and $by \geqslant ax$); and (ii) for any $x$ and $y$ in $X$ and $a$ in $A$, a value of $A$ exists (call it $b$) such that $ax = by$.

In other words, given any three of $a$, $b$, $x$, and $y$, the fourth exists so that the equation

$$ax = by$$

is solved. Hence, the name *solvability*.

Once again, the meaning of this condition can be grasped by considering the conjoint matrix. It is equivalent to the requirement that every value of variable $P$ occur in each row and each column of the matrix.

Thinking in terms of the relationship $P = A + X$, solvability implies that either values of $A$ and $X$ are equally spaced (as are the natural numbers) or else they are dense (as are the rational numbers).

## THE ARCHIMEDEAN CONDITION

Remember that the Archimedean condition, as stated in chapter 3, ensures that no value of a quantitative variable is infinitely larger than any other value. Its meaning here is essentially the same, although in this context its expression is slightly more complex. Thinking in terms of $P = A + X$ again, a general idea of its content may be stated as follows. Conjoint measurement enables quantification of *differences* between values of $A$, between values of $X$ and between values of

$P$. Limiting attention to $A$, the Archimedean condition means that no difference between any two values of $A$ is infinitely larger than the difference between any other two values of $A$.

In order to introduce the concept of a difference between values of $A$ and between values of $X$, attention must be drawn to the fact that if the simple order, $\geqslant$, on $P$ satisfies both double cancellation and solvability, then it entails an ordering on $A$ and $X$. Let $a$ and $b$ be any values of $A$, and $x$ be any value of $X$ such that $ax \geqslant bx$ (this is illustrated in Fig. 4.4). Let $z$ be any other value of $X$. Now, if $\geqslant$ satisfies solvability then there exists a value, $c$, of $A$ such that $bz = cx$.

Also, if $\geqslant$ satisfies double cancellation then both

$$\begin{aligned} ax &\geqslant bx \\ \text{and } bz &= cx \\ \text{entail that } az &\geqslant cx. \end{aligned}$$

(This is an instance of double cancellation that differs from the statement given earlier only in that $y{=}x$). Because $\geqslant$ on $P$ is transitive (this is part of its being a simple order), it follows from the fact that,

$$\begin{aligned} az &\geqslant cx \\ \text{and } cx &= bz \\ \text{that } az &\geqslant bz. \end{aligned}$$

What has been proved here is that for any $a$ and $b$ in $A$, and $x$ in $X$, if $ax \geqslant bx$ then for any $z$ in $X$ $az \geqslant bz$.

This means that the order between $ax$ and $bx$ is the same as that between $ay$ and $by$, and that between $az$ and $bz$, and so on. That is, the order between an $a$-cell and a $b$-cell in the same column of the conjoint matrix, is the same for all columns. In other words it is *independent* of which column we are to inspect (see

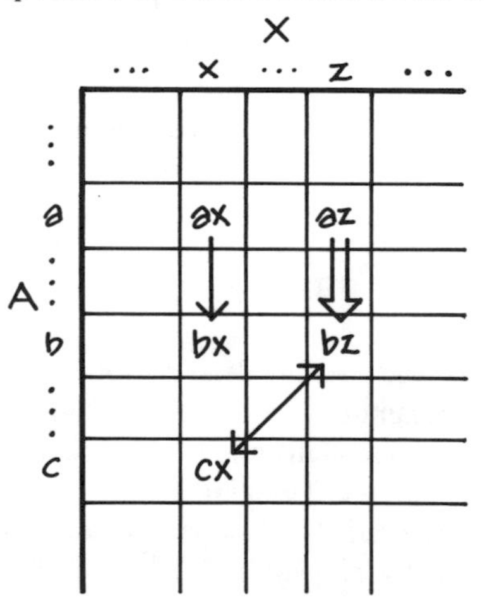


FIG. 4.4 Given that $\geqslant$ on $P$ satisfies transitivity, double cancellation and solvability it follows that it also satisfies independence.

Fig. 4.5). In this sense then, any values, $a$ and $b$, of $A$ are ordered: $a \geqslant b$ if and only if for any (or all) $x$ in $X$, $ax \geqslant bx$.

A similar chain of reasoning applies to any pair of values, $x$ and $y$, of $X$: $x \geqslant y$ if and only if for any (or all) $a$ in $A$, $ax \geqslant ay$.

This property of the order $\geqslant$ on $P$ is called *independence* (cf. Krantz et al., 1971) and its importance is that not only does $\geqslant$ order values of $P$, it may be used to infer an order on the values of $A$ and the values of $X$.

Given the fact that if a simple order on $P$ satisfies double cancellation and solvability, then it also satisfies independence and that, therefore, the order of values of $A$ and $X$ is determined, the concept of the *difference* between values of $A$ and between values of $X$ may be explained. Let $a$ and $b$ be any two values of $A$ such that $a > b$ (i.e., $a \geqslant b$ and not $b \geqslant a$), and let $x$ and $y$ be any two values of $X$ such that $x > y$.

Then, of course, given that $\geqslant$ on $P$ satisfies independence and transitivity it follows that

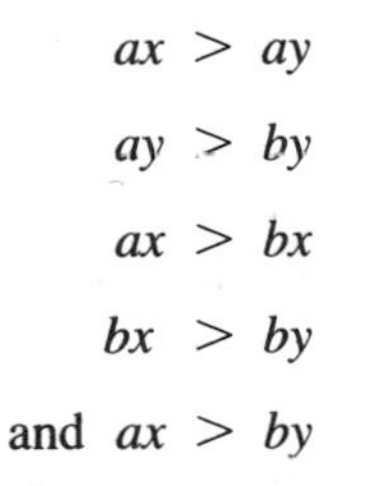

$$ax > ay$$

$$ay > by$$

$$ax > bx$$

$$bx > by$$

$$\text{and } ax > by$$

(see Fig. 4.6) However, what about the order between $ay$ and $bx$? It is not determined by independence, so it may be true that either $ay \geqslant bx$ or $bx > ay$.

Suppose that $bx > ay$. Each of $bx$ and $ay$ differ from $ax$ on only a single component (i.e., on just $A$ or $X$). Thinking in terms of the relationship $P = A + X$ this is clearly seen. That is, if

$$bx = b + x,$$

$$ay = a + y,$$

$$\text{and } ax = a + x,$$

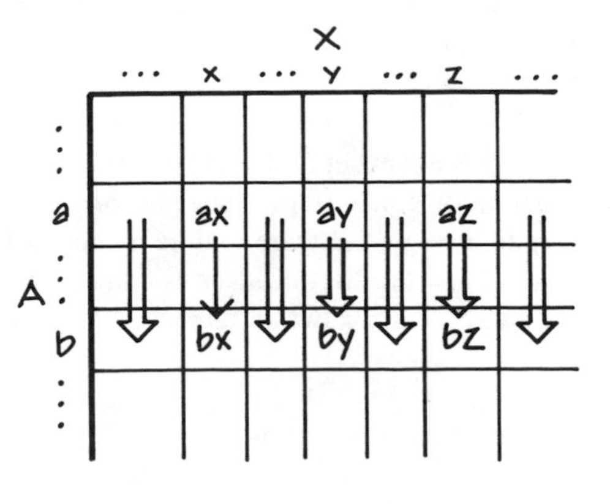


FIG. 4.5 The independence of $\geqslant$ on $A$ from $X$ means that for any $a$, $b$ in $A$ and $x$ in $X$, if $ax \geqslant bx$ then for every other value of $X$, $y$, $z$, $\ldots$, $ay \geqslant by$, $az \geqslant bz$, $\ldots$

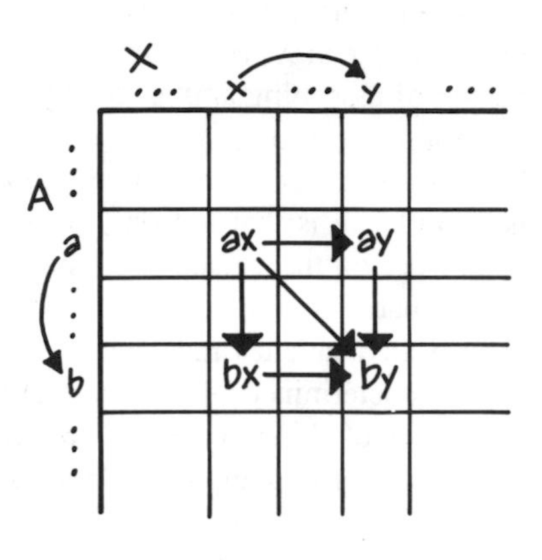


FIG. 4.6 Given independence and transitivity, if $a > b$ and $x > y$ then $ax > ay$, $ax > bx$, $ay > by$, $bx > by$ and $ax > by$.

then the difference between $ax$ and $bx$ is simply $(a + x) - (b + x) = a - b$ and the difference between $ax$ and $ay$ is simply $(a + x) - (a + y) = x - y$.

Now, if $bx > ay$ then the difference between $ax$ and $ay$ must exceed the difference between $ax$ and $bx$ (because $ax > bx > ay$). That is, $x - y > a - b$.

At first sight this claim may seem to be nonsense, for $x - y$ is a difference between values of $X$, $a - b$ is a difference between values of $A$, and different quantitative variables are not commensurate. It is akin to claiming that a weight difference exceeds a length difference. However, just as the ordering of values of $A$ and $X$ is dependent upon the order on $P$, so is the ordering of differences within $A$ and $X$. That is, these orders are relative to their effects on $P$. The claim that $x - y > a - b$ means nothing more in this context other than that the effect on $P$ of moving from $x$ to $y$ in $X$, exceeds the effect on $P$ of moving from $a$ to $b$ in $A$. In conjoint measurement the variables $A$ and $X$ are quantified relative to their effects on $P$.

Considering any interval on, say, variable $A$, such as $a - b$, the solvability condition ensures that, relative to any value, $x$, of $X$, there exists another value of $X$, $z$, such that $a - b = x - z$. That is, $bx = az$.

Thus, relative to $a - b$ of $A$ there will exist a series $x_1, x_2, \ldots, x_n$ of values of $X$ such that

$$a - b = x_1 - x_2 = x_2 - x_3 = \ldots = x_{n-1} - x_n.$$

Such a series Krantz et al. (1971) refer to as a *standard sequence* and it is simply a sequence of equal steps along the ordered values of variable $X$. Similarly, relative to $x - y$ of $X$ there will be a standard sequence of values of $A$: $a_1, a_2, \ldots, a_m$. Now the Archimedean condition can be stated with some precision. If $a - b$ and $c - d$ are two differences between values of $A$ such that

$$a - b < c - d$$

then there exists a natural number $n$ such that

$$n(a - b) \geqslant c - d$$

(where $n(a - b)$ is the standard sequence $a_1, a_2, \ldots, a_{n+1}$, where $a = a_1$, and $b = a_2$). Similarly, any difference between values of $X$, no matter how large, cannot be so great relative to any difference between other values of $X$, that some finite standard sequence based on the smaller difference does not exceed it. No difference within $A$ or $X$ is infinitely larger than any other difference within $A$ or $X$.

## CONJOINT NONINTERACTIVE QUANTITATIVE STRUCTURES

If the variables, $A$, $X$, and $P$ form a conjoint system in which the simple order, $\geqslant$, on $P$ satisfies (1) double cancellation, (2) solvability, and (3) the Archimedean condition, then $A$, $X$, and $P$ are quantitative variables and $P$ is a noninteractive function of $A$ and $X$.

A proof of this claim is given by Krantz et al. (1971). Essentially, the proof involves showing that certain pairs of values of $A$ and $X$ (what might be called "differences" between their values) stand in the ordinal and additive relations necessary for quantity. Likewise, the same may be shown for pairs of values of $P$. Then it is shown that $P$ is a noninteractive function of $A$ and $X$.

This concept of a noninteractive function requires some explanation. The function $f$ such that $P = f(A,X)$ is noninteractive if and only if there exist monotonic functions $f_1$, $f_2$ and $f_3$ such that

$$\begin{aligned} f_1(P) &= f_1(f(A,X)) \\ &= f_2(A) + f_3(X). \end{aligned}$$

That is, $f$ is noninteractive if and only if under some monotonic transformation it reduces to an additive function of $A$ and $X$ (or monotone transformations of them). For example, if

$$\begin{aligned} P &= f(A,X) = A \times X \\ \text{then } \log P &= \log(A \times X) \\ &= \log A + \log X \end{aligned}$$

and because the logarithmic transformation is monotonic, the function $f$ is noninteractive. Of course, the functions

$$P = A + X \text{ and}$$

$$P = A \times X$$

are the simplest of noninteractive functions, and the entire class of such functions is infinitely large. Unless there are special reasons for not doing so, the noninteractive relationship between $P$, $A$, and $X$ may always be expressed in the simple additive or multiplicative forms. Whichever is chosen is merely a matter of convenience.

This may appear to be a strange recommendation. Surely the question of how the variables $A$ and $X$ relate to $P$ is a *factual* matter rather than one of convenience? It is, of course, a factual matter, but the same variable may manifest quite different additive relations. This point is seen more clearly if a variable is distinguished from the quantitative variable of which it is a part. A variable, as already noted, is a class of mutually exclusive properties or relations. A quantitative variable is a variable together with ordinal and additive relations satisfying conditions (1)-(9) for quantity. Then a variable, $V$, might form part of two quite different quantitative variables, $Q+ = (V, \geqslant, +)$ and $Q^* = (V, \geqslant, *)$ (where + and * are distinct ternary relations on $V$ satisfying conditions (4)-(9) for quantity). Indeed, if a variable forms part of *one* quantitative variable, then it forms part of infinitely many.

For example, let $Q+ = (V, \geqslant, +)$ be a continuous quantitative variable and let $U$ be any value of $V$. Then there will exist the relation * such that for any $X$, $Y$, and $Z$ in $V$

$$X*Y = Z \text{ if and only if } (X/U + 1).\,(Y/U + 1) = (Z/U + 1).$$

It can easily be shown that $Q^* = (V, \geqslant, *)$ is also a quantitative variable. Of course, * is not the only other ternary relation on $V$ satisfying conditions (4)-(9) for quantity.

Thus, if $P$, $A$, and $X$ satisfy the conditions for conjoint measurement then $P$ is a noninteractive function of $A$ and $X$, but which noninteractive function is chosen from the infinitely many present is a matter of convenience. It depends on what additive relations within $A$, $X$, and $P$ are identified. It is usually most convenient to choose them such that $P = A + X$, but this is not always the case.

For example, let $P$ be mass, $A$ density, and $X$ volume. In this case the conjoint system satisfies double density cancellation, solvability, and the Archimedean condition and there is a weak order on $P$. Because it is already accepted within physics that mass = density × volume, that would be the most appropriate way to express the relationship between these variables. However, it could be expressed as mass* = density* + volume*, in which case mass and mass*, for example, are the same variable but involve quite different additive relations between values of the variable (i.e., they are different quantitative variables).

## QUANTIFICATION BY CONJOINT MEASUREMENT

Quantification by conjoint measurement involves the development of procedures for testing the hypothesis that a given conjoint system is a noninteractive, quantitative structure. Although it may be difficult to test double cancellation, especially in large matrices (remember that there are six independent tests of double cancellation in each 3×3 matrix and the number of 3×3 matrices in even a small conjoint matrix is large; e.g., in a 5×5 matrix there are 100 different 3×3 matrices) this condition is *directly* testable. This is not the case with solvability and the Archimedean condition.

Consider solvability. Suppose that relative to some $a$ and $b$ in $A$ and $x$ in $X$ no $y$ can be found such that $ay = bx$. This does not mean that there is none, for limitations of time and technology may make it difficult to locate some values of a variable. Thus solvability is not directly falsifiable.

Similarly, for a given difference $x - y$ the standard sequence $a_1, a_2, \ldots, a_i$ may not be able to be shown to be finite. However this again could be due to limitations of time and technology, so the Archimedean condition as well is not directly testable.

This does not mean that these conditions are untestable or "unempirical." They may be tested indirectly, as will be shown. Scott (1964) has shown that any finite subsystem of a noninteractive conjoint structure must satisfy a finite set of generalized cancellation conditions. These, like double cancellation, are directly testable (at least in principle). So if they prove true for any finite set of data (i.e., for any finite conjoint measurement matrix) then this must be indirect evidence that solvability and the Archimedean condition are true. The meaning of this claim will become apparent once the concept of generalized cancellation conditions is explained.

Thus far the concept of double cancellation has been explained. In an earlier section a condition called *independence* was introduced. It may be regarded as *single cancellation*. As well as single cancellation and double cancellation there is triple cancellation. A version of this conditions states that if $a$, $b$, $c$, and $d$ are any values of $A$ and $w$, $x$, $y$, and $z$ are any values of $X$ then $\geqslant$ on $P$ satisfies *triple cancellation* only if

$$\begin{aligned} az &\geqslant by \\ \text{and } cy &\geqslant dz \\ \text{and } dw &\geqslant cx \\ \text{then } aw &\geqslant bx. \end{aligned}$$

An instance of this condition is illustrated in Fig. 4.7.

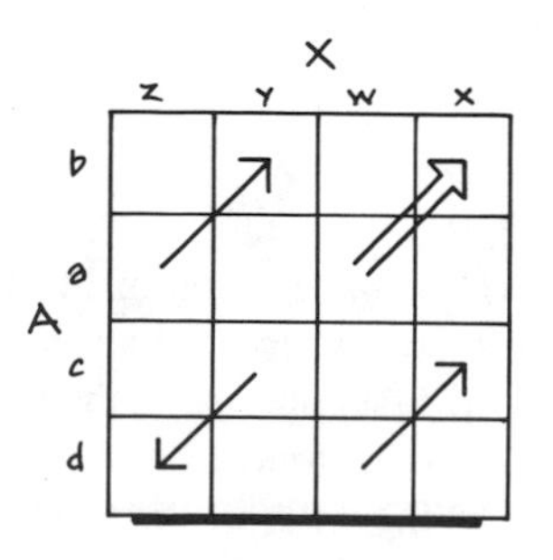


FIG. 4.7 An instance of triple cancellation.

Beyond triple cancellation there is quadruple, or fourth-order, cancellation, and so on. Generally, there is $n$th–order cancellation for any value of $n$. If these cancellation conditions are to be tested then there must be a general statement of $n$th–order cancellation. Such a condition is complex and not easily stated.

Let $a_1, a_2, \ldots, a_i, \ldots, a_{n+l}$ be any $(n+1)$ termed sequence of values of $A$ and $x_1, x_2, \ldots, x_i, \ldots, x_{n+l}$ be any $(n+1)$ termed sequence of values of $X$. A degenerate instance (i.e., a trivially true instance) of $n$th–order cancellation may be expressed as follows:

$$
\begin{array}{llll}
\text{if} & 1. & a_1x_1 \geq a_2x_2 & \text{and} \\
 & \cdot & & \\
 & \cdot & & \\
 & \cdot & & \\
 & i. & a_{i+1}x_{i+1} \geq a_{i+1}x_{i+1} & \text{and} \quad (i = 2, \ldots, n-1) \\
 & \cdot & & \\
 & \cdot & & \\
 & \cdot & & \\
 & n. & a_{n+1}x_{n+1} \geq a_{n+1}x_{n+1} & \text{then} \\
 & & a_1x_1 \geq a_2x_2. &
\end{array}
$$

This condition is trivially true because its logical form is if $p$ and $q_1$ and . . . and $q_n$ then $p$ (which is a tautology) and, incidentally, each of $q_1, \ldots, q_n$ is also a tautology. However, it may be used to provide the basis for a quite general statement of $n$th–order cancellation. The terms within the antecedent of the degenerate condition may be set out in an $n \times 4$ matrix as follows:

$$
\text{Matrix 1} = \begin{bmatrix}
a_1 & x_1 & a_2 & x_2 \\
\cdot & \cdot & \cdot & \cdot \\
\cdot & \cdot & \cdot & \cdot \\
\cdot & \cdot & \cdot & \cdot \\
a_{i+1} & x_{i+1} & a_{i+1} & x_{i+1} \\
\cdot & \cdot & \cdot & \cdot \\
\cdot & \cdot & \cdot & \cdot \\
\cdot & \cdot & \cdot & \cdot \\
a_{n+1} & x_{n+1} & a_{n+1} & x_{n+1}
\end{bmatrix}
$$

If the terms within *any* column of Matrix 1 are permuted then, taking the terms within each row as the terms of an inequality of the form $a_Ix_{II} \geqslant a_{III}x_{IV}$ (where $a_I$ is the term in the first column, $x_{II}$ the term in the second, $a_{III}$ the term in the third and $x_{IV}$ the term in the fourth), a different set of $n$ inequalities will be generated. For example, let the order of the terms in column four of Matrix 1 be reversed. Then Matrix 1 becomes:

$$\text{Matrix 2} = \begin{bmatrix} a_1 & x_1 & a_2 & x_{n+1} \\ \cdot & \cdot & \cdot & \cdot \\ \cdot & \cdot & \cdot & \cdot \\ \cdot & \cdot & \cdot & \cdot \\ a_{i+1} & x_{i+1} & a_{i+1} & x_{n-i+2} \\ \cdot & \cdot & \cdot & \cdot \\ \cdot & \cdot & \cdot & \cdot \\ \cdot & \cdot & \cdot & \cdot \\ a_{n+1} & x_{n+1} & a_{n+1} & x_2 \end{bmatrix}$$

The corresponding set of $n$ inequalities is then,

1. $a_1x_1 \geq a_2x_{n-1}$

$\cdot$
$\cdot$
$\cdot$

$i$. $a_{i+1}x_{i+1} \geq a_{i+1}x_{n-i+2}$ $\quad (i = 2, \ldots, n-1)$

$\cdot$
$\cdot$
$\cdot$

$n$. $a_{n+1}x_{n+1} \geq a_{n+1}x_2$

If $\geqslant$ on $P$ is a noninteractive quantitative, conjoint structure then if each of these $n$ inequalities is true it follows that $a_1x_1 \geqslant a_2x_2$. This argument is nontrivial, for the conclusion is not identical to any of the premises. Similarly, any other permutation of the terms in the columns of Matrix 1 produces a new matrix and, hence, a new set of $n$ inequalities. Each of these sets of $n$ inequalities in turn also implies (given that $\geqslant$ on $P$ is a noninteractive, quantitative, conjoint structure) $a_1x_1 \geqslant a_2x_2$ and providing the intra-column permutations are not all identical, the argument so produced is nontrivial.

It is easy to see that in each case $a_1x_1 \geqslant a_2x_2$ must follow. As noted above, if $\geqslant$ on $P$ is a noninteractive conjoint structure then $P = A + X$. That is, each value of $P$, $ax$, may be expressed as the sum of its row and column factors, that is, as $a + x$. Thus, if $ax \geqslant by$, then $a + x \geqslant b + y$.

Hence, the basic, degenerate $n$th–order cancellation condition may be expressed as,

if 1. $a_1 + x_1 \geq a_2 + x_2$ and

$\cdot$
$\cdot$
$\cdot$

$i$. $a_{i+1} + x_{i+1} \geq a_{i+1} + x_{i+1}$ and

$\cdot$
$\cdot$
$\cdot$

$n$. $a_{n+1} + x_{n+1} \geq a_{n+1} + x_{n+1}$ then

$$a_1 + x_1 \geq a_2 + x_2.$$

Now, as is well known, if

$$p \geqslant q \text{ and}$$
$$r \geqslant s \text{ then}$$
$$p + r \geqslant q + s.$$

Thus, the $n$ antecedent inequalities may be summed, giving

$$a_1 + x_1 + \ldots + a_{i+1} + x_{i+1} + \ldots + a_{n+1} + x_{n+1} \geqslant$$
$$a_2 + x_2 + \ldots + a_{i+1} + x_{i+1} + \ldots + a_{n+1} + x_{n+1}$$

(call this the summed inequality) and if terms common to both sides are cancelled the result is $a_1 + x_1 \geqslant a_2 + x_2$.

When a new set of $n$ inequalities is generated by permuting terms within the columns of Matrix 1 all that is altered is the inequality a given term occurs within. The terms appearing on the left-hand side and the right-hand side of the summed inequality must remain constant. Hence, the same terms will always cancel, leaving

$$a_1 + x_1 \geqslant a_2 + x_2$$
$$\text{i.e., } a_1x_1 \geqslant a_2x_2.$$

So corresponding to each distinct permutation of terms within the columns of Matrix 1 is an $n$th–order cancellation condition, that must be true if $\geqslant$ on $P$ is a noninteractive quantitative conjoint structure. The full set of different $n$th–order cancellation conditions may be generated by permuting just the terms within columns 2, 3, and 4 of Matrix 1. Because the number of permutations within each column is $n!$, there will be $(n!)^3$ $n$th–order cancellation conditions for each different set of values $a_1, a_2, \ldots, a_{n+1}$ and $x_1, x_2, \ldots, x_{n+1}$ of $A$ and $X$, that must all be true within any finite conjoint measurement matrix.

Within this set of cancellation conditions each lower order cancellation condition is subsumed within $n$th–order cancellation. That is, independence (or, single cancellation) is a special case of double cancellation, double cancellation of triple cancellation, and so on. In the case of double cancellation the degenerate schema is,

$$\text{if } a_1x_1 \geqslant a_2x_2 \text{ and}$$
$$a_3x_3 \geqslant a_3x_3 \text{ then}$$
$$a_1x_1 \geqslant a_2x_2.$$

For each different set of values $a_1, a_2, a_3$ of $A$ and $x_1, x_2, x_3$ of $X$ this gives rise to $(2!)^3 = 8$ distinct double cancellation conditions. One of these is the condition stated in the section on "Double Cancellation." This is obtained by permuting only the terms in columns two and three, that is,

$$\text{if } a_1x_3 \geqslant a_3x_2 \text{ and}$$
$$a_3x_1 \geqslant a_2x_3 \text{ then}$$
$$a_1x_1 \geqslant a_2x_2.$$

Another special case of double cancellation is obtained by permuting just the terms in columns three and four. This gives

$$\text{if } a_1x_1 \geqslant a_3x_3 \text{ and}$$
$$a_3x_3 \geqslant a_2x_2 \text{ then}$$
$$a_1x_1 \geqslant a_2x_2,$$

the transitivity of $\geqslant$ on $P$.

Still another version of double cancellation is obtained by permuting only the terms in columns two and four, that is,

$$\text{if } a_1x_3 \geqslant a_2x_3 \text{ and}$$
$$a_3x_1 \geqslant a_3x_2 \text{ then}$$
$$a_1x_1 \geqslant a_2x_2.$$

If $x_1 = x_2$ then this becomes,

$$\text{if } a_1x_3 \geqslant a_2x_3 \text{ and}$$
$$a_3x_1 \geqslant a_3x_1 \text{ then}$$
$$a_1x_1 \geqslant a_2x_1$$

(note that only $a_3$ and $x_3$ are cancelled). This, of course, is logically equivalent to,

$$\text{if } a_1x_3 \geqslant a_2x_3 \text{ then}$$
$$a_1x_1 \geqslant a_2x_1$$

(for the second premise ("$a_3x_1 \geqslant a_3x_1$") is a tautology and, so, may be dropped) that is, independence, or single cancellation. Similarly, double cancellation is a special case of triple cancellation and so on.

In general, when $A$ and/or $X$ are infinite there are infinitely many different cancellation conditions. In practice, however, an application of the theory of conjoint measurement requires operating on finite subsets of values of $A$ and $X$. The prediction is, if $\geqslant$ on $P$ is a noninteractive conjoint structure then all $n$th–order cancellation conditions will be true. This prediction follows from the fact that the simple order, $\geqslant$, on $P$ satisfies double cancellation, solvability and the Archimedean condition. Although the fact that $\geqslant$ is a simple order and satisfies double cancellation is equivalent to certain cancellation conditions, it alone does not entail *all* $n$th–order cancellation conditions. Solvability and the Archimedean condition are premises necessary for that conclusion. Hence, satisfaction of *all*

$n$th–order cancellation conditions in some finite conjoint measurement data matrix provides indirect support for the truth of these two conditions. Thus, they are testable.

The most compelling evidence for $\geqslant$ on $P$ being a noninteractive, conjoint structure is obtained through the construction of standard sequences on both $A$ and $X$. If an $n \times n$ matrix of values of $P$ is constructed where $a_1, a_2, \ldots, a_n$ and $x_1, x_2, \ldots, x_n$ form standard sequences then it is a finite model of a noninteractive conjoint structure. Within that finite model double cancellation, solvability and the Archimedean condition are all obviously true and hence $A$, $X$, and $P$ are readily seen to be quantitative. Furthermore, within such a structure the numerical relationships between values of A and between values of $X$ are transparently obvious. One can see that, for example,

$$a_2 - a_1 = a_3 - a_2 = \ldots = a_n - a_{n-1}$$

and that

$$a_3 - a_1 = 2(a_2 - a_1), \text{ and}$$

$$a_4 - a_1 = 3(a_2 - a_1), \text{ and}$$

$$a_n - a_1 = (n - 1)(a_2 - a_1).$$

Hence, it provides a clear basis for the measurement of $A$, $X$, and $P$. Without such a structure, $A$, $X$, and $P$ cannot be measured with any accuracy. One is reduced to working with methods for solving sets of linear inequalities (e.g., the simplex algorithm) and these are necessarily less precise.

The construction of standard sequences on $A$ and $X$ is no trivial matter. It requires a degree of technological control over $A$ and $X$ that is often difficult to achieve in psychology. This will become evident in later chapters and it suggests that a major obstacle to psychological measurement is the technical control necessary in determining the values of variables.

## THE GENERALITY OF CONJOINT MEASUREMENT

Conjoint measurement is a quite general approach to measurement. As will be indicated in the final chapter, it may be extended forwards beyond the three variable case (i.e., $P = f(A,X)$) to four or more variable cases (i.e., $P = f(A_1, \ldots, A_n)$). In this section it will be shown how conjoint measurement may be extended backwards to cases involving one variable. As such it subsumes extensive measurement.

Extensive measurement is a special case of conjoint measurement. Let $Q$ be the variable involved in extensive measurement. Then, within the conjoint measurement framework, $A = Q$, $X = Q$, and $P = Q + Q$ $(=Q)$. That is, the values of $A$ and $X$ are the values of the variable $Q$ itself and $P$ are these values as combined under the physical operation of addition (see Fig. 4.8). If the simple order on $Q + Q$ satisfies double cancellation, solvability and the Archimedean condition then $Q$ is quantitative (i.e., satisfies conditions (1)-(9) for quantity). This means that satisfaction of the hierarchy of cancellation conditions within a finite substructure of $Q + Q$ supports the hypothesis that $Q$ is quantitative. That is, in particular, it supports conditions (7) and (9), neither of which is directly testable.

However, the application of the theory of conjoint measurement to a single variable under some operation of physical addition is actually a more general notion than extensive measurement. There are variables that are not extensive in the ordinary sense and yet satisfy the conjoint measurement conditions given an appropriate concatenation procedure. One such is *velocity*.

Suppose that the velocity of object $a$ relative to object $b$ is $x$ meters per second, and that the velocity of object $b$ relative to $d$ is $y$ meters per second. What is the velocity of $a$ relative to $d$? According to Newtonian theory it is $x + y$ meters per second. Thus, within Newtonian theory velocity is extensively measurable. However, according to relativity theory the velocity of $d$ relative to $a$ is $(x + y)/(1 + xyc^{-2})$, where $c$ is the velocity of light. So concatenating velocities in this way does not enable extensive measurement of velocity, for the velocity of a concatenation is not the sum of the concatenated velocities.

However, $(x + y)/(1 + xyc^{-2})$ (or $(x + y)/(1 + xy)$ if the unit of velocity is the speed of light) is a noninteractive function of $x$ and $y$. That is, there exists a monotonic function, $f$, such that

$$f((x + y)/(1 + xy)) = f(x) + f(y).$$

Indeed, $f(x)=\tanh^{-1}(x)=1/2\log_e((1+x)/(1-x))$ cf. Krantz et al. (1971). So, in fact, conjoint measurement reveals the additive structure of velocity even though velocity as ordinarily conceived of is not extensively measurable.

| | | ... | x | ... | Q y | ... | z | ... |
|---|---|---|---|---|---|---|---|---|
| | ⋮ | | ⋮ | | ⋮ | | ⋮ | |
| | x | ... | x+x | ... | x+y | ... | x+z | ... |
| | ⋮ | | ⋮ | | ⋮ | | ⋮ | |
| Q | y | ... | y+x | ... | y+y | ... | y+z | ... |
| | ⋮ | | ⋮ | | ⋮ | | ⋮ | |
| | z | ... | z+x | ... | z+y | ... | z+z | ... |
| | ⋮ | | ⋮ | | ⋮ | | ⋮ | |

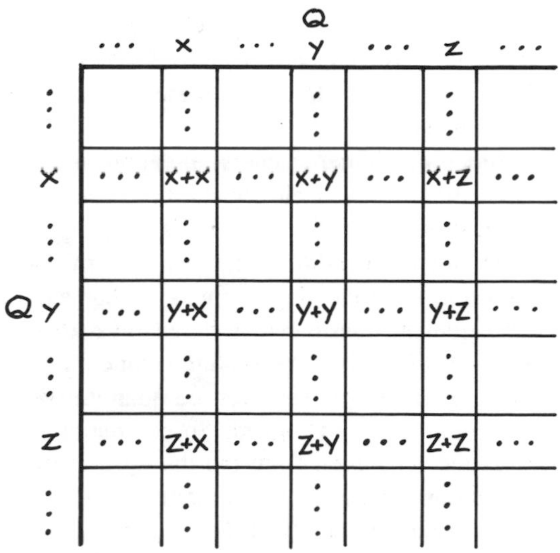

FIG. 4.8 Extensive measurement is a special case of conjoint measurement: variable $Q$ defines the row and column components and their sums (also variable $Q$) form the cell entries.

This kind of generalization of conjoint measurement to a single variable is of special interest to psychology. Although psychologists have not been able to locate suitable concatenation operations on which to base an application of the theory of conjoint measurement, they have been able to locate what they believe are *difference relations* within a single variable. That is, although structures of the kind $Q = Q + Q$ have not been found, it is believed that structures of the kind $Q = Q - Q$ have. Because difference is simply a special case of addition (i.e., since $Q - Q = Q + (-Q)$), it obviously follows that the theory of conjoint measurement can be applied to such structures to test the hypothesis that $Q$ is a quantitative variable. This observation forms the basis for some of the applications of this theory in later chapters of this book.

## CONCLUSION

Quantification in science is inseparable from the experimental method. The hypothesis that a particular variable is quantitative is a substantive hypothesis. It requires that the values of that variable manifest a definite kind of structure. With the possible exception of some quantitative variables open to extensive measurement, evidence for or against the quantitative hypothesis must be gained by experiment. The gathering of such evidence requires a high degree of experimental control and, often, sophisticated apparatus and methods of observation. It is no accident that the extension of quantification in physics from geometry and statics to dynamics, thermodynamics, and electrical phenomena went hand in hand with advances in experimental technique and apparatus. Psychological measurement, if it is to be, requires the same kind of advances.

In this chapter some of the paths to quantification have been considered. In particular, the method of conjoint measurement has been considered in some detail. Its application in psychology requires control over the values of the variables involved and methods for determining order. As will be shown in the following chapter, even these modest requirements present difficulties for psychology.

In the next three chapters, the application of conjoint measurement theory to some attempts at psychological measurement are considered. The logic of these applications is as follows. In this chapter, it has been shown that all variables satisfying the conditions for conjoint measurement are quantitative. What is shown in the following chapters is that each of the attempts at psychological measurement considered is based on a theory that predicts that the variables involved will satisfy the conditions for conjoint measurement. If those predictions are true then those variables are quantitative. This conclusion follows with the iron logic of the syllogism. So our major interest is in showing how, in each case, the prediction from the theory that the variables involved do satisfy the conditions for conjoint measurement, may be tested observationally. Also, in each case a small body of data will be considered in order to illustrate just how such a test may be carried through. The aim is not so much to use this data to accept or reject the quantitative hypothesis. Such a decision remains a long way off. The aim is to acquaint the student with a way of proceeding when faced with the claim that this or that psychological variable is measurable.

# Part II

# Applications

*The logic of application is simply the logic of syllogism.*
*—John Anderson*

# Chapter 5

# Thurstone's Theory of Comparative Judgment

Thurstone's theory of comparative judgment is the first to which the theory of conjoint measurement will be applied. This is fitting, if only because Thurstone's theory is now something of a classic within psychology. Few theories endure within psychology, but interest in Thurstone's theory has been fairly high since it was first proposed in a set of papers published in 1927 (see Thurstone, 1927 a, b, c, and d). Its aim was to explain pair comparison judgments in psychophysics and Luce (1977) has given a recent review of its success in that area. However, Thurstone was keen to apply the theory to the measurement of attitudes and this quickly became the major area of its application. A considerable number of attitude "measurement scales" were consequently constructed (see Shaw & Wright, 1967, for a collection). However, very little foundational research was done into its suitability in this area. Fortunately, the theory of conjoint measurement provides a means of remedying that deficiency.

As already mentioned, the aim of the theory is to explain pair comparison judgments. It may be as well then to begin this chapter with some brief comments about the method of pair comparisons and its significance for psychological measurement.

## THE METHOD OF PAIR COMPARISONS

According to the method of pair comparisons stimuli are ordered pair by pair. Within each pair of stimuli the subjects are instructed to judge which is the greater in some prescribed sense. For example, the stimuli may be lights of different brightnesses and the subjects may be instructed to judge which is the brighter within each pair. Or, the stimuli may be political candidates and the subjects may be asked to judge for each pair which candidate they prefer the most. If there are $n$ stimuli then the complete set of pairs numbers $n \times n = n^2$. This, of course, includes those pairs made up of each stimulus paired with itself. An order on the stimuli is obtained if the judgments prove to be transitive, asymmetric, and connected (or, if the relation being judged includes identity as well as greater than, transitive, antisymmetric, and strongly connected).

There are a number of procedural issues relevant to this method of data collection that must be mentioned. In the first place it is customary not to present the full set of $n^2$ pairs. Obviously, if $n$ is around ten or more the number of judgments to be made is large and extraneous motivational factors will interfere with performance. The reduction in the number of pairs presented generally proceeds as follows. First, all the pairs made up of each stimulus with itself are excluded. This reduces the number of pairs to $n(n-1)$. Second, asymmetry is assumed and so for each couple of stimuli, $x$ and $y$, only one of the pairs $(x,y)$ and $(y,x)$ is presented. This further reduces the number of pairs to be presented to $n(n-1)/2$.

Because asymmetry is assumed true, only transitivity and connexity are open to test. However, a further procedural convention of the method of pair comparisons is to require the subject to make a judgment in relation to each pair. That is, for each stimulus pair the subject is instructed to choose one as the greater in the prescribed sense. So connexity is also assumed, leaving only transitivity to be tested. These assumptions are generally made without empirical support. If there is any doubt about their truth the procedures must be altered in order that these assumptions can be tested.

The method of pair comparisons does not often produce an order on stimuli. Even when the attribute being judged is a physical quantity, such as length or brightness, it often fails. In this case it is because humans find it difficult to perceive small differences between stimuli. Forced choices between stimuli that cannot be clearly distinguished from one another, produce violations of transitivity. This difficulty is compounded with others when the attribute being judged is not of a physical kind (e.g., preference for a political candidate). Then it often is not obvious that the attribute is even ordinal. Nevertheless, psychologists have tended to take the former case as a model for the latter.

In the former case, the subject's confusion increases as the difference between the stimuli decreases. Consider the situation where the same subject repeatedly judges between the same pair of stimuli. If the stimuli cannot be perfectly discriminated from each other then the subject will sometimes judge $x$ greater than $y$ and sometimes $y$ greater than $x$. Assume for the moment that such repeated judgments are independent of each other. Then the proportion of times that $x$ is judged greater than $y$ ($p(x>y)$) should be related to the difference between $x$ and $y$ on the quantitative attribute being judged. As this difference decreases and $x$ and $y$ become more and more similar on the relevant attribute $p(x>y)$ should approach .5. As the difference between $x$ and $y$ increases and $x$ and $y$ become more and more distinct $p(x>y)$ should move from .5 to either 1 or 0, depending on which of $x$ or $y$ is the greater. Hence, in the quantitative case, $p(x>y)$ may be an index of the difference between $x$ and $y$ on the relevant attribute.

In this chapter attention is restricted to a specific version of Thurstone's theory, called "case 5 of the law of comparative judgment." It is this version that has been most widely applied in attempts at psychological measurement. The theory is stated below in seven propositions, which are then discussed in more detail.

## AN OUTLINE OF THURSTONE'S THEORY

(1) The attribute relative to which subjects make their pair comparison judgments (henceforth called the "relevant attribute") is represented psychologically as a quantitative attribute (henceforth called the "psychological quantitative attribute").

(2) On any occasion when a stimulus, $i$, is presented to a subject it gives rise to a representation, $\psi_i$, on the psychological quantitative attribute. (Thurstone calls the $\psi_i$ values "discriminal processes").

(3) Over an infinite number of independent presentations of the same stimulus, $i$, the distribution of $\psi_i$ values is normal with mean $\mu_i$ and variance $\sigma_i^2$.

(4) If on any judgment occasion, any stimulus pair, $i$ and $j$, is presented then the subject will judge $i$ to be greater on the relevant attribute than $j$ if and only if $\psi_i > \psi_j$ (where $\psi_i$ and $\psi_j$ are the discriminal processes produced by $i$ and $j$ on that occasion).

(5) For any stimulus, $i$, the values of $\mu_i$ and $\sigma_i^2$ are constant across subjects.

(6) For all pairs of stimuli, $i$ and $j$, $\sigma_i^2 = \sigma_j^2 = \sigma^2$.

(7) For all pairs of stimuli, $i$ and $j$, the product moment correlation coefficient between $\psi_i$ and $\psi_j$, $\rho_{ij}$, is constant.

Proposition (1) is one of the less plausible features of Thurstone's theory in this context. There is no compelling evidence that attributes like the favorability of attitude statements are quantitative and, if they are not, it does not seem likely that they would be represented psychologically in a quantitative way. But Thurstone's theory needs an underlying quantity in order to explain the $p(x>y)$ values and so it must be introduced. Of course, this need is only relative to his conviction that the processes underlying pair comparison judgments of this kind are analogous to those underlying pair comparisons when the relevant attribute is clearly quantitative.

Proposition (2) has its plausible side. If we are presented with a stimulus, like an attitude statement, and we are comparing its favorability with that of another statement then we must make an assessment of its favorability. This will be its $\psi_i$ value. Of course, we do not seem to be aware that such $\psi_i$ values are quantitative but that need not count against Thurstone's theory. They may be quantitative without us being aware of the fact.

Proposition (3) says that over different occasions the $\psi_i$ values produced by $i$ need not all be the same. That is, for example, our assessment of how favorable an attitude statement is need not always be the same. Indeed, proposition (3) asserts that if the occasions are independent then such assessments will in all probability vary. By "independent" here is meant that the $\psi_i$ value (or discriminal process) produced on any one occasion is not influenced by the value produced on any other occasion. In stating what happens over an infinite number of occasions proposition (3) is clearly hypothetical and it is this hypothesis that gives much of the mathematical strength to Thurstone's theory. It has the consequence that differences between judgments involving the same stimuli are a random, or chance, phenomenon. Coupled with proposition (5) this means that not only differences within the same subject but also differences between subjects are so, as well. Although this is plausible within the context of psychophysics where small differences on some perceptually obvious physical variable are involved, it is much less plausible in the purely psychological areas (like attitude measurement) to which Thurstone's theory has been applied. In that context it is at least possible that differences between subjects in their interests, values, and beliefs contribute to differences between them in pair comparison judgments on attitude statements. This is an issue that could easily be experimentally investigated.

Historically, however, this hypothesis was a virtue for Thurstone's theory because it related it to the statistical theory of normally distributed variables. This is an area of mathematics that psychologists have some familiarity with because of its use in statistical inference. So Thurstone's choice of the normal distribution, from the infinite number that could have been chosen, was largely pragmatic.

Proposition (3) means that the $\psi_i$ value produced by a stimulus, $i$, on any occasion may be regarded as $\mu_i$ plus an error component, $\in_i$, that varies randomly across occasions. That is, $\psi_i = \mu_i + \in_i$ (where $\in_i$ is a normally distributed random variable with a mean equal to zero and a variance of $\sigma_i^2$). The aim of Thurstone's scaling procedure is to estimate the value of $\mu_i$ for each $i$ from the pair comparison judgments.

Proposition (4) gives the principle whereby subjects make pair comparison judgments and the principle whereby the $\mu_i$ values may be estimated. It says that a pair comparison judgment between $i$ and $j$ is based on the order relation between $\psi_i$ and $\psi_j$. Over many independent judgments $p(i>j)$ will be related to the proportion of times $\psi_i$ is greater than $\psi_j$ and this in turn must be related to the order relation between $\mu_i$ and $\mu_j$, the magnitude of the difference between $\mu_i$ and $\mu_j$ and the sizes of $\sigma_i^2$ and $\sigma_j^2$.

Propositions (1) to (4) present the core of Thurstone's theory. Propositions (5) to (7) are introduced to enable the estimation of $\mu_i$ and $\mu_j$. Proposition (5) allows observations from different subjects to be combined and propositions (6) and (7) simplify the equations used, reducing the number of unknown values to a workable few. In some applications of Thurstone's theory all of (5), (6), and (7) are not accepted, other propositions being substituted for them. These differences give rise to the various cases of the "law of comparative judgment" (see Thurstone, 1927a, and Torgerson, 1958).

This so–called "law" (it is really nothing more than a hypothesis) relates the probability of judging stimulus $i$ as greater than stimulus $j$ to the characteristics of the probability distributions associated with $i$ and $j$. The form of this relationship may be understood as follows. Consider the three hypothetical cases illustrated in Fig. 5.1. Here $\mu_i$ and $\mu_j$ are separated by increasingly larger amounts: in (a) $\mu_j - \mu_i = \sigma/2$; in (b) $\mu_j - \mu_i = \sigma$; and in (c) $\mu_j - \mu_i = 2\sigma$. Now imagine taking two values, $\psi_i$ and $\psi_j$, at random from the $i$ and $j$ distributions in each of these three figures. In each case the probability that $\psi_j > \psi_i$ exceeds the probability that $\psi_i > \psi_j$ simply because $\mu_j > \mu_i$. Additionally, moving from (a) to (c), the probability that $\psi_j > \psi_i$ increases and the probability that $\psi_i > \psi_j$ decreases because $\mu_j - \mu_i$ increases. In this way one can easily see an important feature of this version of Thurstone's theory: $\mu_j - \mu_i$ and the probability that $\psi_j > \psi_i$ are monotonically related. Thurstone's theory may be used to predict the precise form of this monotonic relationship.

On any occasion when the subject is presented with $i$ and $j$, $j$ is judged greater than $i$ if and only if $\psi_j - \psi_i > 0$. Because $\psi_i$ and $\psi_j$ fluctuate randomly over occasions so must $\psi_j - \psi_i$ and its probability distribution is also normal with a mean $\mu_j - \mu_i$ and variance $\sigma_j^2 + \sigma_i^2 - 2\rho_{ij}\sigma_j\sigma_i$. For example, if $\mu_j - \mu_i$ equals one standard deviation of the distribution of $\psi_j - \psi_i$ then the situation is as illustrated in Fig. 5.2. Then the probability that $\psi_j > \psi_i$ equals .84 and the probability that $\psi_i > \psi_j$ equals .16.

In this case, if only the probability that $\psi_j > \psi_i$ is known then the value of $\mu_j - \mu_i$ can be derived. The point that cuts the distribution into two parts, with 16% in the lower part, and 84% in the upper, is the $z$ score (or normal deviate) corresponding to this probability. From the table of the normal curve this is found to be $-1.0$. This point is the zero point in Fig. 5.2 and because its $z$ score is $-1.0$, it must be one standard deviation below the mean. That is,

$$z_o = \frac{0 - (\mu_j - \mu_i)}{(\sigma_j^2 + \sigma_i^2 - 2\rho_{ij}\sigma_j\sigma_i)^{1/2}} = -1$$

and therefore

$$\mu_j - \mu_i = -z_o\ (\sigma_j^2 + \sigma_i^2 - 2\rho_{ij}\sigma_j\sigma_i)^{1/2}$$

In more general terms,

$$\mu_j - \mu_i = z_{ji}\ (\sigma_j^2 + \sigma_i^2 - 2\rho_{ij}\sigma_j\sigma_i)^{1/2}$$

(where $z_{ji}$ is the normal deviate corresponding to the value of the probability that $\psi_j > \psi_i$). From propositions (6) and (7) of Thurstone's theory it follows that

$$\begin{aligned} \sigma_j^2 + \sigma_i^2 - 2\rho_{ij}\sigma_j\sigma_i &= 2\sigma^2 - 2\rho\sigma^2 \\ &= 2\sigma^2\ (1-\rho) \end{aligned}$$

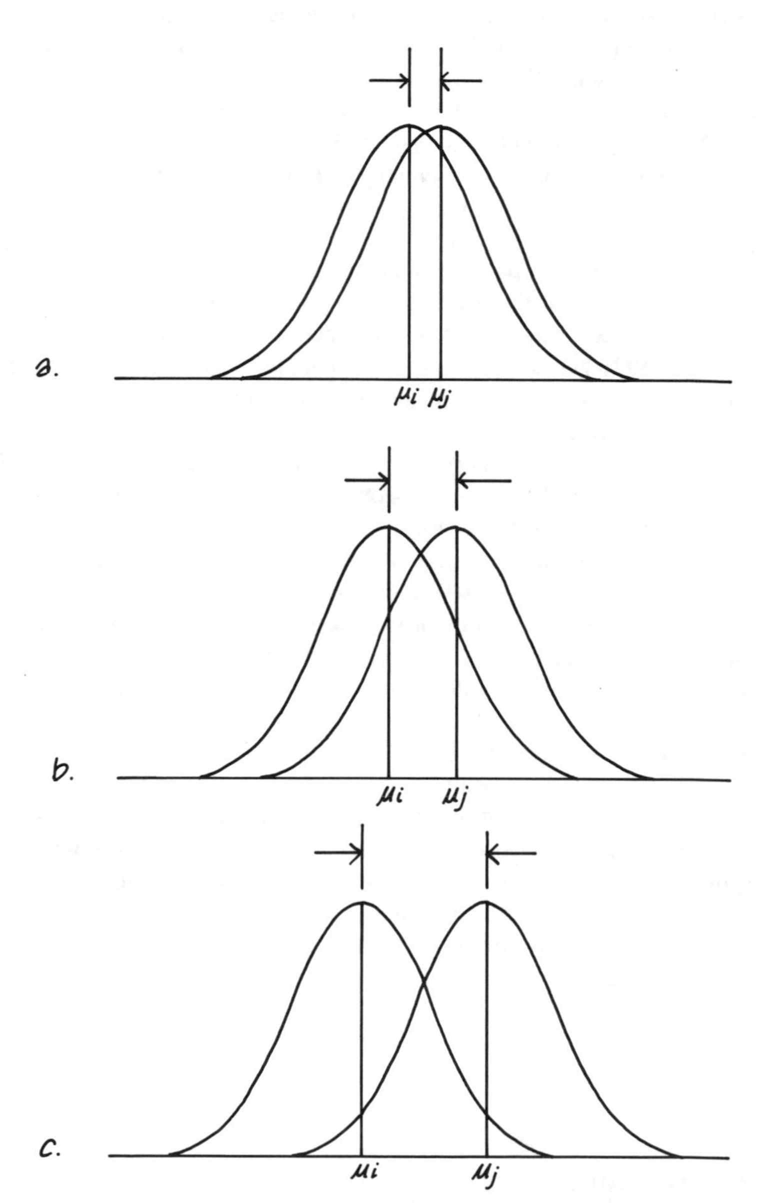


FIG. 5.1 Hypothetical distributions of $\Psi_i$ and $\Psi_j$. When making a comparative judgment between stimuli *i* and *j*, a $\Psi_i$ and a $\Psi_j$ value are randomly sampled from these distributions. As can be seen, the probability that $\Psi_j > \Psi_i$ increases as $\mu_j - \mu_i$ increases.

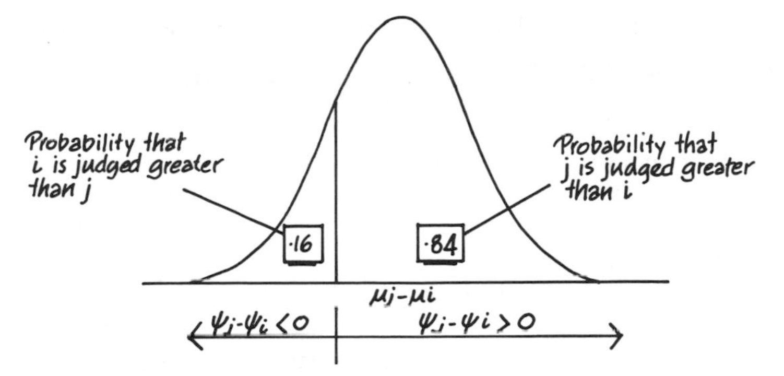


FIG. 5.2 Hypothetical distribution of $\Psi_j - \Psi_i$.

and so

$$(\sigma_j^2 + \sigma_i^2 - 2\rho_{ij}\sigma_j\sigma_i)^{1/2} = \sigma(2(1-\rho))^{1/2}$$

As this value is constant across all stimuli and subjects let it be called $k$. Then,

$$\mu_j - \mu_i = kz_{ji}.$$

By then fixing the unit of measurement at $k$ (and because the unit is always arbitrary it may be fixed at any value) the following result is reached:

$$\mu_j - \mu_i = z_{ji}.$$

So if the probability that $\psi_j > \psi_i$ is known then $\mu_j - \mu_i$ may be deduced because $z_{ji}$ is a direct function of this probability and may be conveniently obtained from the table of the normal curve. That this probability is never known must, of course, be obvious. However this is not a serious impediment. What may be observed is the proportion of times $j$ is judged greater than $i$ over a finite number of independent trials, $p(i>j)$, and this may provide a good estimate of the above mentioned probability. This is the basis of Thurstone's scaling procedure. Torgerson (1958) discussed the analytical procedures for deriving least squares estimates of the values from these sample proportions. If Thurstone's theory is true, then psychological measurement is possible. But this is a big "if."

## THURSTONE'S THEORY AND CONJOINT MEASUREMENT

The central equation of Thurstone's theory, from his point of view, was that $\mu_j - \mu_i = z_{ji}$ because that enabled the values of $\mu_j$ and $\mu_i$ to be assessed. From the point of view of conjoint measurement it is more interesting to remember that $z_{ji}$ and the probability that $\psi_j > \psi_i$ are monotonically related and, therefore, so is that probability and $\mu_j - \mu_i$. It is, thus, a consequence of Thurstone's theory that for any stimuli *h, i, j,* and *k,*

$$\mu_h - \mu_i \geqslant \mu_j - \mu_k \text{ if and only if } P(h>i) \geqslant P(j>k)$$

(where $P(h>i)$ and $P(j>k)$ are the probability that $\psi_h > \psi_i$ and the probability that $\psi_j > \psi_k$ respectively). It is in view of this monotonic relationship that Thurstone's theory is often known as a "monotone theory for pair comparisons" (see Suppes & Zinnes, 1963).

Now if, in terms of the symbolism introduced last chapter, $\mu_h$, $\mu_i$, $\mu_j$, $\mu_k$, . . . , are all values of $A$, $A = X$, and $P = A - A = A+(-A)$, then we have a basis for applying the theory of conjoint measurement to Thurstone's theory. This is because the order of the probabilities, $P(h>i)$, $P(j>k)$, . . . , is the order of $P = A - A$ and the proportions, $p(h>i)$, $p(j>k)$, . . . , are, according to Thurstone's theory, estimates of these probabilities.

It is customary to represent pair comparisons judgments in what is called a *pair comparisons matrix*. This is a table that has a row and a column for each stimulus and $p(i>j)$ is the entry in row j column $i$. Such a matrix is schematically illustrated in Table 5.1.

For any stimulus pair, $i$ and $j$, $p(i>j)$ is set at $1-p(j>i)$ (i.e., these two proportions are not derived from independent judgments), only the top half of the pair comparisons matrix need be inspected.

What the theory of conjoint measurement requires of all monotone theories of pair comparisons is that the probabilities (of which the proportions in the pair comparisons matrix are sample estimates) must satisfy the hierarchy of cancellation conditions. Because the prediction applies to the probabilities and the data are the corresponding proportions, it is necessary to use the methods of statistical inference to test these predictions. Using these methods a series of decisions may be made about the orders of the probabilities corresponding to the proportions. However, we are usually only dealing with the top half of the matrix and it must be 4×4 before independence can be tested, 6×6 before double cancellation can be tested and so on.

So the application of the theory of conjoint measurement to Thurstone's theory of comparative judgment provides a feasible way whereby it may be tested. In fact, as indicated, it provides not only a test of Thurstone's theory but also a test of a much wider class of theories: the class of all monotone theories of pair comparisons. As there are other such theories (e.g., Luce's, 1959, theory of choice), it is quite a useful connection to make.

It is interesting to note how monotone theories differ from one another. Thurstone's hypothesis that for any stimulus, $i$, the distribution of discriminal processes ($\psi_i$ values) is normal (proposition (3) of previous section) leads to the conclusion that for any stimulus pair, $i$ and $j$, the distribution of $\psi_i - \psi_j$ is also normal. Hence, the relationship between $P(i>j)$ and $\mu_i - \mu_j$ is that of the cumulative normal function, as illustrated in Fig. 5.3. This function, of course, is monotonic and it is in virtue of this property that Thurstone's theory is a

TABLE 5.1.
A Schematic Representation of a Pair Comparison Matrix

| | ... | *h* | *i* | *j* | *k* | ... |
|---|---|---|---|---|---|---|
| ⋮ | | ⋮ | ⋮ | ⋮ | ⋮ | |
| h | | . | p(i>h) | p(j>h) | p(k>h) | ... |
| i | | | . | p(j>i) | p(k>i) | ... |
| j | | | | . | p(k>j) | ... |
| k | | | | | . | ... |
| ⋮ | | | | | | |

monotone theory of pair comparisons. Any theory claiming that the relationship between $P(i>j)$ and $\mu_i - \mu_j$ increases from left to right is such a monotone theory, and it is with respect to the shape of this increase that such theories may differ from one another.

Now the possibility that conjoint measurement may be used to measure the differences, $\mu_i - \mu_j$, raises the prospect that the form of this function may be discoverable and so this facet of Thurstone's theory is testable.

The application of conjoint measurement theory to Thurstone's theory illustrates an important aspect of theory testing in experimental science. This is that the failure of the conditions for conjoint measurement (i.e., failure of some of the cancellation conditions to prove true) would not entail that the hypothesized psychological variable involved is not quantitative. Failure could come about for other reasons, for example, the falsity of propositions (5) or (6). If $\mu_i$ and $\sigma_i^2$ are not constant across subjects then proportions based on the judgments of more than one subject will not necessarily conform to the cancellation conditions. Or,

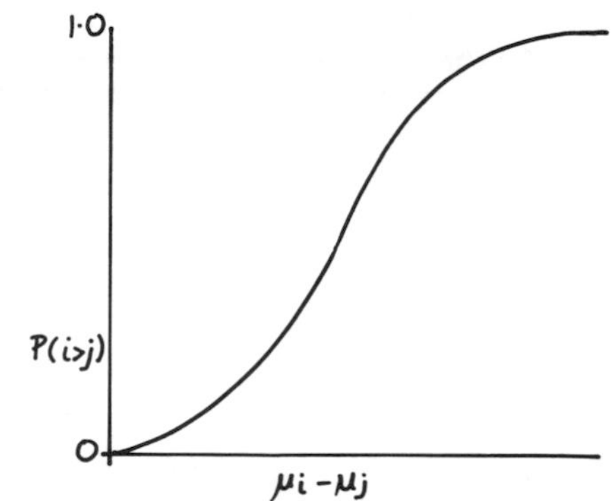


FIG. 5.3 The monotonic relationship between $P(i > j)$ and $\mu_i - \mu_j$.

if the discriminal processes have different variances then for each stimulus pair, $P(i>j)$ is no longer necessarily related to $\mu_i - \mu_j$ by the same monotonic function. Hence, $P(i>j) > P(h>k)$ and $\mu_i - \mu_j < \mu_h - \mu_k$ may both be true. So once again violations of the cancellation conditions would be possible. In complex theories like Thurstone's it is difficult to test the different propositions of the theory independently of one another. One must be prepared to settle for the kind of qualified testing permitted here. In this kind of situation, failure to satisfy the cancellation conditions means that, in the absence of more direct evidence, the hypothesis that the variable involved is quantitative is not proven and may well be false.

## AN EXAMPLE OF CONJOINT MEASUREMENT

The application of the theory of conjoint measurement to Thurstone's theory may be illustrated by considering some data collected by Thurstone (1927d) himself. At the University of Chicago, 266 students made all 171 pair comparison judgments between 19 crimes, the crimes being judged with respect to their seriousness. Thurstone used this data to derive a scale for the "measurement" of the seriousness of these crimes. Our interest, however, is in whether or not his data satisfies the conjoint measurement cancellation conditions. Only a very small subset of Thurstone's data will be considered: a single 3×3 matrix involving the crimes of bootlegging, counterfeiting, libel, perjury, abortion, and kidnapping. This enables tests of single and double cancellations to be illustrated.

The relevant submatrix of Thurstone's data is shown in Table 5.2 below. The cell entries in this table are the proportion of times that the column crime was judged to be more serious than the row crime by Thurstone's subjects. The theory of conjoint measurement states that an order, $\geqslant$, on $P = A \times X$ satisfies single cancellation (or independence) if and only if

(i) for any $a$, $b$ in $A$ and $x$ in $X$, if $ax \geqslant bx$ then for every $y$ in $X$, $ay \geqslant by$; and

(ii) for any $x$, $y$ in $X$ and $a$ in $A$, if $ax \geqslant ay$ then for every $b$ in $A$, $bx \geqslant by$.

TABLE 5.2
A 3 × 3 Submatrix From Thurstone's (1927d) Pair Comparison Matrix Reporting Comparative Judgements about the Seriousness of Crimes

| | Perjury | Abortion | Kidnapping |
|---|---|---|---|
| Counterfeiting | .532 | .756 | .804 |
| Libel | .702 | .809 | .894 |
| Bootlegging | .728 | .872 | .924 |

The meaning of this condition is illustrated in the two 2×2 matrices in Fig. 5.4.

In these matrices the single line arrows represent the antecedent order (the "if" part) and the double line arrows represent the consequent order (the "then" part). Matrix (i) illustrates part (i) of single cancellation and matrix (ii), part (ii). As is evident from Fig. 5.4, single cancellation implies that all rows must be ordered alike and that all columns must be ordered alike. This may be generalized to matrices larger than 2×2. If the rows and columns of a data matrix are permuted so that the cells of the first row and the first column are ordered from least to greatest, (say, from left to right and from top to bottom) then the cells in the other rows and columns must also be ordered from least to greatest in the same way.

In testing Thurstone's theory it is the matrix of probabilities that must satisfy this condition. This hypothesis about the probabilities may be tested statistically via the proportions given in Table 5.2, for if Thurstone's theory is correct, these

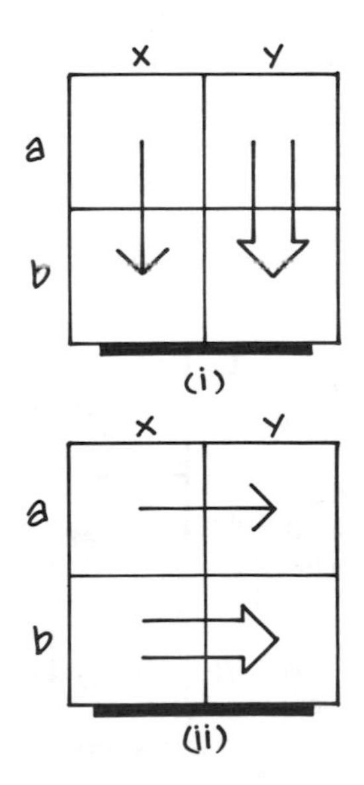


FIG. 5.4 A schematic representation of single cancellation (independence). The single line arrow is the antecedent and the double line arrow, the consequent.

proportions are estimates of those probabilities. For pairs of adjacent cells in the $3 \times 3$ matrix the hypothesis that the two probabilities were equal was tested with type one error rate set at .05. The results are represented in Fig. 5.5. Here, an arrow from one cell to another signifies that the probability in the one cell exceeds that of the other and an equals sign between cells means that the two probabilities are equal.

Obviously, these order relations violate single cancellation and, consequently, this prediction from Thurstone's theory, via the theory of conjoint measurement, is falsified. The extent of the violation of single cancellation may be assessed by counting the number of alterations to the order shown in Fig. 5.5 necessary to satisfy single cancellation. If $CA > LA$, (rather than $CA = LA$) and $LA = BA$ (rather than $LA > BA$) then single cancellation would be satisfied. Hence, Fig. 5.5 deviates from the predicted result with respect to two of the order relations.

As pointed out in the previous chapter, there are eight different versions of double cancellation that might be tested in any $3 \times 3$ matrix. However, these are not all independent of transitivity, or single cancellation, and if these two conditions are taken as true then only one version of double cancellation needs to be tested. This is the version given there in the section on "Double Cancellation." As shown in that section there are six logically independent tests of that version in any $3 \times 3$ matrix. However, again only one of these is independent of single cancellation. This test is illustrated in Fig. 5.6, where it is assumed that the rows are ordered from least to greatest, from left to right, and the columns are ordered from least to greatest, from top to bottom. Here, once again, the single line arrows represent the antecedent inequalities and the double line arrows represent the consequent inequalities. Double cancellation is violated if and only if the antecedent orders hold while the consequent ones do not, so the data patterns leading to a rejection of double cancellation are those illustrated in Fig. 5.7. Anything else confirms double cancellation. Thus, if $\geqslant$ on $P$ satisfies transitivity and single cancellation, then double cancellation may be tested by searching all $3 \times 3$ matrices for one or other of the data patterns illustrated in Fig. 5.7. If either of these do not occur then double cancellation may be accepted.

However, what if single cancellation does not hold within some $3 \times 3$ matrix,

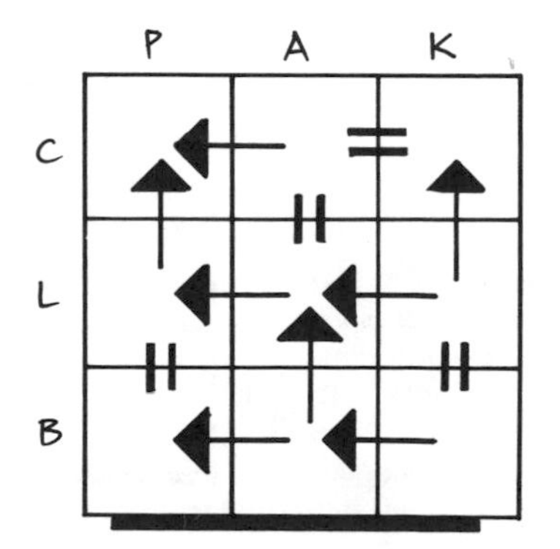


FIG. 5.5 Ordinal relations between the probabilities corresponding to the proportions in Table 5.2. An arrow between two cells means that the probability at the arrow's tail exceeds that at its head; double lines between two cells mean that the probabilities are equal. These ordinal relations are the ones considered in testing single cancellation (independence).

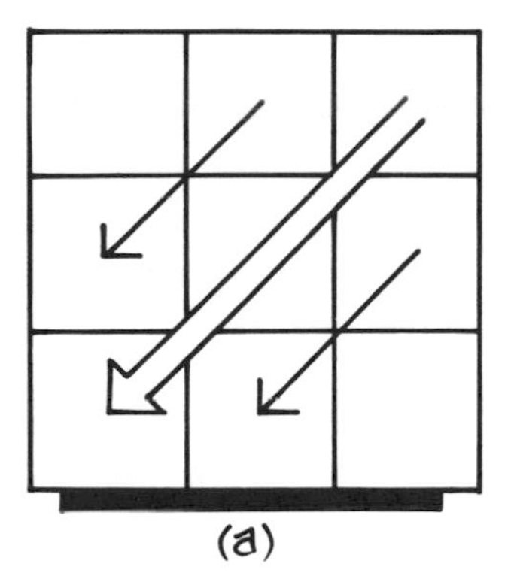


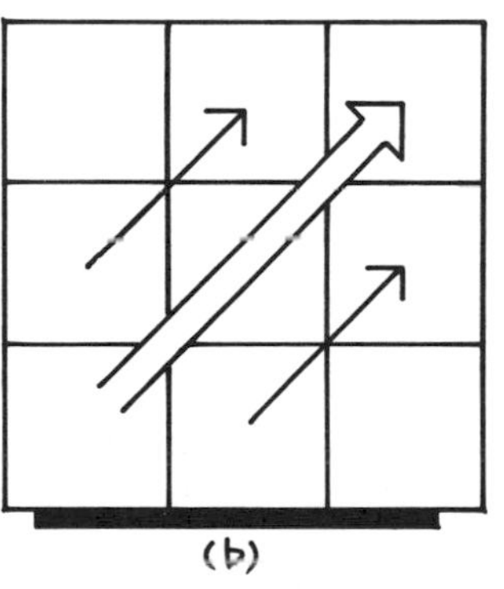


FIG. 5.6 If the rows are ordered from left to right and the columns from top to bottom then the single necessary test of double cancellation is represented in (a) and (b).

as in Fig. 5.5? One could proceed to test double cancellation in all its many versions if one was so inclined. Generally what one wants to know is how far the data under consideration departs from confirming the existence of a conjoint, noninteractive, quantitative structure. In the case of a 3×3 data matrix this may be seen by considering how far the data departs from satisfaction of single cancellation, and considering over and above that how far it departs from satisfying that single test of double cancellation that is independent of single cancellation. This may be assessed by finding the minimum number of alterations to the ordering on the cells necessary to satisfy single and double cancellation (without at the same time violating transitivity). So even if independence is violated, one only need consider that single test of double cancellation illustrated in Fig. 5.6.

The details of this test are as follows. Separating the relation, $\geqslant$, into its components, $>$ and $=$, the relation between any pair of cells may be $>$, $=$ or $<$. Considering the three pairs of cells joined by arrows in Fig. 5.6 the problem is to identify those patterns or orders that satisfy double cancellation and those that do not. Labelling the rows and columns of the 3 × 3 matrix as *a, b, c* and *x, y* and *z* (as before), and calling the order relation between *bx* and *ay* "1", that between *cy* and *bz* "2" and that between *cx* and *az* "3" (as in Fig. 5.8) the logically possible patterns may be indicated as in Table 5.3.

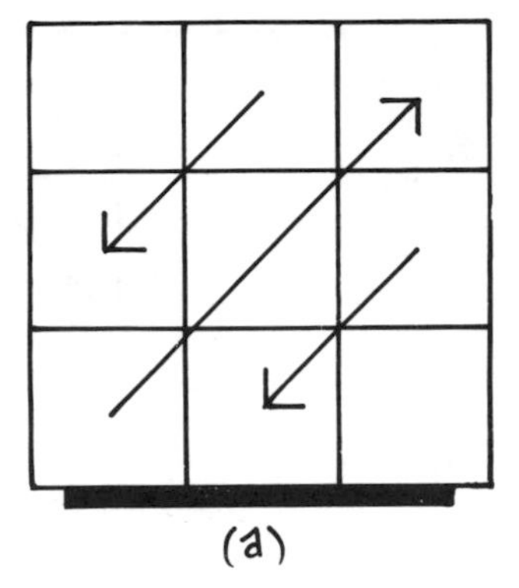


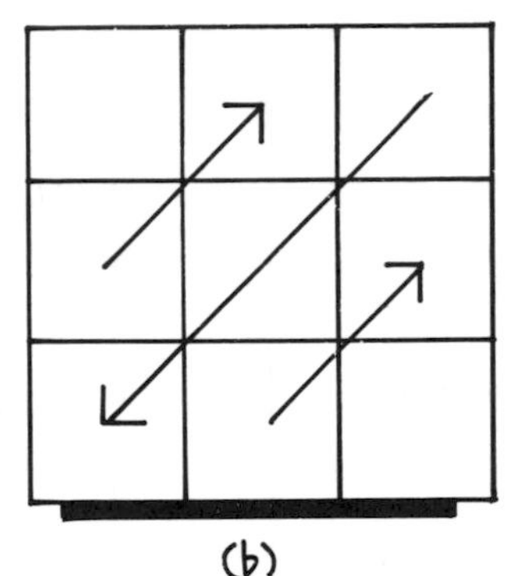


FIG. 5.7 In the test represented in Fig. 5.6, double cancellation is violated if and only if either of the data patterns (a) or (b) occurs.

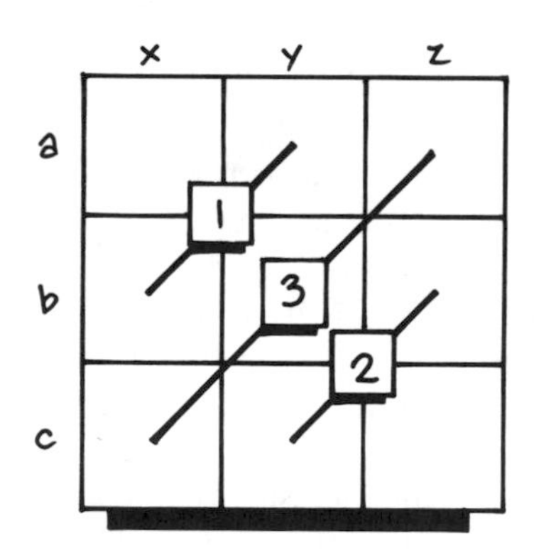


FIG. 5.8 The three order relations to be considered in the test of double cancellation represented in Fig. 5.6. Each relation may be either $<$, $=$ or $>$.

As there are three order relations to consider (1, 2, and 3) and each of these may be $>$, $=$ or $<$, the number of possible patterns is $3^3 = 27$. These are all shown in Table 5.3: 13 patterns satisfy double cancellation and 14 violate it. Despite the claims to the contrary made by Krantz & Tversky (1971), Levelt, et al. (1972), Perline et al. (1979) and van der Ven (1980), none of these 27 possible patterns are indifferent to double cancellation (see also Michell, 1988).

The pattern obtained from the proportions in Table 5.2 after the necessary

TABLE 5.3

Each Relation Identified in Fig. 5.3 is Assigned a Row of This Table (Column R). Each Such Relation May Be Either >, =, or <. All 27 Logical Possibilities are Shown Here: 13 Satisfy Double Cancellation and 14 Violate It. (Adapted from Michell (1988, Table 1). Adapted by permission of Academic Press.)

| | *PATTERNS SATISFYING DOUBLE CANCELLATION* | | | | | | | | | | | | | *PATTERNS VIOLATING DOUBLE CANCELLATION* | | | | | | | | | | | | | |
|---|---|---|---|---|---|---|---|---|---|---|---|---|---|---|---|---|---|---|---|---|---|---|---|---|---|---|---|
| R | 1 | 2 | 3 | 4 | 5 | 6 | 7 | 8 | 9 | 10 | 11 | 12 | 13 | 14 | 15 | 16 | 17 | 18 | 19 | 20 | 21 | 22 | 23 | 24 | 25 | 26 | 27 |
| 1 | < | < | < | < | < | = | = | = | > | > | > | > | > | < | < | < | < | = | = | = | = | = | = | > | > | > | > |
| 2 | < | = | > | > | > | < | = | > | < | < | < | = | > | < | < | = | = | < | < | = | = | > | > | = | = | > | > |
| 3 | < | < | < | = | > | < | = | > | < | = | > | > | > | = | > | = | > | = | > | < | > | < | = | < | = | < | = |

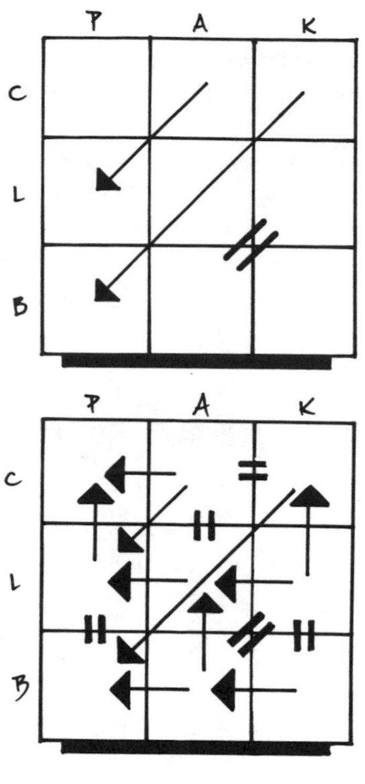


FIG. 5.9 Ordinal relations between the probabilities corresponding to the proportions in Table 5.2.

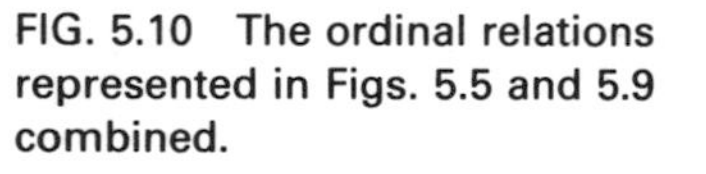

FIG. 5.10 The ordinal relations represented in Figs. 5.5 and 5.9 combined.

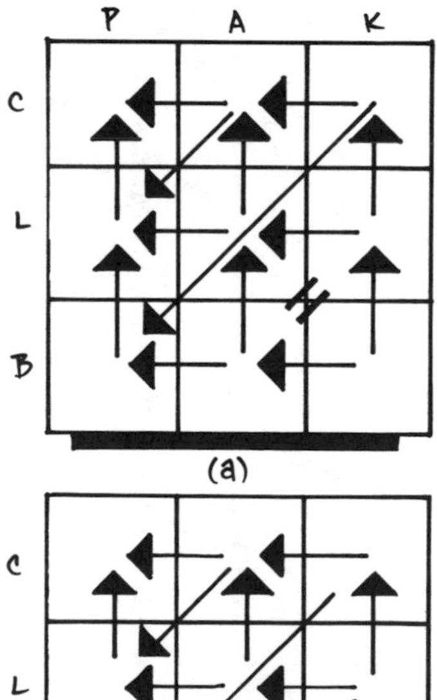




FIG. 5.11 Two sets of ordinal relations in a 3×3 matrix which satisfy both single and double cancellation. The relations represented in Fig. 5.10 approximate these.

statistical tests is shown in Fig. 5.9 and that is pattern 2 in Table 5.3. This satisfies double cancellation.

If the orders in Figs. 5.5 and 5.9 are then combined, the result is shown in Fig. 5.10. This contains the violations of single cancellation mentioned above together with a violation of transitivity: $BA = LK$ and $LK = BK$, by transitivity implies that $BA = BK$, however, in fact, $BA > BK$. The minimum number of alterations necessary for the order on the cells to satisfy both single and double cancellation (together with transitivity) is three (Figs. 5.11a and b). This illustrates how single and double cancellation may be tested in a 3×3 matrix. In this instance single cancellation and transitivity (a special case of double cancellation) were violated, suggesting that either seriousness of crimes is not a quantitative variable or else some other part of Thurstone's theory of comparative judgment is false.

Chapter 6

# The Theory of Multidimensional Scaling

Though widely used until the 1950s, Thurstone's approach to psychological measurement gradually gave way in the late 1960s to a new approach: *Multidimensional scaling*. One of the features that came to disturb psychologists about Thurstone's theory was its commitment to unidimensionality. Although in relatively well controlled psychophysical experiments the unidimensionality of the stimulus set could be ensured, in other areas, like social psychology, there was little control over the dimensionality of the stimulus set. Here the stimuli were attitude statements, political candidates, and so on. It was difficult to identify the relevant dimensions, let alone control them. The methods of multidimensional scaling had the advantage of leaving the issue of dimensionality open, it was one of the parameters determined by the data rather than by the researcher.

This shift in method also involved a change in the kind of judgments used. Thurstone's method made use of pair comparison judgments and his theory was a theory of such judgments. Multidimensional scaling makes use of similarities data. The most common form of similarities data used are direct judgments of similarity or dissimilarity between stimulus pairs, although other, less direct kinds of data may also be used. For example, a theory may prescribe that the time taken to discriminate between a pair of stimuli is an index of their dissimilarity, or that the proportion of times two stimuli are confused is an index of their similarity.

The concept of similarity is a commonly used one and, at first sight, seems clear enough. We often make judgments of similarity, for example, the judgment that the English language is more similar to German than to Russian or, that the music of Mozart is more like that of Bach than like that of Delius. Such judgments are taken to be facts. That is, similarity is taken to be an objective relation between things. If it were not such an objective relation then there would be no reason to suppose that in judging similarity any two people would be judging the same kind of thing. This would make construction of a theory of similarities judgments a difficult business.

The theory of multidimensional scaling offers a simple explanation of similarities judgments. The similarity of one thing to another is said to be inversely related to the distance between them in a multidimensional attribute space. All things possess attributes, and their similarity or difference to other things is related to the difference between them on these attributes. Each attribute may be thought of as a dimension in a multidimensional space, and each object as a point whose location is defined by the object's value on each attribute. The closer two objects are in this attribute space the more similar they are and vice versa. Hence, judgments of similarity are monotonically related to distance in the multidimensional attribute space. The theory says that $x$ will be judged more similar to $y$ than $w$ is to $z$, if and only if the distance from $x$ to $y$ in this space is less than that from $w$ to $z$.

Simple as this idea is, it was not until the early 1960s that methods were devised for multidimensional scaling. Such methods take as their starting point the judgments of similarity or dissimilarity, and conclude by constructing a space wherein the objects judged may be located, so that judged similarity and distance within the space are inversely monotonically related. The major external constraint is to keep the dimensionality of the space as low as possible and most methods allow some slippage in the monotonicity requirement in order to attain a solution of satisfactorily low dimensionality. The methods most commonly used (due to Guttman, 1968, Kruskal, 1964 a & b, & Shepard, 1962 a & b), are complex, lengthy, and best implemented via electronic computers. No account of them will be given in this book and the interested student is referred to these articles. Simple sketches of some of the methods are given in Baird and Noma (1978) and van der Ven (1980). Our interest here is in the theory behind the method, for it is (i) only if this theory enables measurement, and (ii) only if its quantitative aspects can be experimentally tested, that the methods of multidimensional scaling will be of any value to psychology.

An illustration of the application of multidimensional scaling is the study by Wish, Deutsch, and Biener (1970) (also reported in Carroll & Wish, 1974). In that study the subjects were instructed to rate the similarities of each pair of 12 nations on a 9 point rating scale. This gave a 12 × 12 matrix of similarities ratings for each subject, which the multidimensional scaling method was then applied to. The particular method used in this study was one devised by Carroll and Chang (1970) called INDSCAL. It produces different configurations of stimuli in multidimensional space for different subjects. The presumption is that while all subjects judge similarity on the basis of the same attributes, they may differ in the importance they attach to different attributes. Figure 6.1 shows the two-dimensional solutions obtained for two of the subjects in this study (from Carroll & Wish, 1974).

Dimension one was interpreted by the authors as reflecting how procommunist

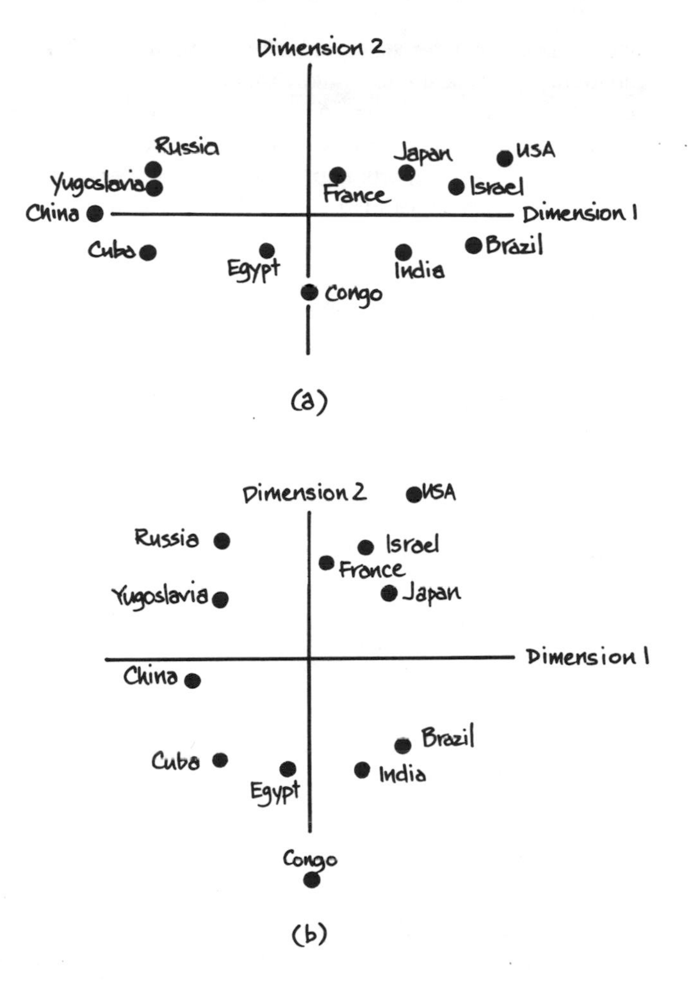


FIG. 6.1. Two dimensional solutions for two subjects (a and b) of their judgments about the relative similarities of 12 nations, using the INDSCAL program. (Based upon Fig. 10 in Carroll and Wish (1974). Adapted by permission of Academic Press and the authors.)

or prowestern the nations were; dimension two as how economically developed or underdeveloped they were. The two subjects differed according to how much importance they attributed to these different dimensions in judging similarity. Subject (a) saw the USA as being more similar to Brazil than to Russia because he gave more weight to political than to economic differences, whereas (b) reversed the weights and, saw the USA as more like Russia than like Brazil.

The appeal of multidimensional scaling resides in its reduction of a matrix of data to a simple geometric picture that allows one (after interpretation) to see at a glance, both the dimensions used and the similarities relations involved. Such matters of apparent convenience, however, cannot hide the substantive questions that such pictures pose. Are broad political and economic differences between nations quantitative? Is similarity really like distance in a multidimensional space? Because the methods of multidimensional scaling always ensure a solution, answers to these questions must depend on research into the theory underlying the method. The fact that an interpretable solution is obtained, given a set of similarities data cannot, itself, validate the method.

## THE THEORY OF ORDINAL MULTIDIMENSIONAL SCALING

The theory may be summed-up in the following five propositions.

(1) There are $k$ variables relevant to the judgments of similarity (where $k$ is some natural number).

(2) All of these $k$ variables are quantitative.

(3) These $k$ quantitative variables form a space.

(4) The distance between any pair of points, $x$ and $y$, in this $k$-dimensional space ($d(x,y)$) is given by the following expression:

$$d(x, y) = \left[ \sum_{i=1}^{k} |x_i - y_i|^r \right]^{1/r}$$

(where $x_i$ and $y_i$ are the values of $x$ and $y$ on the $i$th dimension and $r$ is a real number greater than or equal to one).

(5) Judged similarity or dissimilarity between any two stimuli, $x$ and $y$, is monotonically related to the distance between them in the $k$ dimensional space ($d(x,y)$) as follows:

(a) the judged similarity of $x$ to $y$ increases as $d(x,y)$ decreases;

(b) the judged dissimilarity of $x$ to $y$ increases as $d(x,y)$ increases.

The significance of each of these propositions will be discussed in turn. In proposition 1 the $k$ variables relevant to the judgments of similarity will, of course, be variables upon which the objects judged possess values. That proposition, is then, hardly a startling hypothesis. Every object possesses many, if not an infinite number of attributes. However, not all of these are relevant to judgments of similarity. At least two factors restrict the relevant attributes to a relatively small class. First, because of the limitations of our sensory systems, we are only sensitive to a small number of attributes possessed by objects. For example, by looking at an object we cannot usually directly perceive its temperature or density and so when judgments are based on vision only, these attributes would not be relevant. Second, whatever personal interests dominate our judgments of similarity, these may further restrict the class of relevant variables: We will attend only to some of the features we might have sensed, ignoring the rest. For example, in judging the similarities of different cheeses we might attend only to attributes of flavor, odor and texture, ignoring color, weight, and temperature. So a complete theory of similarities judgments would specify which attributes are relevant in which contexts. This the theory of multidimensional scaling does not yet attempt to do. Rather the method is seen as a means whereby these relevant attributes may be discovered.

Proposition 2 limits the range of application of the theory to situations where the $k$ variables involved are all quantitative. Because some of the variables upon which similarity judgments are based are not quantitative (e.g., hue and texture), the theory is not completely general. This, of course, has not prevented psychologists from applying methods of multidimensional scaling in contexts where the variables involved are not quantitative, or have not been shown to be quantitative. In fact it is within this latter context that multidimensional scaling is thought to be able to make a contribution. It is felt by many psychologists that lying behind judgments of similarity between many stimuli (such as political candidates, attitude statements, word meanings, etc.) are unmeasured quantitative variables of a psychological kind. So it is supposed that multidimensional scaling provides a means not only of identifying, but also, of measuring them. Certainly, if there are such quantitative variables and the theory of multidimensional scaling is true then this supposition is true. These, however, are big "ifs" and they are precisely the ones in which we are interested. As will be shown in the next section, the theory of conjoint measurement shows how we may come to grips with them.

Proposition 3 is one that is rarely brought into the open. It is, of course, implicit in Proposition 4, for the concept of distance relative to more than one variable, only has meaning if the variables jointly constitute a space. The mere fact that objects differ on $k$ quantitative variables does not itself imply that each object has a location in a $k$-dimensional space. That conclusion requires the existence of quantitative relations *between* the $k$ variables. These quantitative relations must be of a particular kind if the concept of distance is to be applicable. Distance between points in a space is always a function of component distances within each of the dimensions. If $V$ is any quantitative variable and $x$ and $y$ objects possessing values of $V$, then the distance between $x$ and $y$ on variable $V$ is $|x_v - y_v|$, the absolute value of the difference between $x$ and $y$ on $V$. Now, the multidimensional or spatial concept of distance is some function of these component distances and so, since a function is a kind of relation, there must be some relation between the component distances. In the case of the theory of multidimensional scaling the distance is an additive power function of the component distances and this requires that the component distances stand in some kind of additive relation to one another. That is, it requires for any two variables involved, $U$ and $V$, that any difference, $s_u - t_u$, on $U$ be $r$ times any difference on $V$, $p_v - q_v$ (where $r$ is some real number).

This is easily seen by considering a hypothetical space constituted by the variables height and weight. Each person, possessing both a height and a weight, will have a point in this space. But how are distances within the space related to distances within height and weight. If we let a difference of one inch equal a difference of one pound, then the distance between points *a* and *b* equals that between points *c* and *d* (see Fig. 6.2a). However, if the space is reconstituted so that a difference of one centimeter equals a difference of one kilogram then, as Fig. 6.2b shows, the distance from *c* to *d* exceeds that from *a* to *b*. As is obvious from this figure, in order to have a height/weight space (and hence height/weight distances between people) differences in height must equal some factor times difference in weight.

The physical space wherein we live, is of course, our paradigm of a space, and within that space the three dimensions, height, width, and depth, are quantitatively comparable because they each involve the same quantity (length) and differ only in direction. In recent times, it has been discovered that these three dimensions are yoked with time to form a four dimensional space. That is, the spatial dimensions (height, width, and depth) and time are interrelated so that there is such a thing as the space–time distance between any two events. Similarly, if attribute spaces for similarity judgments exist then the attributes (or variables)

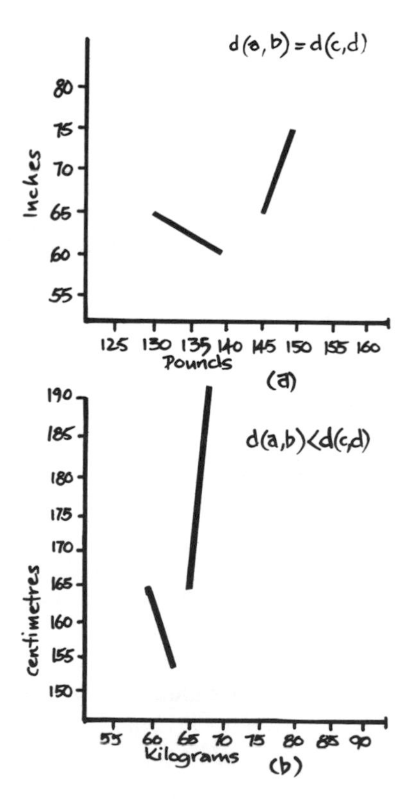


FIG. 6.2. (a) A height-weight space in which 1 inch equals 1 pound. Then $d(a,b) = d(c,d)$. (b) A height-weight space in which 1 centimeter equals 1 kilogram. Then $d(a,b) < d(c,d)$. Since the heights and weights of *a*, *b*, *c* and *d* remain unchanged, this illustrates the fact that in such spaces distance is relative to the quantitative relationship between height and weight.

involved must be interrelated so that there is a similarity-distance between any two objects. Of course, it may be that such attributes are only interrelated via the subject who makes similarities judgments: The subject's mind or nervous system interrelates the attributes. But then there would be no objective similarity which the subject was judging and it would be a strange coincidence if all subjects were then judging in the same way. Perhaps such thinking lay behind Carroll and Chang's INDSCAL method (mentioned earlier). It allows for subjects to weigh attributes differently. But if similarity is a thoroughly subjective concept, more leeway than this might be needed to account for all individual differences in its judgment.

Proposition 4 construes the concept of distance in multidimensional space in accordance with what Beals, Krantz, and Tversky (1968) called *the power metric*. This relates the distance between any points, $x$ and $y$, to the values that $x$ and $y$ have upon the dimensions involved. The power metric relation has three components.

(i) *Intradimensional Subtractivity:* The distance between $x$ and $y$ is related to *the difference between x and y within each dimension.*

(ii) *Interdimensional Additivity:* Each dimension makes a contribution to distance (viz. $|x_i - y_i|^r$) and distance is a function of the *sum* of these dimensional contributions.

(iii) *Power:* The distance between $x$ and $y$ is related to *the intradimensional differences raised to some power* (equal to or greater than one) and *the interdimensional sum raised to the inverse power.*

Of course, the familiar Euclidean distance concept is the special case of the power metric resulting when the power exponent is two. That is,

$$d(x, y) = \left[ \sum_{i=1}^{k} |x_i - y_i|^2 \right]^{1/2}.$$

So the power metric is really a generalization of this familiar distance concept, in that 2 is replaced by $r(\geqslant 1)$.

Does this very general distance concept exhaust all the possibilities? This depends on what properties the distance between any two points is expected to have. Generally, it is expected to have three properties, that are taken to be the defining properties of a distance metric (or measure). These are:

(a) *Positivity:* for any points $x$ and $y$, $d(x,x) = 0$ and if $x = y$ $d(x,y) > 0$;

(b) *Symmetry:* for any two points $x$ and $y$, $d(x,y) = d(y,x)$; and

(c) *The Triangle Inequality:* for any three points $x$, $y$ and $z$, $d(x,y) + d(y,z) \geqslant d(x,z)$.

Now Beals, Krantz, and Tversky (1968) note that the power distance metric is not the only possible distance relation between two points in a multidimensional space. Another possibility is what they call the *exponential metric:*

$$d(x, y) = \log_p \left[ 1 + \sum_{i=1}^{k} (p^{|x_i - y_i|} - 1) \right]$$

(where $p$ is a real number greater than one). This distance measure also satisfies (a), (b), and (c) above and so one would like to know if anything other than unfamiliarity caused its exclusion from the theory of multidimensional scaling. These authors go on to state that one major difference between the power and exponential metrics is that the power metric satisfies a condition they call *segmental additivity* while the exponential does not. The idea behind this condition is that the power metric distance between any two points is composed of additive parts or segments. Taking any two points $x$ and $y$ and the path between them whose distance is $d(x,y)$ then segmental additivity means that for any point $z$ on that path $d(x,z) + d(z,y) = d(x,y)$. Given the exponential metric, no two points satisfy segmental additivity unless they differ on only one dimension. So as long as segmental additivity is thought to be important the power metric will be preferred to the exponential. Interestingly, Tversky and Krantz (1970) have proved that given segmental additivity and both (i) and (ii) above, the power distance relation is the only distance metric available.

Proposition 5 links distance to similarity and dissimilarity judgments and so completes the psychological theory. Because the core of the theory is Proposition 4, it is interesting to observe what implications 4 has for judgments of similarity and dissimilarity given 5. Beals, Krantz, and Tversky (1968), Tversky and Krantz (1970), and Tversky and Gati (1982) have traced many of these implications. Some of the simpler points they make are mentioned here to give something of the flavor of multidimensional scaling as a psychological theory.

Consider the three components of the power metric, (i), (ii), and (iii) above. The implication of intradimensional subtractivity for judgments of similarity and dissimilarity is that it is the *differences* between things that are all important rather than what things have in common. This is brought out clearly by considering a simple unidimensional example. In Fig. 6.3 the difference between lines $a$ and $b$ equals that between lines $c$ and $d$.

FIG. 6.3. According to the principle of intradimensional subtractivity similarity depends only on differences and not on common features. Hence, line *a* is as similar to line *b* as *c* is to *d*, for the difference between *a* and *b* equals that between *c* and *d*, even though *c* and *d* have more in common than do *a* and *b*.

This means that *a* is as similar to *b* as *c* is to *d*. This is despite the fact that *c* and *d* have much more in common (the length *c*) than do *a* and *b*. If judgments of similarity did not conform to this expectation then intradimensional subtractivity would be refuted as a basis for similarities judgments. Tversky (1977) has proposed another theory of similarities judgments which takes common features as well as differences into account.

Interdimensional additivity means that the contribution of any one dimension (i.e., the difference between *x* and *y* on that dimension) to judged similarity or dissimilarity is independent of the contribution of each other dimension. These contributions merely add together. They do not interact or modify each other. Now interaction between the dimensions in producing judgments of similarity is a logical possibility. In Fig. 6.4, interdimensional additivity implies (granting that height and width are the relevant dimensions) that *a* and *b* are as similar to one another as are *c* and *d*, and that *a* and *c* are as similar to one another as are *b* and *d*. Yet it is conceivable that these two dimensions could interact: for example, as width is increased (from 2 to 5 cm) a fixed height difference (4cm−3cm) contributes more to dissimilarity. Then *a* and *b* would be judged as being more similar than are *c* and *d*. Krantz and Tversky (1975) present some

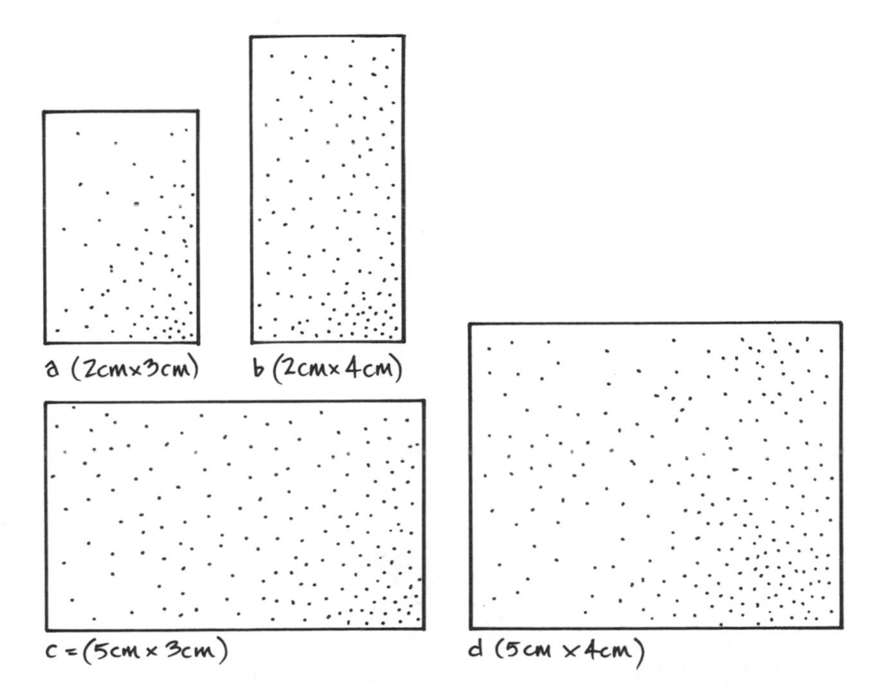


FIG. 6.4. According to the principle of interdimensional additivity the contributions from different dimensions to similarity do not interact with one another. Hence, if in the case of the similarity of rectangles width and height are the relevant dimensions, the similarity of *a* to *b* equals that of *c* to *d* and the similarity of *a* to *c* equals that of *b* to *d*.

experimental results that suggest that in judgments of the similarity of rectangles, the two dimensions of height and width do interact rather than simply add together.

Component (iii) of the power metric has interesting implications for judgments of similarity. The effect of the exponent, $r$, is to weight each of the intradimensional differences by an amount equal to that difference raised to the power of $r - 1$. That is, $|x_i - y_i|^r = |x_i - y_i|^{r-1} \times |x_i - y_i|$. Now, the larger $|x_i - y_i|$ is, the larger $|x_i - y_i|^{r-1}$ will be (for $r \geq 1$), so larger differences get weighted by proportionally larger weights. That is, the effect of $r$ is to give more weight to big intradimensional differences in producing

$$\sum_{i=1}^{k} |x_i - y_i|^r.$$

When $r = 1$ all weights are equal (i.e., 1) but as $r$ approaches infinity the weight given to larger differences increases. Some idea of this effect may be obtained by considering the set of all points, $y$, such that $d(x,y) = 1$ in two dimensional space, for some different values of $r$ (Fig. 6.5) (Coombs, Dawes, and Tversky, 1970). Or, another way is to consider two points, $x$ and $y$, in two dimensional space, and compute the distance between them for various values of $r$ (Fig. 6.6). Obviously, as $r$ increases, so $d(x,y)$ approaches 4 which equals $|x_1 - y_1|$, the larger of the two differences, that is, the contribution of $|x_1 - y_1|^r$ to $d(x,y)$, relative to that of $|x_2 - y_2|^r$, becomes progressively greater. This also shows how quickly, in two dimensions, the value of $r$ reaches a point where increments have an insignificant impact.

The power metric requires that $r \geq 1$ and Tversky and Gati (1982) have shown an interesting implication of this. Given four points in two dimensional space, as shown in Fig. 6.7, the fact that $r \geq 1$ means that $d(c,e) + d(e,a) \geq d(c,a)$ (if $r = 1$ then $d(c,a) = d(c,e) + d(e,a)$), so it cannot be true that either

$$d(c,b) > d(c,e) \text{ and}$$

$$d(b,a) > d(e,a)$$

$$\text{or } d(c,b) > d(e,a) \text{ and}$$

$$d(b,a) > d(c,e).$$

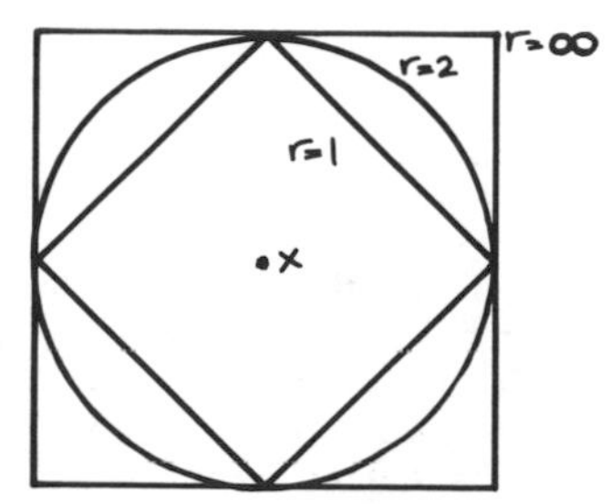


FIG. 6.5. The locus of points $y$ such that $d(x,y) = 1$ for $r = 1$, $r = 2$ and $r = \infty$ using the power metric. (Based upon Fig. 3.16 in Coombs, Dawes, & Tversky, 1970. Adapted by permission of authors.)

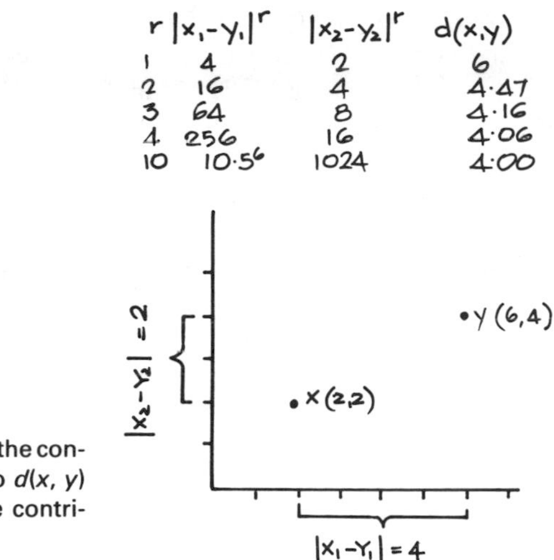


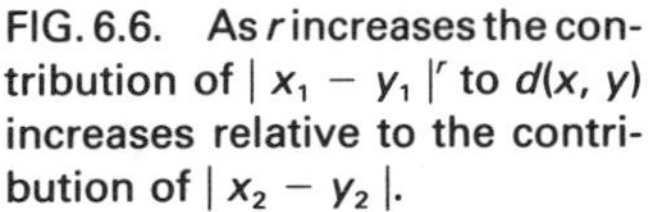
FIG. 6.6. As $r$ increases the contribution of $|x_1 - y_1|^r$ to $d(x, y)$ increases relative to the contribution of $|x_2 - y_2|$.

That is, as Tversky and Gati (1982) put it, the center path cannot exceed the corner path. If $r < 1$ then it will and in so doing the triangle inequality is violated. This means that one of the conditions that a distance metric must satisfy is false in this context and so similarity judgments no longer behave as if reflecting such a metric. So if $a$, $b$, $c$, and $e$ represent stimuli in a two dimensional attribute space then the dissimilarity of $c$ to $b$ cannot exceed that of $c$ to $e$, while the dissimilarity of $b$ to $a$ exceeds that of $e$ to $a$, and neither can the dissimilarity of $b$ to $a$ exceed that of $c$ to $e$, while that of $c$ to $b$ exceeds that of $e$ to $a$. Tversky and Gati (1982) review a number of experiments in which this prediction has been falsified.

If similarity and dissimilarity are monotonically related to $d(x,y)$ further consequences flow from the fact that $d(x,y)$ is a metric. First, in accordance with (a), the similarity of all things to themselves must be equal and greater than the similarity of any two different things. Second, in accordance with (b) similarities

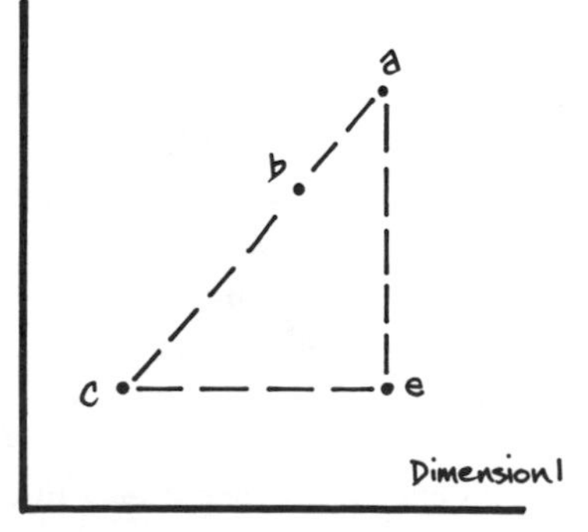


FIG. 6.7. In this two dimensional attribute space $a$ and $e$ take the same value on dimension 1 and $c$ and $e$ take the same value on dimension 2. Hence, if $r \geq 1$ then $d(c, e) + d(e,a) \geq d(c, b) + d(b, a)$.

must be symmetric: The similarity of object $x$ to $y$ must equal the similarity of $y$ to $x$. Tversky and Gati (1978) present evidence suggesting the occurrence of systematic asymmetries in certain kinds of similarities judgments.

Anyone proposing to use the methods of multidimensional scaling should be aware of these predictions and the experimental evidence relating to them. Here, however, it is not my aim to review this evidence, but to show how the theory of conjoint measurement may be applied to the theory of multidimensional scaling. This provides theoretical justification for the methods of multidimensional scaling as measurement procedures and also, shows how the specifically quantitative parts of the theory may be tested.

## THE APPLICATION OF CONJOINT MEASUREMENT

There are two applications of the theory of conjoint measurement to multidimensional scaling. The first is to each dimension separately and it tests two things: (i) that the dimension is quantitative and (ii) the proposition of intradimensional subtractivity. The second application is to dimensions pair by pair and, subject to confirmation of the first test, it tests interdimensional additivity, so that the dimensions together form a space.

Note that these tests require the prior identification of the dimensions or relevant stimulus attributes. However, they require no more than that values of these attributes be classifiable. It is not necessary that they be ordered.

### Test 1

The first test of the theory of multidimensional scaling using conjoint measurement is similar in form to the test of Thurstone's theory described in the last chapter. If a set of stimuli are chosen such that they differ with respect to just one of the relevant attributes (i.e., they differ along just one of the dimensions), then the distance between any two of them, $x$ and $y$, is

$$d(x, y) = \left( |x_i - y_i|^r \right)^{1/r}$$
$$= |x_i - y_i|$$

(where $i$ is the dimension along which they differ). For any other dimension $j$, the value of $|x_j - y_j|$ is zero, for by hypothesis the stimuli do not differ on that dimension. Hence, $|x_i - y_i|$ is the only nonzero difference contributing to distance and thus the only one to count.

Given a set of dissimilarities (or similarities) judgments on such a set of stimuli, the order of the stimuli along the dimension (i) may be inferred. Let $a$ and $b$ be the most dissimilar pair of stimuli. Then the order of the dissimilarities from $a$ (or, alternatively, from $b$), from least to most dissimilar, gives the order of the stimuli along the dimension (see Fig. 6.8a). This is because the order of the dissimilarities between stimuli is the same as the order of the distances between them (Proposition 5 of the theory). While this does not enable one to infer direction along the dimension (i.e., which end is the greater and which the lesser), this is not important for this particular test of the theory.

Given, then, that the stimuli are ordered, they may be partitioned into two disjoint subsets, the first *n* and the last *m* (for completeness of testing *n* and *m* should be as large as possible, and the difference between *n* and *m* should be as small as possible). An $n \times m$ dissimilarities matrix may then be constructed in which the rows are the first *n* stimuli and the columns the last *m*. The dissimilarities judgments within this matrix should satisfy the hierarchy of cancellation conditions. The reason why is as follows.

Let the distance between any stimulus pair, *x* and *y*, be $d(x,y)$. Because of the method of construction, either *all* row stimuli are greater on dimension *i* than *any* column stimulus or vice versa. Without loss of generality assume the former (i.e., $x_i > y_i$). Then

$$\begin{aligned} d(x,y) &= x_i - y_i \\ &= x_i + (-y_i). \end{aligned}$$

Hence, the distance between row and column stimuli is an additive function of their values on dimension *i* and so these distances must conform to the hierarchy of cancellation conditions. However, according to Proposition 5, judgments of dissimilarity are monotonic with distance, so the corresponding dissimilarities matrix must also satisfy this hierarchy of ordinal conditions.

These predictions depend not only on the assumption that dimension *i* is quantitative (2) (and, of course, 5 as already mentioned), but also upon the assumption of intradimensional subtractivity, one of the three components of the power metric (4).

The kind of situation envisaged here is illustrated in Figures 6.8 (i), (ii), and (iii). Fig. 6.8(i) shows that $d(a,f)$ is the largest distance and the order of the stimuli along the dimension is given by the order of their distances from *a*. Figure 6.8(ii) illustrates single cancellation or independence. In row *a* the order of the columns must be *f, e, d* (from greatest to least). Similarly, the same order on the columns must prevail in the other rows (*b* and *c*). Finally, Fig. 6.8 (iii) illustrates double cancellation. If $d(c,e) > d(b,d)$ and $d(b,f) > d(a,e)$ then, of course, $d(d,f)$ must exceed $d(a,c)$ and so, $d(c,f) > d(a,d)$. These two cancellation conditions are also illustrated in Fig. 6.9, which shows the order relations in the resulting dissimilarities matrix.

## Test 2

The second application of conjoint measurement to the theory of multidimensional scaling requires a set of stimuli differing with respect to just two relevant dimensions. Call these dimensions *i* and *j*. Then the distance between any two of these stimuli, *x* and *y*, is

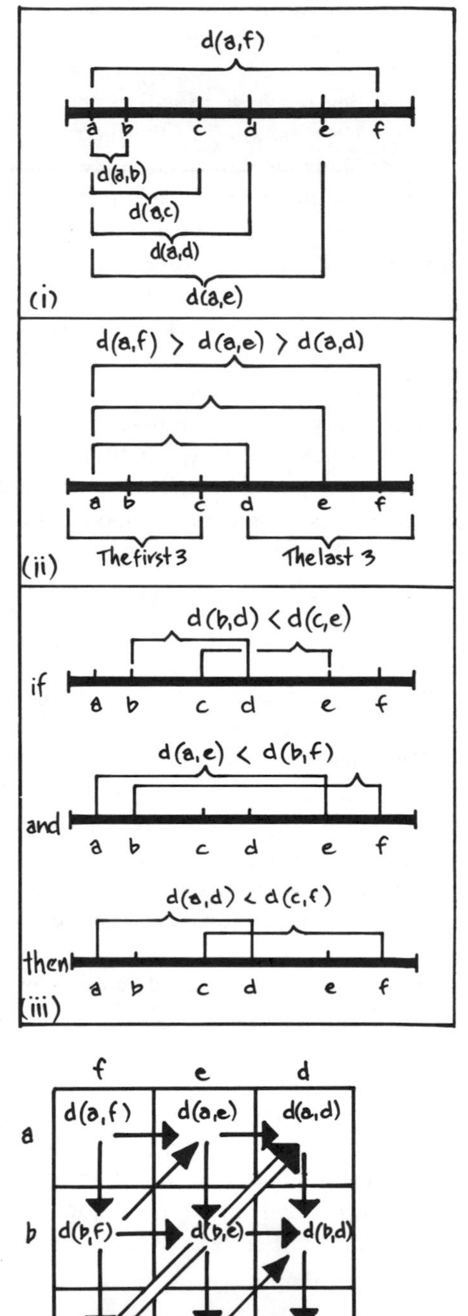


FIG. 6.8. (a) If *a, b, c, d, e* and *f* are points along a single dimension and *d*(*a, f*) is the greatest distance between any pair of these points then the order of the points along the dimension is given by the order of their distances from *a* (or *f*). If the order of the first 3 points from *a* is *a, b, c* and the order of the last 3 from *f* is *f, e, d* then (b) from single cancellation it follows that $d(a,f) > d(a,e) > d(a,d)$, etc.; and (c) from double cancellation it follows that whenever $d(b,d) < d(c,e)$ and $d(a,e) < d(b,f)$ then $d(a,d) < d(c,f)$.

FIG. 6.9. If *a, b, c, d, e,* and *f* are points along a single dimension in that order then these are the order relations upon the distances between them, the double cancellation prediction, of course, being a conditional statement.

$$d(x, y) = \left( |x_i - y_i|^r + |x_j - y_j|^r \right)^{1/r}.$$

Each dimension contributes its own component to the distance between $x$ and $y$, the contribution of dimension $i$ being $|x_i - y_i|^r$ and the contribution of dimension $j$ being $|x_j - y_j|^r$. The components contributed by $i$ may be thought of as a variable in their own right (call this variable "$A$") and likewise the components contributed by $j$ (call that variable "$X$"). Then, labeling the distance resulting from the power metric "$D$", the relationship between these three variables is

$$D = (A + X)^{1/r}$$

$$\text{or } D^r = A + X.$$

That is, $D^r$ is an additive function of the $i$ and $j$ components and, hence, must conform to the hierarchy of cancellation conditions. Since for the power metric, $r \geq 1$, it follows that $D^r$ is an increasing monotonic function of $D$ (i.e., the order upon $D$ and $D^r$ must be the same). Furthermore, it follows from Proposition 5 that judged dissimilarities and distances must be in the same order. Hence, judged dissimilarities must also conform to the hierarchy of cancellation conditions.

This prediction depends on $i$ and $j$ being quantitative variables (2), on distance, and dissimilarity being monotonically related (5), and on two components of the power metric, intradimensional subtractivity and interdimensional additivity. While it was assumed that $r \geq 1$, this component of the powermetric is not actually required. Providing $r \neq 0$ the above mentioned prediction follows.

The kind of situation that might be used to test this prediction is illustrated in Fig. 6.10. The nine stimuli $F$, $G$, $H$, $I$, $J$, $K$, $L$, $M$, and $N$ form a rectangular array in which $F$, $G$, and $H$ are the same on dimension 2, as are $I$, $J$, and $K$, and

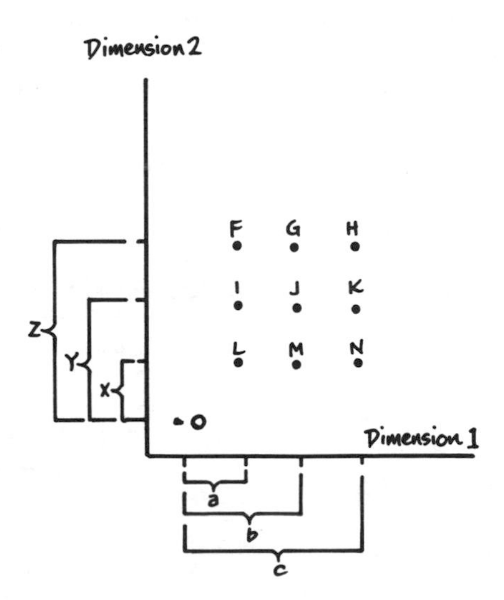


FIG. 6.10. The nine stimuli, *F, G, H, I, J, K, L, M,* and*N,* form a rectangular array in a two dimensional attribute space, with the stimuli within each triple *(F,I,L)*, *(G,J,M)*, and *(H,K,N)* having the same value on dimension 1 and the stimuli within each triple, *(F,G,H)*, *(I,J,K)*, and *(L,M,N)* having the same value on dimension 2. Hence, the distance between each of these nine and *O* is an additive function of one of *a, b, c* (to the power of *r*), and one of *x, y,* or *z* (to the power of *r*).

*L, M,* and *N*. Also, *F, I,* and *L* are the same on dimension 1, as are *G, J,* and *M,* and *H, K,* and *N*. Thus, the proximity of these nine stimuli to one outside of the rectangle, such as *O* (whose values on dimensions 1 and 2 are both lower than that of any of the stimuli in the rectangle), is determined by the requisite composite of one of *x, y,* and *z* with one of *a, b,* or *c*. For example,

$$d(O,L)^r = a^r + x^r$$

$$d(O,J)^r = b^r + y^r$$

$$\text{and } d(O,H)^r = c^r + z^r.$$

Thus, the dimensional components constituting the set of distances are, for dimension 1, $a^r$, $b^r$, and $c^r$, and for dimension 2, $x^r$, $y^r$, and $z^r$. Each dissimilarity judgment then is monotonically related to the sum of a dimension 1 component plus a dimension 2 component, as shown in Table 6.1.

It is the order relations between the cells of a dissimilarities matrix such as this that must satisfy the cancellation conditions (in this case single and double cancellation).

## AN EXAMPLE OF CONJOINT MEASUREMENT

As an illustration of these two tests of multidimensional scaling theory a sample of 130 psychology students at the University of Sydney were instructed to make the appropriate dissimilarities judgements about pairs of stimuli from Fig. 6.11. These stimuli are schematic pictures of flower pots and they vary systematically along two dimensions: leaf size/shape and pot size/shape. They have been so contrived that judgments on pairs within the subset, *E, F, G, H, I,* and *J* enable Test 1 to be carried out. These six stimuli differ only according to leaf size/shape and dissimilarity judgments based on these differences should conform to single and double cancellation. A similar prediction applies to judgments on the set *B, D, H, K, M,* and *P*. Finally, the differences between each of the nine stimuli *A,*

TABLE 6.1
The Distance Between Each of the Nine Stimuli in Fig. 6.10 and *O* is an Additive Function of a Row Component (From Dimension 2) and a Column Component (From Dimension 1)

| | | *Dimension 1 components* | | |
|---|---|---|---|---|
| | | $a^r$ | $b^r$ | $c^r$ |
| *Dimension 2 components* | $x^r$ | $d(O,L)^r$ | $d(O,M)^r$ | $d(O,N)^r$ |
| | $y^r$ | $d(O,I)^r$ | $d(O,J)^r$ | $d(O,K)^r$ |
| | $z^r$ | $d(O,F)^r$ | $d(O,G)^r$ | $d(O,H)^r$ |

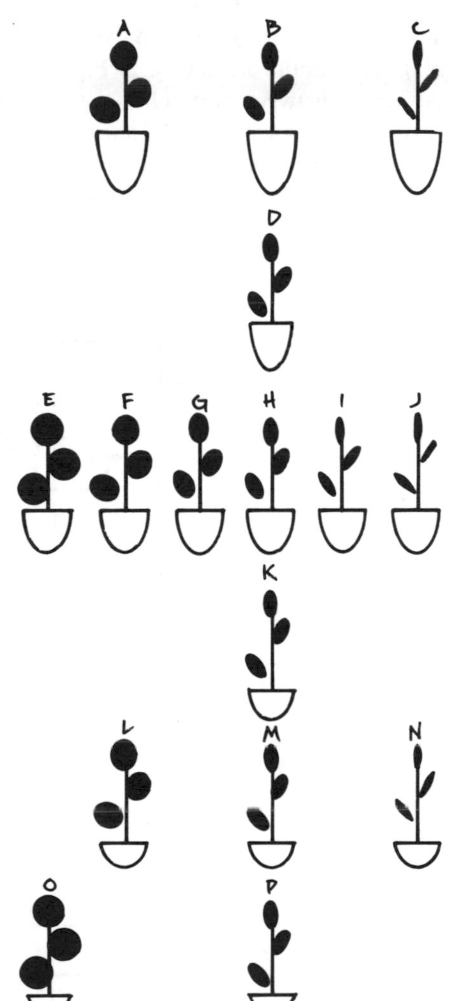


FIG. 6.11. The schematic flower pots used as stimuli in the test of the theory of multidimensional scaling.

*D*, *C*, *F*, *H*, *J*, *L*, *M*, *N*, and stimulus *O* form a matrix like that illustrated in Table 6.1 and, so, enable Test 2 to be conducted.

The relevant pairs of stimuli were presented to the subjects in a test booklet and the subjects were instructed to indicate the degree of dissimilarity between each stimulus pair on a 21-point rating scale. In order to test the conjoint measurement conditions various pairs of ratings must then be compared. For example, one may be interested in how the pair (*G*,*J*) is rated compared to the pair (*G*,*I*). Within each subject's data, the difference between the ratings on these two stimulus pairs were classified as "greater than 0" (>), "equal to 0" (=) or "less than 0" (<), and then across subjects the frequencies within these categories were obtained ($N_>$, $N_=$, $N_<$) relative to these two pairs of stimuli. The significance of the difference between such ratings across all subjects was then assessed by performing sign tests (i.e., $\chi^2$ tests on the difference between the two frequencies $N_>$ and $N_<$). The results are shown in Fig. 6.12. Part (i) shows the results for Test 1. An arrow between two cells (e.g., between *EJ* and *EI*) indicates that significantly more subjects rated the stimulus pair at the arrow's tail (e.g., *EJ*), as more dissimilar than the stimulus pair at the arrow's head (e.g., *EI*) than did vice versa. On the assumption that individual differences are due to error, the

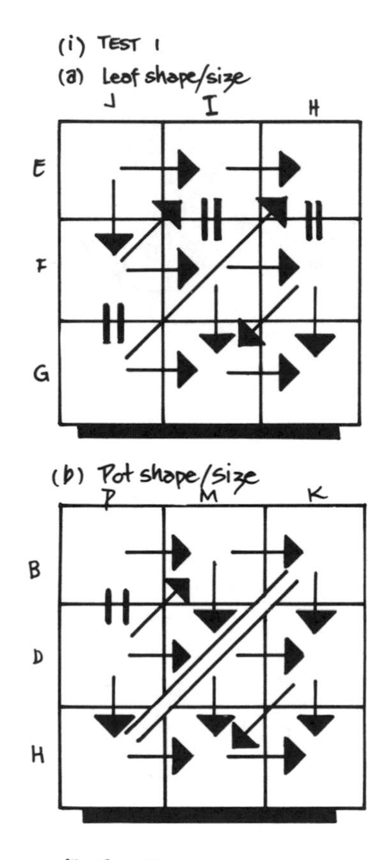

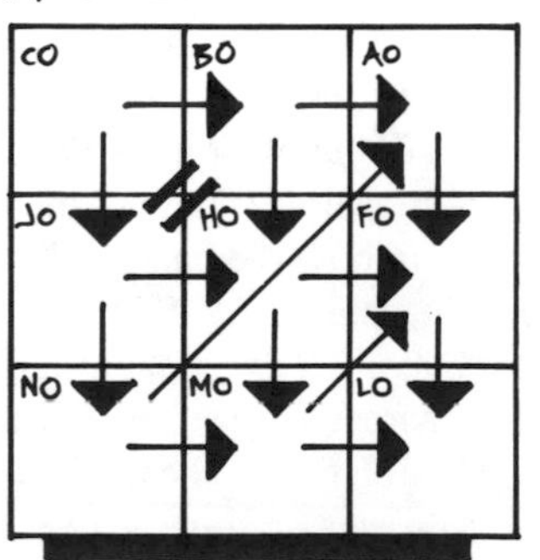


FIG. 6.12. The order relations inferred from the dissimilarity judgments of the 130 subjects used. (i)(a) fails single cancellation but satisfies double cancellation (pattern 3 of Table 5.3); (i)(b) also fails single cancellation and satisfies double cancellation (pattern 4 of Table 5.3); and (ii) satisfies both single and double cancellation (pattern 6 of Table 5.3).

arrows in Fig. 6.12 may be taken as indicative of the true dissimilarity ordering for the population.

The orders given in (i)(a) and (b) depart from that required by single cancellation. However, two alterations to the order in (i)(a) (replacing the arrow between *EJ* and *FJ* by "=" and the "=" between *FJ* and *GJ* by an arrow) and one alteration to the order in (i)(b) (replacing the "=" between *BP* and *DP* by an arrow), produces orders consistent with single cancellation. Neither (i)(a) nor (i)(b) violated double cancellation. Hence, for Test 1, the order obtained from the subjects' judgments departed from that predicted on three occasions. This may be taken to indicate that at least one of the assumptions underlying this prediction is false. Which one(s), of course, it is not possible to tell from these results.

The order shown in Fig. 6.12(ii) conforms to both the single and double cancellation conditions. Remembering that Test 1 is based on Propositions 2, 5, and intradimensional subtractivity and Test 2, on these propositions together with interdimensional additivity, these results indicate that at least one of the first three of these propositions is false.

Of course, one would not reject the theory of multidimensional scaling on the basis of such a disconfirmation. In testing any theory other propositions must always be assumed to be true and, therefore, the failure of a prediction may reflect on these propositions as much as on the theory. For example, in this instance, it was assumed that all subjects attended only to the dimensions of pot/shape size and leaf shape/size, and that all subjects were able to rate their degrees of judged dissimilarity in a consistent way. Also, it was assumed that the stimuli were sufficiently distinct from one another to prevent confusions. It may have been that the pairs *E* and *F*, and *B* and *D*, were too similar to enable a reliable test of the theory of multidimensional scaling.

Whatever the cause of the disconfirmations here, evidence against the theory of multidimensional scaling has been accumulating over the last 20 years (cf. Krantz & Tversky, 1975; Tversky & Krantz, 1969; Tversky & Gati, 1982; Wender, 1971; & Wiener-Ehlich, 1978). This evidence calls into question the current attitude towards multidimensional scaling within psychology. At present it is used indiscriminately, without first testing the applicability of the theory to the stimulus domain involved. Here, it has been illustrated how the theory of conjoint measurement may be used to make such tests in certain stimulus domains.

Chapter 7

# Coombs' Theory of Unfolding

Coombs' theory is similar to Thurstone's in that it also was proposed in order to support a scaling procedure (in this case the "unfolding" procedure, from which the theory derived its name). Hence, it presumes the existence of quantitative variables of a psychological kind. It differs from Thurstone's theory in two important respects. In the first place it concerns a special category of pair comparison judgments, namely, preferences. Second, it lacks the probabilistic mechanism inherent to Thurstone's theory. Consider the situation where a person is making pair comparison preference judgments on a set of attitude statements. The subject is not judging which statement within each pair is the more favorable; he is indicating his preference (i.e., which statement within each pair he agrees with most). Assume that the statements lie along a single relevant quantitative dimension (e.g., the pro-anti dimension). Let each person have a point of maximum preference on this dimension. Then according to Coombs' unfolding theory a person will prefer statement $x$ to statement $y$, if and only if he perceives his point of maximum preference to be nearer to $x$ than to $y$ along this dimension. Thus each pair comparison preference judgment provides information about the relative distances between a subject's point of maximum preference and the stimuli used. Because the theory postulates that all subjects agree about the location of the stimuli on this dimension, even though they might have different points of maximum preference, pair comparison preference judgments from different subjects may be pooled to provide enough distance information to infer something of the quantitative structure of this dimension. Ideally, both the location of the stimuli and the subjects' points of maximum preference may be inferred. Something of the flavor of this procedure is given in this chapter, although the primary concern is with the logic of the theory: its assumptions, testability, and use as a basis for psychological measurement.

The theory and its associated method were first proposed by Coombs in 1950. He subsequently integrated it into a much broader theory of judgmental behavior in his book, *A Theory of Data* (1964). The procedure was moderately well received and included amongst the prescribed methods of psychological measurement (e.g., Green, 1954; & Torgerson, 1958). It has the advantage of fitting very neatly into the representational measurement theory framework. A description of the procedure is included in a number of recent scaling text books (e.g., Dawes, 1972 & van der Ven, 1980). At first sight it is somewhat surprising then that in the last 30 or more years the number of its applications is very few. Its inclusion in the books mentioned is based more on promise than performance. The reason is not hard to find and it provides an interesting commentary on the attitude of psychologists towards measurement. The successful application of Coombs' theory demands that the stimuli used actually be unidimensional. That is, that there be only a single variable relevant to the subjects' judgments. Thus, its application requires careful stimulus control in contexts where such control is very difficult to attain. This in turn requires intensive research into relevant stimulus attributes. In general psychologists have shied away from that daunting task and found refuge in quantitative methods that, because they assume more, demand less foundational research as the basis for their application. Methods that always yield a scaling solution, like the method of summated ratings, are almost universally preferred to methods which, like Coombs', do not produce a scaling solution when they are falsified by the data. Surprisingly, vulnerability to falsification is commonly deemed by psychologists to be a fault rather than a virtue.

## AN OUTLINE OF THE THEORY

Coombs' theory may be summed-up in the following five propositions.

(1) There is a single stimulus variable relevant to the preference judgments.
(2) That variable is quantitative.
(3) Each subject has a single point of maximum preference on that variable.
(4) A person's degree of preference for any stimulus, $x$, decreases as the distance between $x$ and the person's point of maximum preference increases.
(5) All subjects agree about the location of the stimuli on the relevant dimension.

Coombs calls a person's point of maximum preference his or her *ideal point* and he calls a person's preference ordering of the stimuli an *I scale* (the "I" indicating that it is the order of an individual subject). The use of the term "scale" to denote an ordering is too grandiose. Hence, the more accurate descriptive phrase "individual preference order" is used here instead.

The kind of situation the theory covers is illustrated geometrically in Fig. 7.1. In that figure there are four stimuli, *A, B, C,* and *D* and their values on the relevant variable are represented as points on a line. Person *i's* point of maximum preference on the variable is indicated by the arrow. Coombs calls such a geometric representation of both stimuli and individuals a *J scale* (the "J" indicating the diagram's *joint* accommodation of stimuli and individuals). Person *i's* preference ordering of the four stimuli would be *BACD,* because that is the order of their proximity to *i's* ideal point. On the other hand, another person, *j,* whose ideal point is to the right of the *CD* midpoint, would give *DCBA* as their order of preference. Coombs suggests that a person's preference order may be obtained by folding the line representing the variable at the person's ideal point so that one is left with a single line, as in Fig. 7.2. Then the person's preference order is simply the order of the stimuli down this line. Because one does not know the locations of the stimuli on the variable this is not, of course, a real possibility. The aim of Coombs' procedure is to discover something of these locations from the individual preference orderings that constitute the data. However, at the theoretical level, these preference orderings are "foldings" of the J scale. Coombs' procedure, he suggests, may be thought of metaphorically as a simultaneous "unfolding" of them. Hence, the name given to his procedure and the theory sustaining it.

Before considering the application of conjoint measurement theory to unfolding theory, the five propositions constituting the theory will be considered in more detail. Proposition 1 locates the type of stimulus domain to which the theory applies. It applies only to undimensional stimuli, that is, to stimuli varying along a single dimension relevant to the preferences of the subjects involved. If the stimuli vary along more than one relevant dimension then the theory does not apply. Thus, Proposition 1 is not so much a part of the theory as a boundary condition necessary for its application. In multidimensional contexts a different, though related, theory might be contemplated and, indeed, Coombs (1964) has done just that.

Proposition 2 requires that the relevant variable on which the stimuli differ be a quantitative variable. As with 1, this may also be regarded as setting a boundary condition for the application of the remainder of the theory. Thus, an adequate test of Coombs' theory would require construction of stimuli satisfying these two conditions. Then, failure of the theory's predictions would imply its falsity. Many

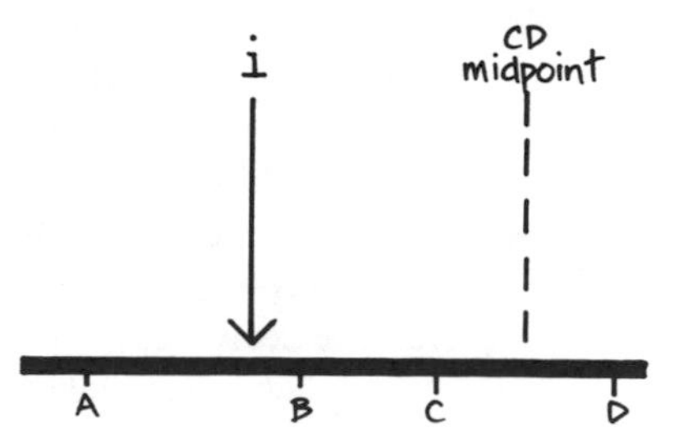


FIG. 7.1. Four stimuli differing along a single dimension relevant to person *i*'s preferences. According to Coombs' theory *i*'s order of preference will be: *BACD*. Another person, to the right of, say, the *CD* midpoint would give *DCBA* as their preference order.

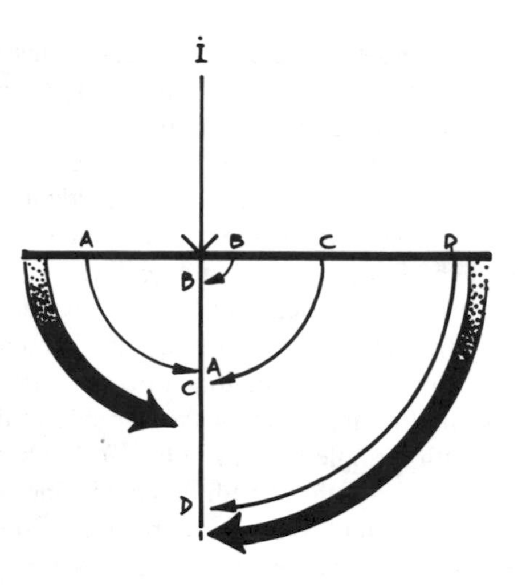


FIG. 7.2. *i*'s preference order may be obtained by folding the relevant dimension at *i*'s ideal point to form a single vertical line. *i*'s order of preference is the order of the stimuli down this line.

of its current applications within psychology, as in attitude measurements for example, beg Propositions 1 and 2.

Proposition 3 requires that each subject has a *single* point of maximum preference on the relevant variable. This is a simple and attractive hypothesis but by no means logically necessary. It is false, for example, if a subject has *no point* of maximum preference. Suppose a subject is choosing between the members of a set of paintings. Further suppose that this person is a complete philistine for whom the only relevant variable is monetary value. Then he may not have a single point of maximum preference simply because there is no greatest monetary value. Another person may not have a point of maximum preference on this variable because he completely disregards this variable in making his choices. However in that case it is not a relevant variable for him.

Proposition 3 is also false if any subject has more than a single point of maximum preference. This is a real possibility. Proposition 3 denies the complexity of human beings; the fact that we are often torn between competing interests. For example, in choosing something as simple as a cup of tea a person might have two quite distinct points of maximum preference. Imagine a set of cups of tea that differ only with respect to quantity of sugar. The same person may maximally prefer tea with no sugar (because of his dietary interests), and tea with two teaspoons of sugar (because of taste). Could such a person make a choice? A prediction would depend on our theory and it's not clear what Coombs' theory would predict. Clearly, this is an important issue and one that requires a deeper analysis of just how our preferences are determined by our interests, and recognition of the fact that interests within the same person often conflict.

Proposition 4 assumes the truth of 3 and relates degree of preference to distance from the subject's point of maximum preference. It has two important facets. First, the degree of preference decreases as distance from the point of maximum preference increases. Second, because it makes no mention of direction it follows

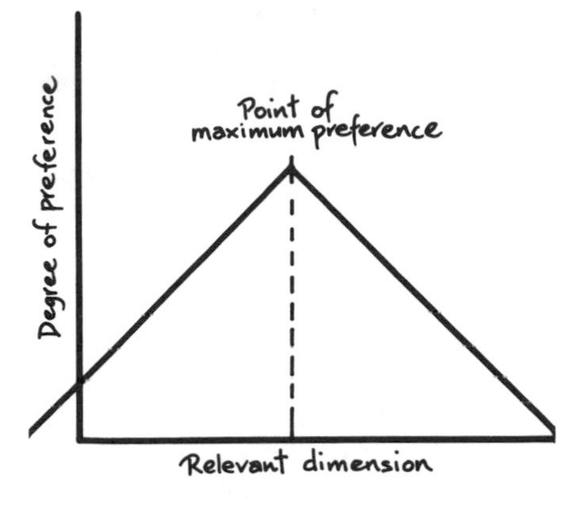


FIG. 7.3. Degree of preference is monotonic decreasing and symmetric about the point of maximum preference (ideal point) according to Coombs' theory.

that the rate of decrease must be the same on either side of the point of maximum preference (as shown in Fig. 7.3). Of course, the decrease need not be linear but it must be symmetric.

Proposition 5 is necessary because the location of the stimuli on the relevant dimension is inferred from the judgments of a number of different subjects. Hence, they cannot disagree about where the stimuli are located, or else the stimulus locations inferred will not necessarily be representative of the subjects. For example, if one was attempting to locate political candidates on the left-right political dimension, and the subjects disagreed about the location of different candidates, then there would be no common scale that represented the views of all subjects. Obviously, this proposition is the most tenuous of all when the stimulus variables are of a psychological nature.

## THE APPLICATION OF CONJOINT MEASUREMENT

Coombs' theory may be expressed as follows. Let $S$ be a set of stimuli varying with respect to a single relevant dimension which is quantitative. Then for any person, $a$,

$$P(a, s, t) \text{ if and only if } |a - s| < |a - t|$$

(where $P(a, s, t)$ is the ternary relation, person $a$ prefers $s$ to $t$, and the values of $a$, $s$, and $t$ on the dimension are symbolized by those letters). The form of the inequality on the right is similar to that mentioned in relation to the application of conjoint measurement to the postulate of intradimensional subtractivity in the last chapter. It may be thought that conjoint measurement applies to Coombs' theory in a similar way. However, there are some complications in this approach and a simpler line will be taken. This simpler alternative depends on the fact that given any body of data (i.e., preference orderings from a group of subjects), Coombs' theory implies an ordering on the interstimulus midpoints, and because these midpoints are an additive function of the stimulus values, this ordering must satisfy the hierarchy of cancellation conditions.

Let $S$ be a set of $n$ stimuli differing with respect to a single relevant quantitative variable. Let $A$ be a group of subjects and let each subject produce a preference ordering of the stimuli in $S$. For the moment the possibility of ties in these preference orderings will be ignored, and it will be assumed that for each subject, $a$, there is a preference ordering of the $n$ stimuli, $P_a=\{s,t,...\}$, such that any stimulus, $x$, comes before any other stimulus, $y$, if and only if $P(a,x,y)$.

If there are $n$ stimuli then $n!$ different preference orders are possible. Coombs' theory, however, predicts that no more than $\frac{1}{2}n(n-1)+1$ of these will occur. The reason is as follows. First, consider a simple illustration. Figure 7.4 shows the location of four hypothetical stimuli, $A$, $B$, $C$, and $D$ along the relevant dimension. It also shows the interstimulus midpoints (the bisectors have been drawn in). Because there are four stimuli there are $\frac{1}{2}n(n-1) = \frac{1}{2}.4(4-1) = 6$ interstimulus midpoints and they partition the dimension into $6 + 1 = 7$ intervals. Associated with each interval is a unique preference order because if the points of maximum preference from any two subjects fall within the same interval then the relative proximity of the stimuli to their points of maximum preference is the same. Hence, in this case there must be only seven different preference orders allowed by Coombs' theory. More generally, if there are $n$ stimuli at various different points along a single dimension then there must be $\frac{1}{2}n(n-1)$ interstimulus midpoints, and so $\frac{1}{2}n(n-1) + 1$ intervals separated by the midpoints. Each interval has associated with it its own preference order. Hence, there are no more than $\frac{1}{2}n(n-1) + 1$ allowed.

Not only does Coombs' theory predict that no more than $\frac{1}{2}n(n-1) + 1$ of the $n!$ possible preference orders will occur, it also predicts that those that do occur have a special structure. Note that in Fig. 7.4 as one moves from left to right each new preference order differs from the preceding one by just the inversion of a single pair of stimuli, and this pair is just those whose midpoint was last crossed. This pattern continues until all midpoints are crossed and the final preference order becomes the complete reversal of the first. So the $\frac{1}{2}n(n-1) + 1$ permissible preference orders must have that kind of structure.

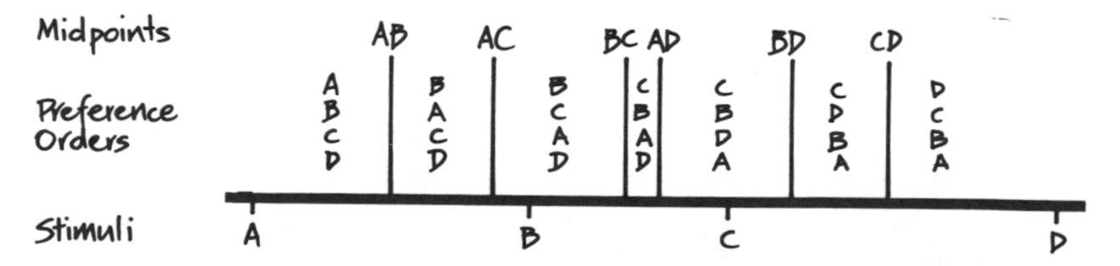


FIG. 7.4. The position of four hypothetical stimuli along the relevant dimension. Also shown are the six dashed lines bisecting the distances between the pairs of stimuli; the seven intervals so created; and the preference orders that, according to Coombs' theory, belong to any person whose point of maximum preference falls within any such interval.

More can be said about this structure. Notice that in Fig. 7.4 the only two preference orders that are complete reversals of each other are the first and last. Notice also that each of these gives the order of the stimuli along the dimension, either from right to left, or from left to right. So, according to Coombs, if any body of preference data contains such a pair of orders then they give the order of the stimuli along the dimension. In turn, the order of the stimuli along the dimension gives part of the order of the interstimulus midpoints along the dimension. For example, if, as in Fig. 7.4, the order of the stimuli along the dimension is *A, B, C,* and *D* then it follows that the order of the midpoints must include $AB < AC < AD$ and $BC < BD$ (where "*AB*", "*AC*", . . . etc. refer to midpoints and "$<$" means "comes before"). This can be illustrated in Fig. 7.5, where there is a matrix whose rows and columns are the four stimuli listed in their order along the dimension and the cell entries (above the diagonal) refer to the midpoints. These cells must be ordered from left to right, and from top to bottom. Hence, they will satisfy single cancellation (or independence). Of course, this does not completely order all of the midpoints, the order between the *BC* and *AD* midpoints being unstated. But that order is settled by the fact that the preference order *CBAD* is present, rather than *BCDA:* the *AD* midpoint comes before the *BC* midpoint.

The preference orders satisfying the constraints illustrated in Fig. 7.5 are set out in Fig. 7.6. The are joined by arrows and beside each arrow is the stimulus pair reversed in moving from the preference order above to the one below. Note that when we get to *BCAD* there are two possibilities: either *AD* or *BC* may be reversed. The path we take depends on the data. If *CBAD* is given by some subjects then $BC < AD$ and if *BCDA*, then $AD < BC$. Coombs' theory predicts that both cannot occur.

In general terms then, if $x_1, x_2, \ldots, x_n$ is the order of the $n$ stimuli along the relevant dimension, then for any $j, k = 1, 2, \ldots, n$ $(j \neq k)$:

$$x_j < x_k \text{ if and only if } x_i x_j < x_i x_k$$

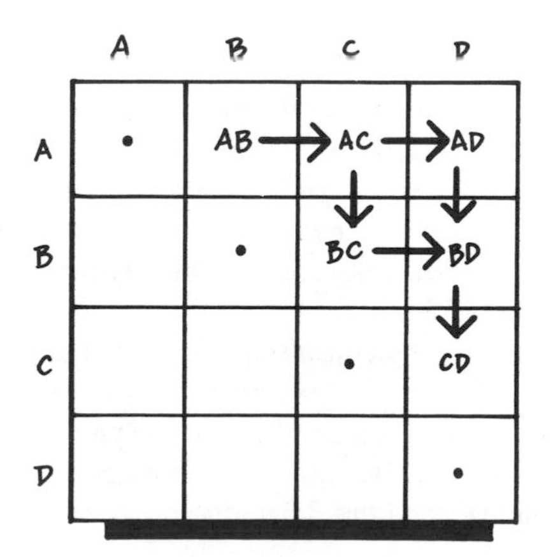


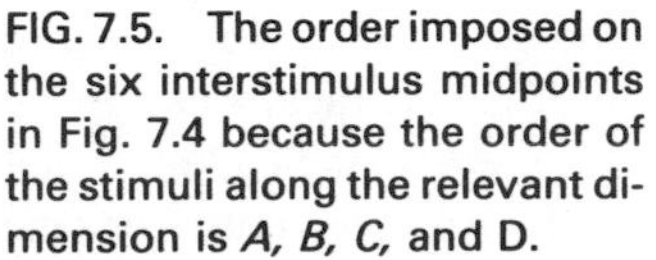
FIG. 7.5. The order imposed on the six interstimulus midpoints in Fig. 7.4 because the order of the stimuli along the relevant dimension is *A, B, C,* and D.

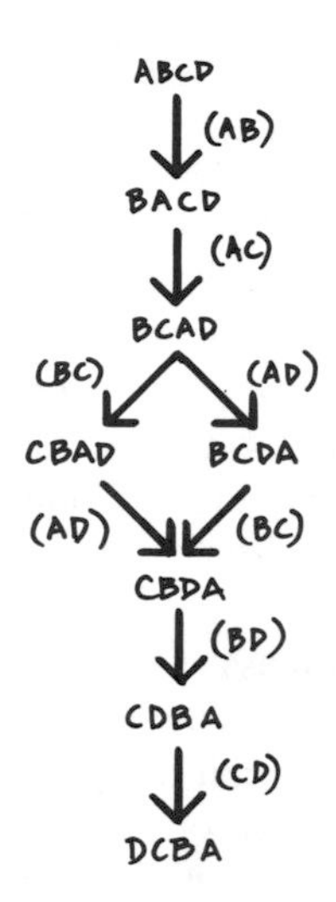


FIG. 7.6. The preference orders allowed by Coombs' theory form a single descending path through this graph, given that the order of the stimuli along the relevant dimension is *A, B, C,* and *D.*

(for any $i = 1, 2, \ldots, n$, $i \neq j$, $i \neq k$ and where $x_ix_j$ ($= x_jx_i$) denotes the interstimulus midpoint between $x_i$ and $x_j$). This is equivalent to the conjoint measurement condition of independence, because it means that all rows will be ordered parallel to one another and so will all columns. It leaves undetermined the order on the midpoints of all pairs $x_hx_k$ and $x_ix_j$, where $x_h < x_i < x_j < x_k$. The order upon these midpoints follows from the presence or absence of certain preference orders in the data (as illustrated in Fig. 7.6).

Not only must the order on the interstimulus midpoints satisfy single cancellation, it must satisfy the entire hierarchy of cancellation conditions. This follows from the fact that the midpoint is an additive function of the stimulus values, i.e., Midpoint $(X, Y) = \frac{1}{2}(X + Y)$ and the order on $\frac{1}{2}(X + Y)$ must be the same as that on $X + Y$. Of course, in Fig. 7.5 there is no opportunity to test any of the cancellation conditions beyond independence. This only becomes possible with six or more stimuli.

With six stimuli, for example, where the order along the dimension is discovered to be *A, B, C, D, E,* and *F,* any set of $\frac{1}{2}.6(6 - 1) + 1 = 16$ preference orders falling on any one of the paths through Fig. 7.7 will satisfy independence. It remains to be seen, however, whether or not it will satisfy double cancellation. For example, if a set of preference judgments on these six stimuli include the following three orders, then the order on the midpoints is as shown in Fig. 7.8, and that violates double cancellation. These preference orders are: *BCDEAF, DCBEAF, DCEFBA.*

As can be seen by consulting Fig. 7.7, the presence of *BCDEAF* means that the order of *AE* is reversed before *BD*. Similarly, the presence of *DCBEAF* means that *CD* is reversed before *AF*. And the presence of *DCEFBA* means that *BF* is reversed before *CE*. Hence, the *AE* midpoint precedes the *BD,* the *CD* midpoint precedes the *AF,* and the *BF* midpoint precedes the *CE*. As is obvious from the

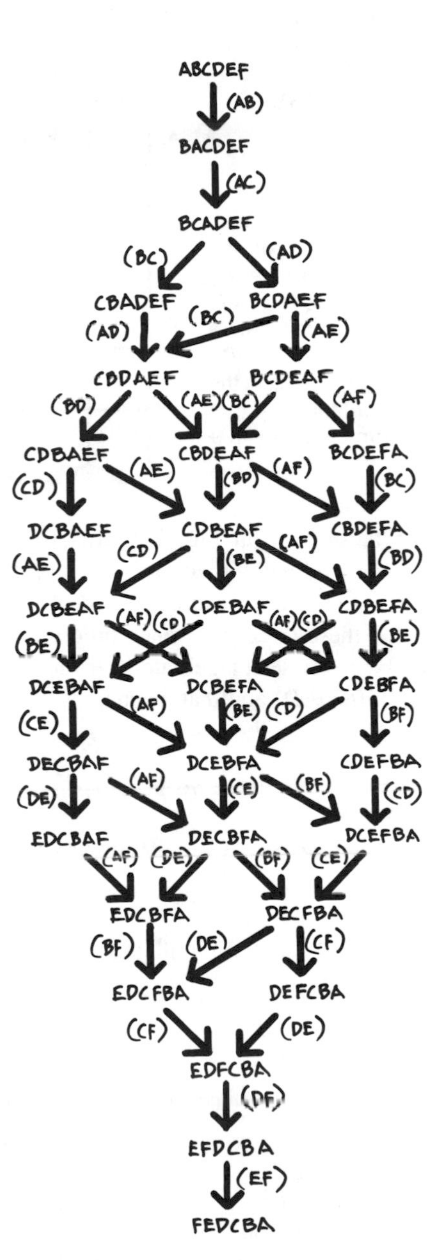


FIG. 7.7. The preference orders allowed by Coombs' theory form a single descending path through this graph, given that the order of the six stimuli along the relevant dimension is *A, B, C, D, E,* and *F.*

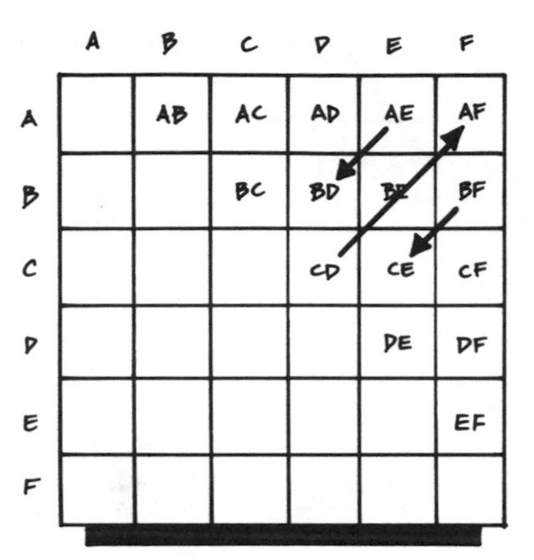


FIG. 7.8. If the order of the stimuli along the relevant dimension is *A, B, C, D, E,* and *F,* then the preference orders *BCDEAF, DCBEAF,* and *DCEFBA* jointly imply this order upon the interstimulus midpoints (the arrow goes from earlier to later values).

direction of the arrows in Fig. 7.8, this means that the double cancellation condition is violated and violation of that condition means that there is no way that $A$, $B$, $C$, $D$, $E$, and $F$ can be placed along the relevant dimension (in that order), so that these three preference orders can be accommodated.

This can be easily seen algebraicly. If the *AE* midpoint precedes the *BD* then $\frac{1}{2}(A + E) < \frac{1}{2}(B + D)$ and that means,

$$A + E < B + D$$

$$\text{i.e. (i) } E - D < B - A.$$

Similarly, $\frac{1}{2}(C + D) < \frac{1}{2}(A + F)$ implies that

$$\text{(ii) } C - A < F - D$$

and $\frac{1}{2}(B + F) < \frac{1}{2}(C + E)$ implies that

$$\text{(iii) } F - E < C - B.$$

But given that the order long the dimension is $A$, $B$, $C$, $D$, $E$, $F$ it follows that

$$C - A = B - A + C - B$$

$$\text{and } F - D = E - D + F - E,$$

so, as shown in Fig. 7.9, if (i) and (iii) are satisfied (ii) cannot be.

What now must be obvious is that if any of the hierarchy of cancellation conditions fails then Coombs' theory proves false. So conjoint measurement provides an ideal way to test the theory. As well, given that Coombs' theory is true and the requisite degree of stimulus control attained, it would prove the ideal way to quantify psychological variables lying behind preferences. This would involve the construction of standard sequences of stimuli based on equality of midpoints of nested pairs. In Fig. 7.9 for example, the *BC* pair is nested between the *AD* pair. If their midpoints coincided then $D - C = B - A$. A complete

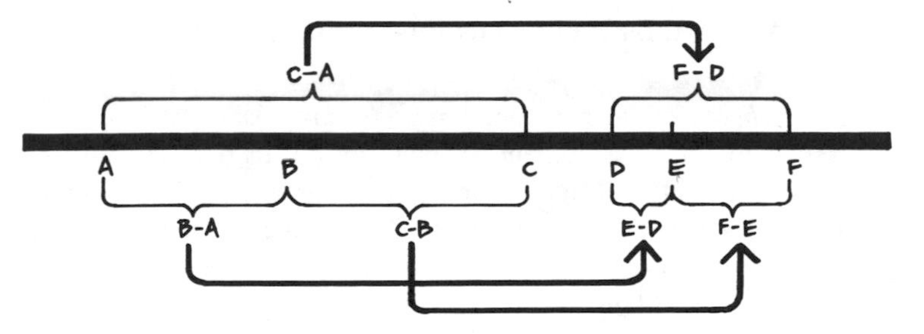


FIG. 7.9. If $B - A$ exceeds $E - D$ and $C - B$ exceeds $F - E$ then $C - A$ must exceed $F - D$.

standard sequence for the six stimuli $A, B, C, D, E$, and $F$ is shown in Fig. 7.10. Here the coincidence of the $AF$, $BE$, and $CD$ midpoints implies that

$$E - D = C - B,$$

$$\text{and } F - D = C - A,$$

$$\text{whence } F - E = B - A.$$

Also, the coincidence of the $AD$ and $BC$ midpoints means that $D - C = B - A$ and the coincidence of the $CF$ and $DE$ midpoints means that $F - E = D - C$. Finally, the coincidence of the $BD$ and $AE$ midpoints means that $E - D = B - A$ and the coincidence of the $CE$ and $BF$ midpoints means that $F - E - B - C$. Thus, $B - A = C - B = D - C = E - D = F - E$. That is, we have a standard sequence.

In the case of Coombs' theory evidence for a standard sequence is obtained by getting fewer than the allowed number of individual preference orders. Note that in Fig. 7.10, only 10 of the 16 permitted orders is present. So the existence of a standard sequence puts further constraints on the occurrence of individual preference orders.

I am not suggesting that the construction of such sequences would be easy. Far from it. The important point is that their construction would provide compelling evidence that the variable involved is quantitative.

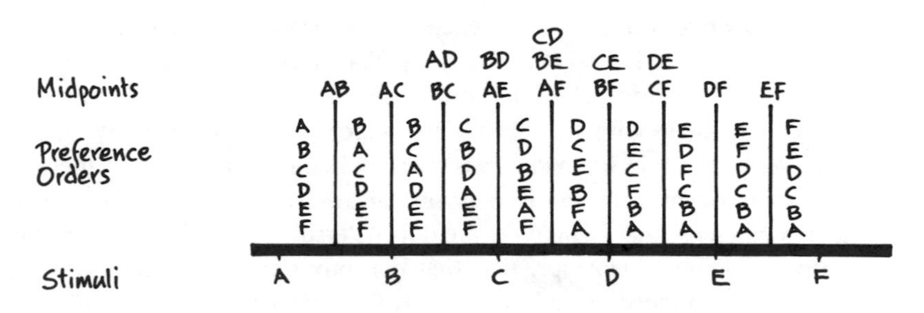

FIG. 7.10. A hypothetical standard sequence of six stimuli.

## AN EXAMPLE OF CONJOINT MEASUREMENT

In his book *A Theory of Data,* Coombs reports some data which will suffice to illustrate the conjoint measurement analysis of his theory. He instructed 62 students at the University of Michigan to make judgments on all pair comparisons on the letter grades $A+$, $A$, $A-$, $B+$, $B$, $B-$, $C+$, which were grades they might get in their course. For each pair comparison the students were asked which they thought they were more likely to get. 58 of the students gave transitive judgments, while four did not. The data from these four subjects consequently violates Coombs' theory, because it predicts that each subject's judgments will be transitive. However, each intransitivity could have resulted from just one error. In that case, there would be four errors out of 1302 pair comparison judgments and any theory can live with that.

For ease of presentation, let the grades $A+$ to $C+$ be represented by the symbols $A$ to $G$ in the obvious order. If the order of the stimuli along the dimension is $A$, $B$, $C$, $D$, $E$, $F$, $G$ then Coombs' theory predicts that each preference order will be consistent with that ordering, in the sense that it can be produced by "folding" that order at some point, and interleaving the stimuli in the two folded arms.

This sense of consistency is worth stating precisely. Let $x_1, x_2, \ldots, x_n$ be the order of the stimuli along the relevant dimension (i.e., $x_1 < x_2 < \ldots < x_n$). Let the preference ordering for any subject, $a$, be $P_a = x_i, \ldots, x_j, \ldots, x_k, \ldots$. Then Coombs' theory implies that for each preference order, $P_a$,

(i) for all $j, k > i$, $x_j$ comes before $x_k$ in $P_a$ if and only if $j < k$; and
(ii) for all $j, k < i$, $x_j$ comes before $x_k$ in $P_a$ if and only if $j > k$.

In general, if there are $n$ stimuli, there will be $2^{n-1}$ preference orders consistent with any given ordering of those stimuli along the dimension. In this case $2^{n-1} = 2^6 = 64$ and the set of 64 preference orders consistent with the stimulus order, $A$, $B$, $C$, $D$, $E$, $F$, and $G$ along the dimension is shown in Fig. 7.11. Those preference orders obtained by Coombs are shown in Fig. 7.12 (with their frequencies of occurrence in parentheses). All of the 58 subjects whose preference orders were transitive produced preference orders that were consistent with the stimulus order mentioned. This result suggests that all of the subjects agreed that was the order of the stimuli along the dimension.

It is also worth mentioning that each of the preference orders given by the four intransitive subjects could be made transitive, and converted to one of these 64 permitted orders by an alteration to only one of the pair comparison judgments made. It is in this sense that so far there are only 4 "errors" out of 1302 judgments.

Of course, Coombs' theory predicts that not only must the preference order produced come from those listed in Fig. 7.11, they must all fall on a single path through that diagram. Each path through this figure accommodates no more

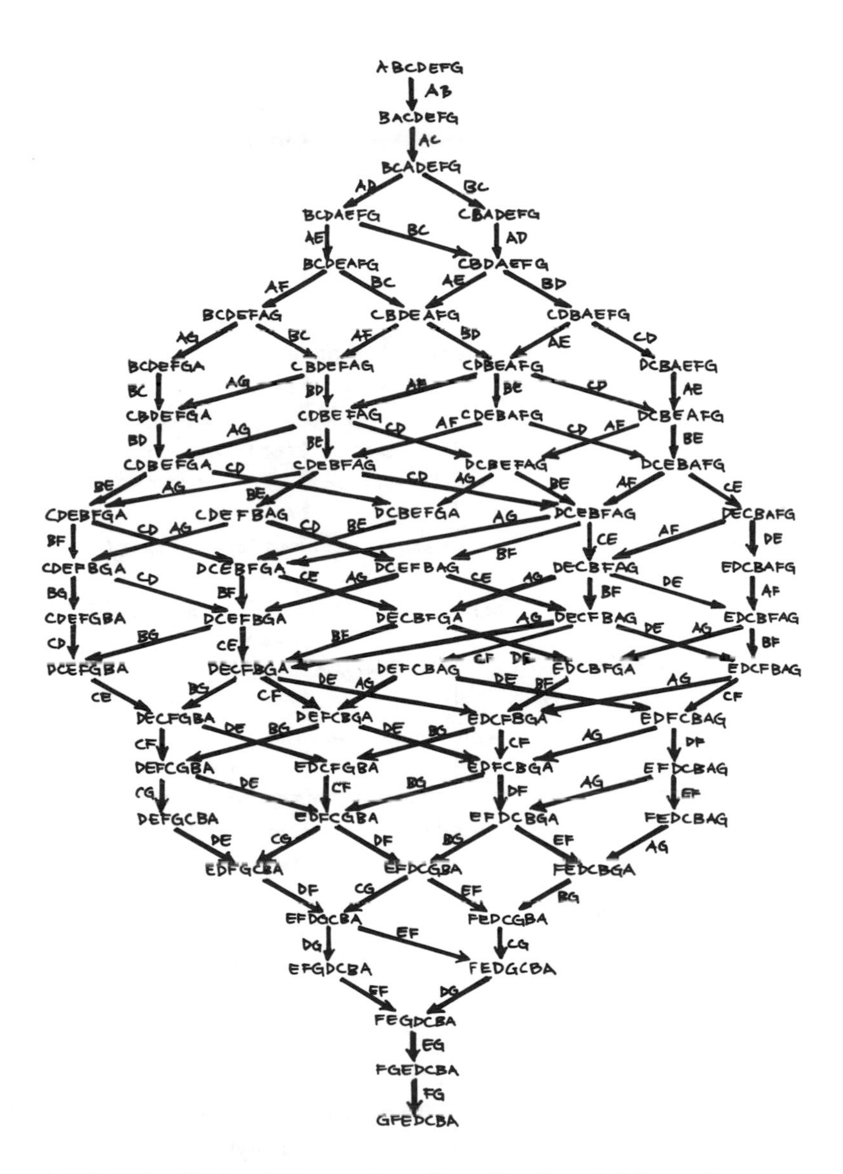


FIG. 7.11. The preference orders allowed by Coombs' theory form a single descending path through this graph, given that the order of the six stimuli along the relevant dimension is *A, B, C, D, E, F,* and *G.*

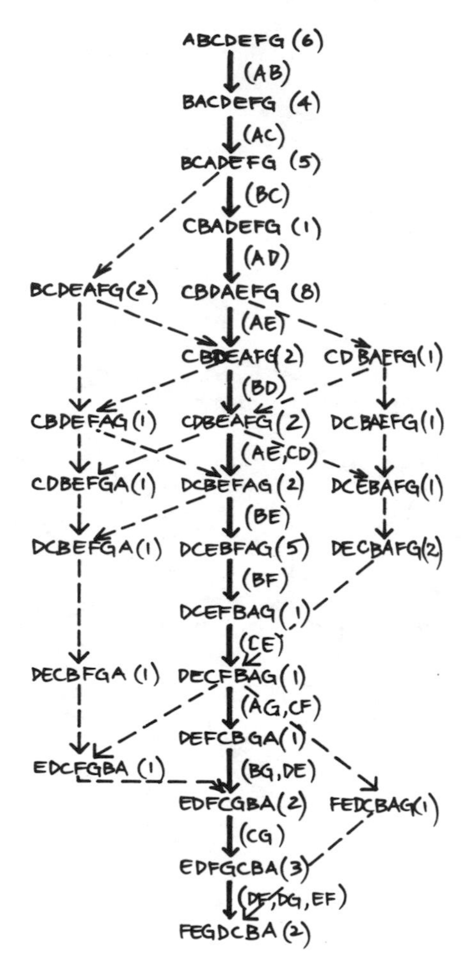


FIG. 7.12. The preference orders obtained by Coombs (with associated frequencies in parentheses). The solid arrows trace the dominant path through this graph.

than $\frac{1}{2}n(n - 1) + 1 = \frac{1}{2}.7(7 - 1) + 1 = 22$ different preference orders. Not counting the four intransitive orders, the remaining 58 subjects produced 26 different preference orders. Hence, without further analysis we know that they cannot all fit onto the same unidimensional scale. Further analysis shows that the path through Fig. 7.11 accounting for the highest frequency of subjects (45) accommodates only 15 of the preference orders given. The remaining 11 preference orders given (by 13 subjects) fit onto alternative paths through Fig. 7.11. That fragment of Fig. 7.11 containing all of the 26 transitive preference orders given (by the 58 subjects) together with their connections is shown in Fig. 7.12. The path marked by the solid arrows is the one accounting for the greatest number of subjects (the *dominant* path).

Before examining this dominant path and its satisfaction of the cancellation conditions, it is instructive to consider the orders from the 13 subjects that fail to fit onto it. In each case it is possible to find the minimum number of reversals necessary to relocate that preference order on the dominant path. Because each reversal corresponds to one pair comparison judgment made, this gives the minimum number of "errors" made by these subjects. This turns out to be 17. Three of the four "corrected" intransitive preference orders also fit the dominant path, the fourth requiring another two reversals. Hence there are 17 + 3 + 2 = 22 "errors." That is, if the dominant path satisfies the cancellation conditions then this accounts for 1280 out of the 1302 pair comparison judgments made.

As explained in the last section, any path through Fig. 7.11 entails an order on the interstimulus midpoints. Coombs' theory predicts that this order must satisfy the hierarchy of cancellation conditions. The order on the midpoints entailed by the dominant path through Fig. 7.12 may be read off by following the solid arrows. Because some preference orders that could have been included on the path were not given by any subjects, the order of certain pairs of interstimulus midpoints cannot be deduced. These are printed on the same level, on either side of the arrow, in Fig. 7.12. For example, this applies to the pairs *CD* and *AF*, *CF* and *AG*, *BG* and *DE*, *EF* and *DG*. The order entailed by the dominant path is shown in Fig. 7.13, where the order on the cells must go from left to right, and from top to bottom.

Given this order one can begin to test the hierarchy of cancellation conditions. Independence is already satisfied. This leaves double cancellation and any higher order cancellation conditions. Tests of double cancellation require a 3 × 3 matrix, and, as already noted, if independence is satisfied only one test of double cancellation needs to be made in any such matrix. Considering Fig. 7.13, it can be seen that it contains seven different 3 × 3 matrices: *ABC* × *DEF*, *ABC* × *EFG*, *ABC* × *DEG*, *ABC* × *DFG*, *ACD* × *EFG*, *BCD* × *EFG*, and *ABD* × *EFG*. The tests of double cancellation in these matrices are illustrated in Fig. 7.14. In each matrix the premises of the double cancellation condition are represented by a single line arrow and the conclusion by a double line arrow, the arrow going from the earlier

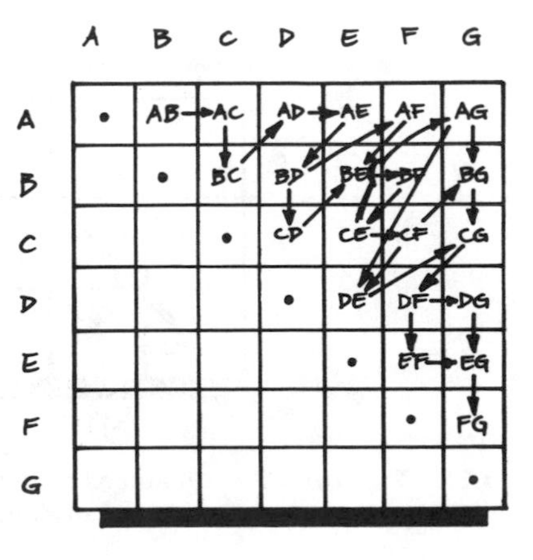


FIG. 7.13. The order on the interstimulus midpoints entailed by the dominant path in Fig. 7.12, according to Coombs' theory.

to the later midpoint. The direction of the arrows is determined by their direction in Fig. 7.13. Note that in (a) and (f), the direction of the conclusion is not known because the order of those interstimulus midpoints was not determined by the data. Consequently, these two matrices do not permit a test of the theory. The other five, however, do and reference to Table 5.3 shows that they all satisfy that condition. Fig. 7.14 (b) and (c) are instances of pattern 9 in Table 5.3, (d) is an instance of pattern 1 and (e) and (g) are instances of pattern 13. These are all confirmatory patterns.

It is interesting to note a special feature of the matrix in Fig. 7.12, a feature which has implications for the testing of double cancellation. This feature is that the same seven stimuli define both the rows and the columns. Whenever this

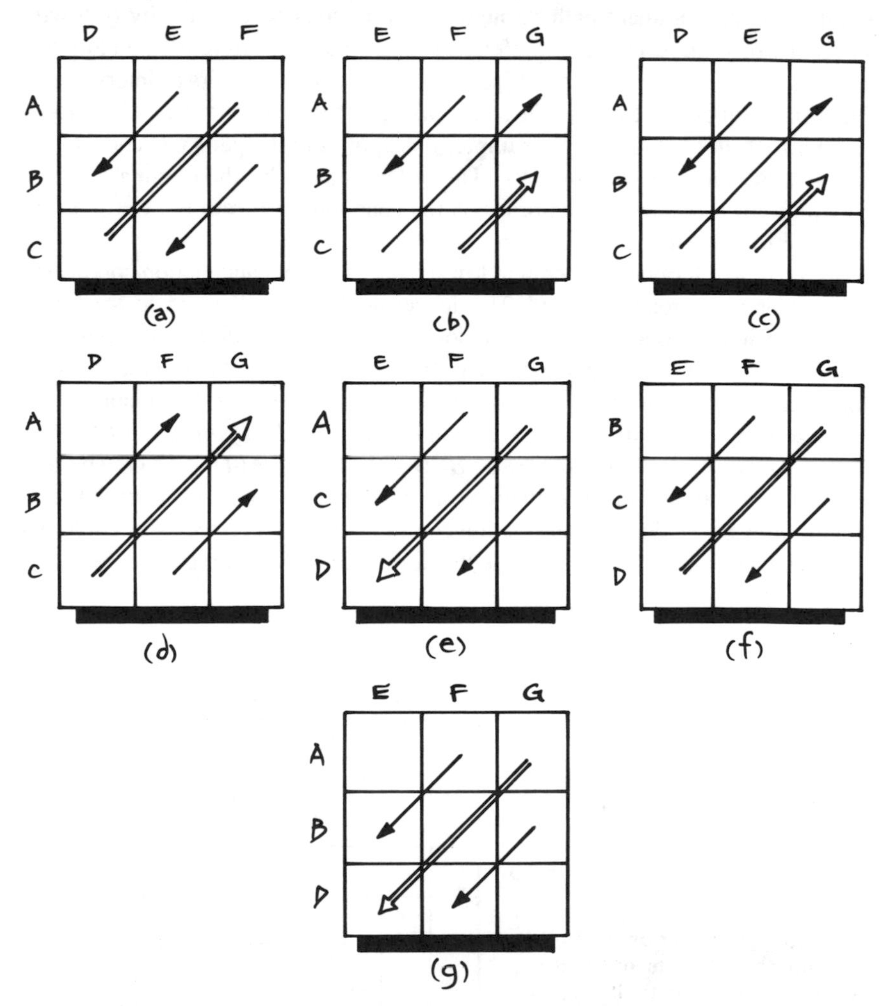


FIG. 7.14. The seven 3 × 3 matrices contained within the upper half of Fig. 7.13 and the associated tests of double cancellation.

happens it implies the existence of additional tests of double cancellation. These additional tests are illustrated in Fig. 7.15. They include no violations of double cancellation.

Satisfaction of both single and double cancellation in the data shown in Fig. 7.13 raises the question of whether or not any further tests of higher order cancellation conditions must be performed. While the matrix, $ABCD \times DEFG$, within that figure is not a complete $4 \times 4$ matrix (the order of the $D,D$ cell relative to the others is not known), it is possible to test triple cancellation in $3 \times 4$ or $4 \times 3$ matrices, and there are two such matrices in Fig. 7.13. At this point in the testing procedure it would be helpful to know exactly which tests of triple cancellation are logically independent of double cancellation. It would then be known which tests of triple cancellation, if any, need to be performed in order to verify or falsify the claim that the data in Fig. 7.13 satisfies the hierarchy of cancellation conditions. However, as the answers to these questions are not known, a different approach must be used.

One approach that may be used is relatively simple and convenient. It involves making numerical estimates of the stimuli ($A, B, C, D, E, F, G$) on some arbitrary scale that are consistent with the order on the midpoints given in Fig. 7.13. If such estimates can be made then the order in Fig. 7.13 must satisfy the hierarchy of cancellation conditions. There are a variety of techniques that produce such estimates. Coombs (1964, pp. 96–102) explains one (see also McClelland & Coombs, 1975) that may be conveniently done by hand. The values he obtained for this particular set of data are shown in Table 7.1.

The numerical order on the cells in Table 7.1 does not contradict the order shown in Fig. 7.13, though necessarily it is not exactly the same because some midpoints unordered in Fig. 7.13 are ordered in Table 7.1. However, this result is sufficient to show that the data in Fig. 7.13 must satisfy all the cancellation conditions that apply to it.

Simple as this procedure may be, it suffers two drawbacks. First, if a numerical solution consistent with the prescribed order on the midpoints does not exist, then it is not known which, or how many, independent tests of the cancellation conditions fail. Although some numerical estimation procedures do provide a solution of "best fit" in such circumstances (and some even provide a "measure" of how close this solution is to the prescribed order) it would be useful to know just which cancellation conditions fail.

Second, there is a temptation to regard these numerical estimates as genuine measurements. However, to treat them as measurements is premature, for they are only measurements if the variable involved is quantitative and Coombs' theory is true. In this particular instance 98% of the pair comparison preferences agreed with Coombs' theory. This may be taken as confirmation of the theory. However, the theory requires a more searching experimental analysis than this before being accepted as true, and until such an analysis is made any numerical estimates made must not be thought of as measurements. To do so is to succumb to wishful thinking.

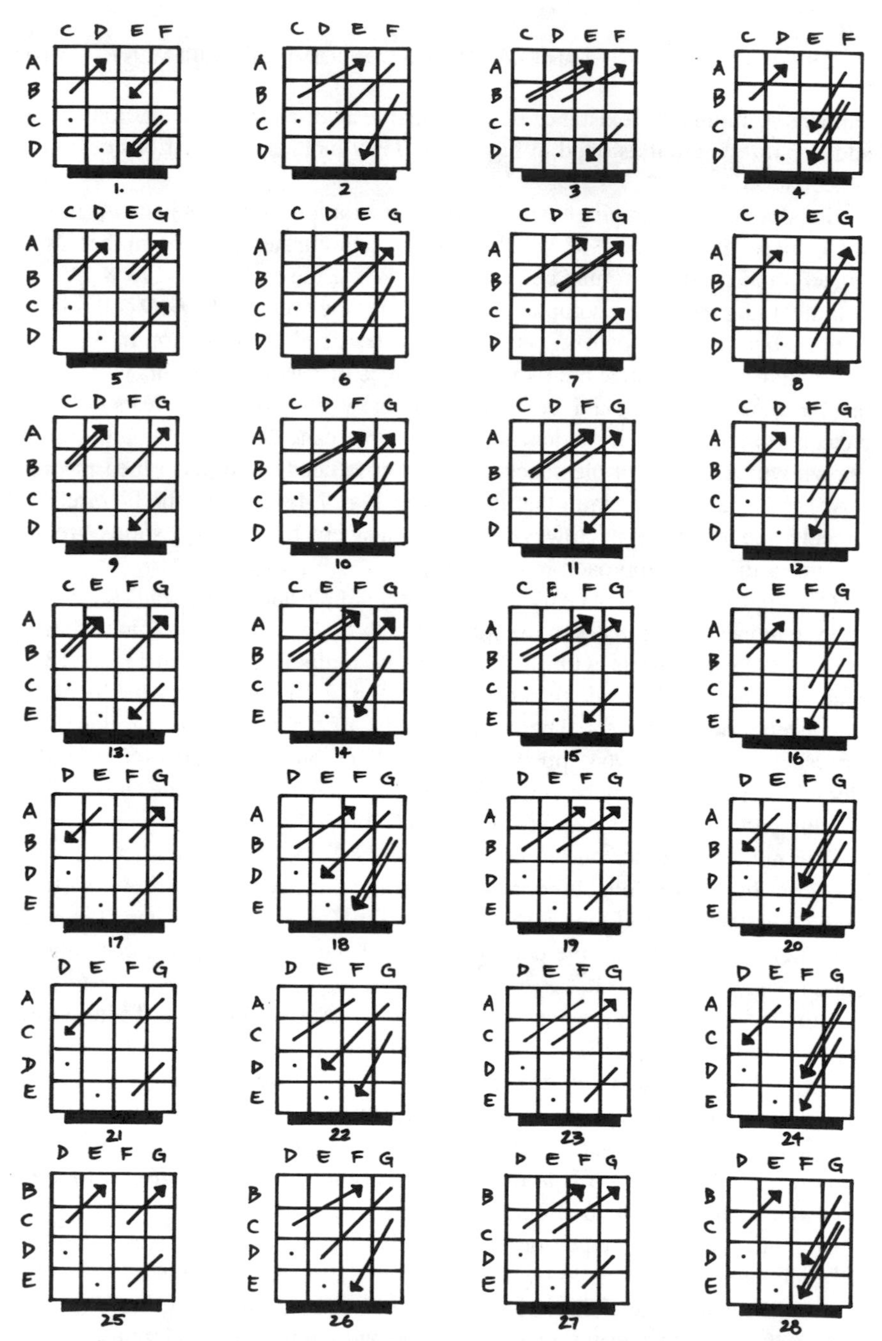


FIG. 7.15. Twenty-eight additional tests of double cancellation required of the order upon midpoints shown in Fig. 7.13. These additional tests are required in the special case where the values defining the six rows and columns are the same. As with other tests of double cancellation, the condition is falsified if and only if the middle arrow points in a direction opposed to both outside arrows.

TABLE 7.1
Numerical Estimates of *A, B, C, D, E, F,* and *G* and the Resulting Numerical Values of the Midpoints Between Them, Consistent With the Order Upon the Midpoints Shown in Fig. 7.13

| | $A=0$ | $B=5$ | $C=8$ | $D=16$ | $E=20$ | $F=22$ | $G=29$ |
|---|---|---|---|---|---|---|---|
| $A=0$ | • | 2.5 | 4 | 8 | 10 | 11 | 14.5 |
| $B=5$ | | • | 6.5 | 10.5 | 12.5 | 13.5 | 17 |
| $C=8$ | | | • | 12 | 14 | 15 | 18.5 |
| $D=16$ | | | | • | 18 | 19 | 22.5 |
| $E=20$ | | | | | • | 21 | 24.5 |
| $F=22$ | | | | | | • | 25.5 |
| $G=29$ | | | | | | | • |

What has been shown in this chapter is how the theory of conjoint measurement may be applied to Coombs' unfolding theory and an illustration of such application has been given. Should Coombs' theory prove true for at least certain stimulus domains, the theory of conjoint measurement could be used to establish standard sequences of stimuli that could then be used as a basis for psychological measurement.

# Chapter 8

# Prospects for the Development of Psychological Measurement

One of the theses argued in this book is that the theory of conjoint measurement opens the way to measurement in psychology, providing, of course, that psychology actually deals with quantitative variables. In the preceding chapters three theories of psychological measurement have been considered, and it was shown how they each entail the existence of structures of the kind treated by the theory of conjoint measurement. That is nothing but the first step down a long and difficult road. In this chapter let us consider some later steps in a general and schematic way.

## THE NEED FOR STIMULUS CONTROL

The obvious second step, and one stressed throughout this book, is the need to develop technologies of stimulus control. In so far as stimuli are physical objects or events, and primary interest is in purely physical attributes of such stimuli, the technology exists. So the possibility of developing psychophysics using the theory of conjoint measurement is a practicable one (see Falmagne, 1986). However, in so far as the attributes of interest are nonphysical (for example, the favorability of attitude statements; the right or left wing tendencies of a political statement; the authoritarianism of a political candidate; even, the difficulty of an intellectual problem) there is little in the way of any technology of stimulus control.

So far in the history of psychological measurement there has been little attempt to achieve this kind of control. The aim has been to use techniques like Thurstone's scaling procedure, multidimensional scaling and to a lesser extent, Coombs' unfolding procedure, in the hope that they would identify the relevant stimulus dimensions. This is a fatuous hope in the absence of evidence to show that these techniques are based on true theories. This approach shows the influence of operationism on attempts at psychological measurement. It is thought that these procedures must measure something and it is simply a matter of deciding what. As I have argued, this is not so. They may not measure anything. The experimental method must be applied to the underlying theories before that issue can be resolved. And to apply the experimental method, as shown in earlier chapters, the stimuli used must be carefully controlled.

My plan in this section is to give an illustration of how this might be approached by taking an area notorious for lack of such control, the area of attitude measurement. The stimuli in this case are attitude statements, and the relevant dimension is considered to be the favorability of such statements towards the object of the attitude. The aim is to develop procedures whereby statements may be constructed that vary on no other relevant variable than this. This involves clarifying precisely what properties of statements fix their value on the favorability variable, and what properties locate them on other possibly relevant variables. To do this one needs to characterize the favorability variable.

The concept of attitude is a poorly defined one and, yet, a consistent thread of meaning can be detected. It runs from Thurstone's (1931) definition of attitudes as "affect for or against a psychological object", through Katz's and Stotland's (1959) definition as "an individual's tendency or predisposition to evaluate an object or a symbol of that object in a certain way", to the more recent definitions of Fishbein, (1967), Maze, (1973) and Rokeach, (1968), who all agree that the concept of evaluation is central to that of attitude. This common thread is that an attitude towards some object or policy is necessarily evaluative and, thereby, has a location on a dimension running from pro (or favorable) to anti (or unfavorable). This I take to be the core of the concept and, thus, define an attitude towards person or policy $x$ as an evaluation of $x$.

So it follows, then, that an attitude statement is an evaluative statement. If the concepts of good, bad, right, and wrong are taken as paradigmatic evaluative concepts then a necessary and sufficient condition can be stated for a statement's being evaluative.

A statement, $S$, is *evaluative* if and only if it implies that some object or policy is either good or not good, right or not right.

Applying this conception to the statements used in, so-called, attitude scales it is obvious that many of them are not evaluative. Consider, for example, some of the statements in Thurstone and Chave's (1929) study on attitudes towards the church. They included the following statement:

(1) I believe the church is losing ground as education advances.

Such a statement, of itself, does not imply that the church is either good or not good. Implicit, of course, is the idea of a causal connection between education opening people's eyes and their seeing the teachings of the church as false, but even that, itself, is nonevaluative. It becomes evaluative when conjoined with certain value judgments about education, enlightenment and believing falsehoods. Indeed, because value judgments of that kind vary amongst social groups, judgments about how favorable or unfavorable (1) is towards the church may vary from person to person. On the other hand, a statement such as

(2) The church is an evil institution

(not, incidently, one of Thurstone's and Chave's) is intrinsically evaluative, for it implies that the church is not good.

What is required, then, in order to test theories like Thurstone's, Coombs' and that of multidimensional scaling in the attitude area, are intrinsically evaluative statements that do not differ on other relevant dimensions. What the other relevant dimensions of a statement are, of course, is a matter to be investigated. I will assume that purely grammatical attributes are not relevant and that the only relevant features have to do with meaning. Then a necessary and sufficient condition for a statement's having nonevaluative content may be given.

A statement, *S*, possesses nonevaluative content if and only if it implies some nonevaluative statement.

Thus, for example, (2) above implies that the church is an institution and so possesses nonevaluative content. A unidimensional set of attitude statements could then be constructed by ensuring that the statements differ only with respect to their evaluative content. For example, consider the following statements,

*A*. Bob Hawke is a perfect Prime Minister.
*B*. Bob Hawke is an extremely good, but not perfect, Prime Minister.
*C*. Bob Hawke is a good, but not extremely good, Prime Minister.
*D*. Bob Hawke is a bad, but not very bad, Prime Minister.
*E*. Bob Hawke is a very bad, but not absolutely deplorable Prime Minister.
*F*. Bob Hawke is an absolutely deplorable Prime Minister.

They all contain precisely the same nonevaluative content (viz., Bob Hawke is a Prime Minister) and differ only with respect to their evaluative content. Furthermore, in so far as their evaluative content is concerned they are ordered from favorable to unfavorable (from *A* through *F*). This has been achieved by so wording them that if any one of them is true all the rest are false. Hence, they must each occupy a different value or position on the dimension of evaluations of Bob Hawke as Prime Minister. Such a carefully worded set of statements, differing only with respect to a single semantic dimension, may then provide a basis for testing theories like the ones considered in earlier chapters. More than that, such theories, if true, provide a basis for testing the hypothesis that such semantic dimensions are quantitative.

By way of illustrating these points, 103 psychology students at the University of Sydney made pair comparison preference judgments on all 15 pairs of these six statements. The aim was to show that for carefully constructed sets of attitude statements, Coombs' unidimensional unfolding theory provides a basis for attitude measurement. Two subjects failed to complete the 15 pair comparison judgments and their data were excluded. Of the remaining 101 subjects, the judgments from ten were not transitive and a complete preference ordering of the six statements was not entailed. However, in most cases only one or two violations of transitivity were involved.

Given the order of the statements along the dimension of favorability, Coombs' theory predicts that the preference orders produced by the subjects should fall on a single path through the graph displayed in Fig. 7.7. 90 of the 91 preference orders produced were those given in that figure. The subgraph produced by this data is shown in Fig. 8.1. The dominant paths are shown by the solid arrows and as can be seen there are two dominant orderings of the interstimulus midpoints (Fig. 8.2). These both satisfy double cancellation (Fig. 8.3).

When the subjects whose data did not conform to Coombs' theory are taken into account the solution of best fit is that shown in Fig. 8.4 and it accounts for 1488 out of the 1515 pair comparison judgments made by the 101 subjects (i.e., 98.2% of the judgments). This result confirms the hypothesis that the subjects are able to discern the single relevant attribute in this case. That is, the method of constructing the stimuli was successful. Furthermore, satisfaction of double cancellation confirms the hypothesis that this attribute is quantitative, though clearly, *that* is an hypothesis that requires further research. This illustration shows that with careful construction, stimuli of a psychological kind can satisfy the boundary conditions for the application of Coombs' theory.

## EXTENDING APPLICATIONS OF CONJOINT MEASUREMENT

Another step towards the achievement of psychological measurement is the extension of conjoint measurement theory to other attempts at psychological measurement. Some suggestions are included in Krantz et al. (1971) and Krantz (1972), showing how the theory may be applied to Stevens' theory of magnitude estimation and cross modality matching (Stevens, 1986). This is a significant application because of the prominent place of Stevens' methods within modern psychophysics. Magnitude estimation is one of the most widely used methods in the attempt at psychophysical measurement and it is, therefore, important that it be subjected to experimental examination. Two other very widely used methods in the quest for psychological measurement are the ability test and the rating scale. Indeed, it is no exaggeration to claim that between them they would account for the majority of attempts at psychological measurement. How conjoint measurement may be applied to the theory of abilities is explored in the following paragraphs.

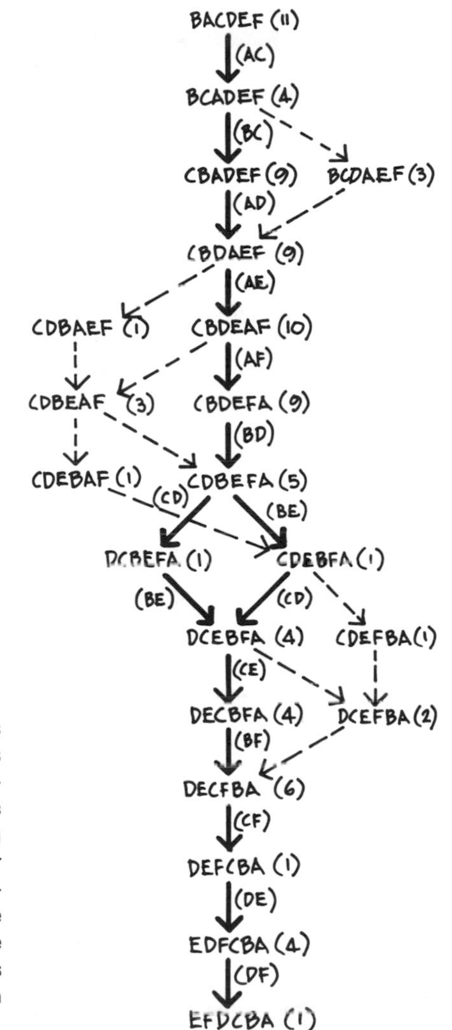


FIG. 8.1. The preference orders obtained from the 90 students who gave transitive pair comparison preference judgments to the statements evaluating Bob Hawke as Prime Minister and whose judgments were consistent with the order of the statements along the evaluative dimension. The solid arrows trace the dominant path through the graph shown in Fig. 7.7.

The suggestion that collections of intellectual tasks may be used to measure intellectual abilities is one that has permeated much of modern psychology, and found wide acceptance within schools, and other institutions with an interest in intellectual abilities. However widely accepted this suggestion is, it is at present no more than a hypothesis, and indeed, one that is widely accepted more because of its usefulness to those who believe it, than because of the evidence in support of it. Consequently, there is an urgent scientific need to extend conjoint measurement theory to the theories used in support of this hypothesis, so that its truth can be assessed.

The most important of such theories are the factor analytic theories stemming

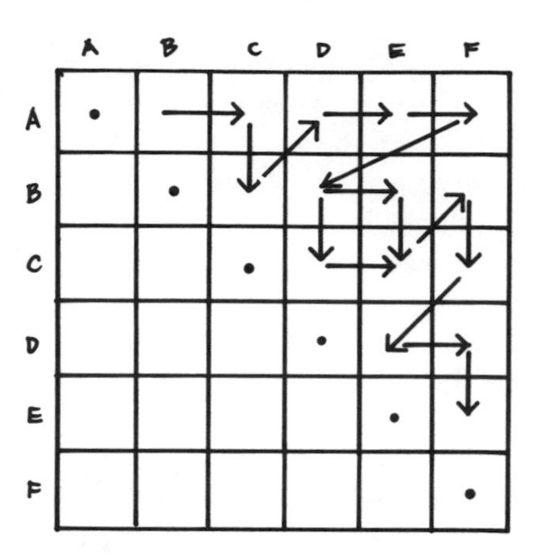


FIG. 8.2. The order on the midpoints entailed by the dominant path shown in Fig. 8.1.

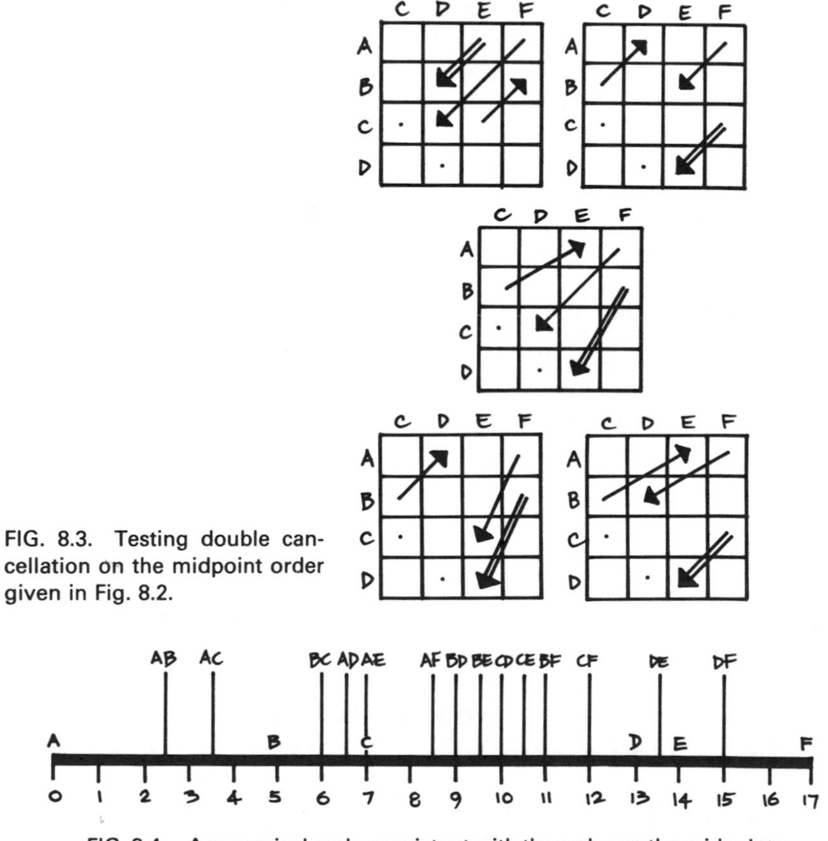


FIG. 8.3. Testing double cancellation on the midpoint order given in Fig. 8.2.

FIG. 8.4. A numerical scale consistent with the order on the midpoints in Fig. 8.2.

from Cattell, (1971), Spearman, (1904) and Thurstone, (1935). These theories postulate that a person's score on an ability test is a function of his abilities and the extent to which the test measures them. These abilities are hypothesized to be quantitative variables. It is thought that the factor analytic method provides a way of identifying them from the patterns of intercorrelations between test scores. However this method, whatever its merits, presumes that abilities are quantitative, and it is precisely this presumption that must be put to some kind of experimental test. Unfortunately, most factor analytic theories of ability are of such a level of complexity that they are not easily reduced to the kind of structure that conjoint measurement deals with. However, the least complex of them all, Spearman's so-called "two-factor" theory, does entail such a structure.

Spearman's theory was that if a test made up of intellectual tasks, all of *one kind,* is considered then a person's performance on such a test is determined by two variables, general ability (g), and the specific ability (s) suited to tasks of that kind. Each specific ability was thought of as a "mental engine" for solving problems of a particular kind, and general ability was thought of as the "mental energy" that drove those engines. People were thought to differ in both the competence of their "engines" and in the quantity of their "energy", and this accounted for their different performances on ability tests. The theory is today regarded as false because the factor analytic pattern it predicts does not generally occur. There are also other predictions, like that of zero tetrad differences, that are now also believed to be generally false. However, in Spearman's defense it must be said that the theory has never been satisfactorily tested. The issue of whether any existing test ever contains tasks of only *one* kind is one that has never been settled. To do so would require a theory specifying the different cognitive processes involved in solving intellectual tasks of various kinds. Given such a theory, genuinely unidimensional sets of test items may be able to be constructed. The issue again is one of stimulus control. Cognitive psychology is yet to furnish the necessary theory.

Mathematically, Spearman's theory may be expressed as

$$z_{ij} = g_j g_i + s_j s_i$$

(where $z_{ij}$ is the z-score of person $i$ on test $j$; $g_i$ is $i$'s measure of general ability; $s_i$ is $i$'s measure of specific ability; $g_j$ is the extent to which test $j$ measures general ability; and $s_j$ is the extent to which test $j$ measures specific ability). If the test to be used is fixed then $g_j$ and $s_j$ become constants across all subjects. Thus, the $j$ subscript may be ignored, whence,

$$z_i = g \cdot g_i + s \cdot s_i.$$

For each subject, $i$, $g_i$ and $s_i$ are simply being multiplied by the constants $g$ and $s$, so $g \cdot g_i$ and $s \cdot s_i$ may simply be regarded as rescalings of $g_i$ and $s_i$. Letting $g \cdot g_i = G_i$, and $s \cdot s_i = S_i$, the equation becomes,

$$z_i = G_i + S_i.$$

This equation in turn implies that for any two persons, $i$ and $k$,

$$z_i \geqslant z_k \text{ if and only if } G_i + S_i \geqslant G_k + S_k.$$

This proposition is a weaker theory than Spearman's (even though it is entailed by it) because it no longer implies that a person's $z$-score *equals* $G_i+S_i$, but merely that it be monotonic with that sum. Since $z$-scores and raw scores are monotonic with each other, this theory is equivalent to

$$X_i \geqslant X_k \text{ if and only if } G_i + S_i \geqslant G_k + S_k$$

(where $X_i$ and $X_k$ are $i$'s, and $k$'s raw scores on test $j$). Here we have a theory of the kind amenable to conjoint measurement analysis.

What such an analysis requires, of course, is that levels of the variables $G$ and $S$ be identifiable independently of test scores. Here is where the factor analytic theories of ability fail, for they use test scores as the sole criterion for identifying values of such variables. However, it is just here that the recent *rapprochement* between the areas of individual differences and cognitive psychology may help. An example of what I mean is Hunt's (1980) suggestion that Spearman's $g$ may be identified with attentional resources, and his $s$ with problem solving strategies. If each of these variables can be experimentally manipulated it may be possible to test Spearman's theory. Of course, the value of such a test would be contingent on the truth of Hunt's suggestion, and that may be false. However, this kind of approach is the only one that is going to show whether or not abilities are quantities and how they combine to determine performance. Progress can only be made in this area of psychology by linking the hypothetical quantitative variables of the factor analytic theories (the abilities), to experimentally controllable variables. This requires bold hypotheses similar to Hunt's and while such hypotheses may be false, it is better to show an hypothesis to be false than not to be able to test it at all.

This sketchy analysis of Spearman's theory shows the direction in which research must go if attempts at measurement in this area are to work. First, there needs to be a theory in terms of which tasks or items of a given *kind* can be identified. Two items will be of the same kind when they can be solved using the same family of cognitive processes. Second, there needs to be a theory relating abilities of different kinds to cognitive processes of different kinds (such as Hunt's). Only when these steps are taken can the issue of whether or not ability tests measure anything be experimentally evaluated.

## EXTENDING THE THEORY OF CONJOINT MEASUREMENT

A third area where progress has been made in the quest for psychological measurement is in the mathematical development of the theory of conjoint measurement. As expounded in Chapter 4 the theory covers the case where two quantitative variables ($A$ and $X$) combine noninteractively to produce a third ($P$). Already the theory has been developed significantly beyond that point. Krantz and Tversky, (1971) and Krantz et al., (1971) explore certain cases where three quantitative variables ($A$, $B$, and $C$), combine to produce a fourth ($D$) and show how these cases may be distinguished from one another by the character of the order upon $D$. In particular they show how the following four composition rules in three variables may be distinguished:

(1) $D = A + B + C$ (Additive)

(2) $D = (A + B)C$ (Distributive)

(3) $D = A \cdot B + C$ (Dual- distributive)

(4) $D = A \cdot B \cdot C$ (Multiplicative).

The importance of this is that it allows experimental differentiation between rival theories which postulate different composition rules. For example, Hull's learning theory states that habit strength ($H$), drives strength ($D$), and incentive motivation ($K$), combine multiplicatively to produce reaction potential ($E$): $E = H \cdot D \cdot K$.

Spence's theory, on the other hand, has it that the distributive rule applies: $E = H(D + K)$.

Given that none of these variables can be measured, but that they may be ordered, it follows that conjoint measurement theory is necessary to distinguish between them experimentally. An experimental application of this development in conjoint measurement theory in another area of psychology is given by Coombs and Huang, (1970).

Extending this theme, Krantz (1968) shows how the four variable combination rule $A = B \cdot C + D \cdot E$ may be handled within the conjoint measurement framework. This is interesting because that is the general form Spearman's two-factor theory of abilities takes (i.e., without holding the test constant) and so it opens the possibility of a more complete test than permitted in two-variable conjoint measurement theory.

These extensions to the theory of conjoint measurement consider the effects of increasing the number of variables involved. There is another possible extension to the theory and that is to consider the effects of increasing the complexity of the composition rule with two variables. That is, to extend conjoint measurement theory to include interactive compositions. One such interactive composition rule often considered in the context of analysis of variance is $P = A + X + A \cdot X$ and, as noted by Krantz et al., (1971), a theory for this special case would be of interest.

## DEEPENING THE UNDERSTANDING OF QUANTITY

Another area of theoretical activity over recent years has significantly advanced the understanding of what it means for a variable to be quantitative. This is research by R. D. Luce (1986, 1987) and L. Narens (1981, 1985) into the mathematical foundations of measurement theory. Though highly technical, some of the major results can be explained in less technical terms.

The background to this work is in the theory of scale types. As expounded in earlier chapters of this book, since Stevens' (1946, 1951, 1959) liberalization of the representational theory, psychologists have accepted the view that there are four types of measurement scales: nominal, ordinal, interval, and ratio. These are normally distinguished from one another via the admissible scale transformations involved. However, as became increasingly obvious following Suppes' and Zinnes' (1963) axiomatic reformulation of Stevens' theory, the differences between different scale types must ultimately reside in some intrinsic property of the empirical relational systems involved. For example, an empirical relational system capable of a ratio scale representation, must differ in some fundamental way from an empirical relational system enabling only an ordinal scale representation. Attempts to characterize this difference led to the discovery of the properties called *homogeneity* and *uniqueness* (Narens, 1981). In turn, the concept of homogeneity has enabled the essential nature of quantity to be discerned more clearly.

The concepts of homogeneity and uniqueness have been defined via the concept of an *automorphism*. An automorphism is an isomorphism (or one-to-one mapping) between a relational system and itself. Let $X$ be some nonempty set of empirical entities of some kind. Let $R_1, \ldots, R_j$ be empirical relations upon $X$. Let $f$ be a one-to-one function mapping each element of $X$ onto some other element of $X$. Then $f$ is an *automorphism* if and only if for any relation, $R_i$ $(i = 1, \ldots, j)$, and ordered set of elements of $X$, $\langle x_1, x_2, \ldots, x_n \rangle$,

$$R_i(x_1, x_2, \ldots, x_n) \text{ if and only if}$$

$$R_i(f(x_1), f(x_2), \ldots, f(x_n))$$

(where "$R_i(x_1, x_2, \ldots, x_n)$" means that the set of objects, $x_1, x_2, \ldots, x_n$, (in that order) stand in the relation $R_i$). That is, in words, a one-to-one function mapping elements of $X$ onto other elements of $X$ is an automorphism if whenever some elements of $X$ stand in a particular relation, $R_i$, then so do the elements that $f$ maps them into, and vice versa.

An example will make this concept clearer. Suppose that our empirical relational system consists of a set of rods of various lengths and that we have two relations, $R_1$ and $R_2$, where $R_1(x,y)$ means that rod $x$ is not shorter than rod $y$, and $R_2(x,y,z)$ means that rods $x$ and $y$ linearly concatenated end to end equal rod $z$ in length. Now, suppose the function $f$ maps each rod into another one twice its length, i.e., for any rods, $x$ and $y$, $f(x) = y$ if and only if $R_2(x,x,y)$.

Then $f$ is an automorphism if and only if for any rods $x$, $y$, *and* $z$

(i) $R_1(x,y)$ if and only if $R_1(f(x), f(y))$, and

(ii) $R_2(x,y,z)$ if and only if $R_2(f(x), f(y), f(z))$.

Obviously, (i) and (ii) are both true, because (i) if $x$ is not shorter than $y$, then a rod twice $x$'s length will not be shorter than one twice $y$'s (and vice versa); and (ii) if the length of $x$ concatenated with $y$ equals the length of $z$, then the concatenation of rods twice the lengths of $x$ and $y$ will equal the length of a rod twice $z$ and vice versa. So, in this case $f$ would be an automorphism.

The importance of automorphisms is this. Consider any empirical relational system that is at least ordinally scalable. It may be represented numerically in many different ways, each different way being a distinct numerical scale, and each at least positively monotonically related to the others. Indeed, there are infinitely many distinct mappings of a structure that is at least ordinal into the real numbers. If we allow that $X$, the empirical set involved, is unbounded, dense and continuous (relative to the ordering relation involved), then corresponding to each numerical scale for this empirical relational system there exists an automorphism and vice versa. That is, there is an isomorphism between the set of all numerical scales representing some (unbounded, dense, continuous) empirical relational system and the set of all automorphisms on that system. Hence, any property that the scales possess (such as being ordinal, interval, or ratio scales) must have its analogue in the set of automorphisms for that system. Thus, what it is for an empirical relational system to be ratio scalable (or quantitative, in my terms) can be defined as a property of the automorphisms of such systems. All such systems must have a common automorphic structure. As we shall see later, R. D. Luce has precisely defined this structure and, hence, Luce's definition can be used to give a precise characterization of what it is for a variable to be quantitative.

Let me return to the claim made earlier in the last paragraph, that there is an isomorphism between the set of all numerical scales representing some (unbounded, dense and continuous) empirical relational system, and the set of all automorphisms on that system. Its truth can easily be illustrated for the case of the ratio scale.

Consider two numerical scales of length, say the Imperial scale (where the yard is the unit), and the metric scale (where the meter is the unit). We take any rod, $x$, and find the number that is its length in yards, call it $y(x)$, and then we find the rod $z$ (I am assuming for simplicity that each rod is a different length and the set of rods is unbounded, dense and continuous), such that the number equal to $z$'s length in meters, $m(z)$, equals $y(x)$. Here we have an isomorphic mapping from lengths of rods to lengths of rods via numerical measurements. That is,

$$x \text{ maps to } y(x) = m(z) \text{ maps to } z.$$

Furthermore, this mapping must be an automorphism because it is simply the composition of two isomorphisms. So that procedure gives us one automorphism. Others may be obtained by varying the Imperial scale (or, alternatively, the metric scale) as the first step in establishing the automorphism. Select any length ratio scale from the infinite set possible. Find the numerical value of $x$ on that scale, call it $l(x)$. Then we have a new automorphism because,

$$x \text{ maps to } I(x) = m(z) \text{ maps to } z.$$

And for each numerical scale there will be an automorphism and vice versa.

If for any empirical relational system that is at least ordinal, unbounded, dense and continuous, there is an isomorphism between scales of the same kind (i.e., isomorphisms into the real numbers) and automorphisms (i.e., isomorphisms onto itself), then it simply remains to specify the property or properties of automorphisms that correspond to scale type. Narens (1981) identified two properties of automorphisms that jointly characterize the scale type of measurements of such empirical relational systems. These he called *n–point homogeneity* and *n–point uniqueness*. He defined these properties as follows.

Let $< X, \succcurlyeq, R_1, R_2, \ldots >$ be a relational system, $\succcurlyeq$ a simple order on $X$ (which is unbounded, dense, and continuous) and $R_1, R_2, \ldots$ other relations on $X$. Let $A$ be a set of automorphisms of this system. $A$ satisfies *n–point homogeneity* (for some nonnegative integer $n$) if and only if for each $x_1, \ldots, x_n$ and $y_1, \ldots, y_n$ in $X$ (where $x_1 > x_2 > \ldots > x_n$ and $y_1 > y_2 > \ldots > y_n$) there exists an automorphism $a$ in $A$ such that $a(x_i) = y_i$ (for $i = 1, \ldots, n$). $A$ satisfies *n–point uniqueness* if and only if for each $a$ and $b$ in $A$, if $a$ and $b$ agree at least at $n$ distinct elements of $X$ then $a = b$. Now, if $A$ is the set of all automorphisms of this relational structure, then this relational structure satisfies $n$-point homogeneity if and only if $A$ is $n$–point homogeneous, and this relational structure satisfies $n$–point uniqueness if and only if $A$ is $n$–point unique.

We can easily see that as an extensive structure length satisfies 1–point homogeneity but not 2–point homogeneity. No matter what elements $x_1$ and $y_1$ are of the length variable, there will be an automorphism, $a$, for which $a(x_1) = y_1$. For, suppose on the meter scale that $m(x_1) = r \cdot m(y_1)$ (where $r$ is some positive real number), then $a$ will be the function mapping each length into another, $r$ times as large and therefore for any lengths $x$, $y$, and $z$, $x > y$ if and only if $m(x) > m(y)$, if and only if $r \cdot m(x) > r \cdot m(y)$, if and only if $a(x) > a(y)$; and relative to the concatenation relation $x \circ y \sim z$, if and only if $m(x) + m(y) = m(z)$, if and only if $r \cdot m(x) + r \cdot m(y) = r \cdot m(z)$, if and only if $a(x) \circ a(y) \sim a(z)$.

Hence, $a$ is an automorphism. Therefore, length is 1–point homogeneous. However, it is not 2–point homogeneous, for letting $x_1 > x_2$ and $y_1 > y_2$ be any lengths whatsoever, we know values can be chosen such that

$$m(x_1) = r_1 \cdot m(y_1),$$

$$m(x_2) = r_2 \cdot m(y_2), \text{ and}$$

$$r_1 \neq r_2.$$

For example, suppose $r_1 = 2$ and $r_2 > 2$. Suppose $x_2 \circ x_2 \sim x_1$, then it cannot be that $a(x_2) \circ a(x_2) \sim a(x_1)$, if and only if $y_2 \circ y_2 \sim y_1$, for $y_2$ is more than double $x_2$, while $y_1$ is twice $x_1$. So there will be values of the length variable for which 2–point homogeneity fails.

As well, as an extensive structure, length is 1–point unique. If $a(x_1) = y_1$ and $b(x_1) = y_1$, then $a = b$. It is, of course, also 2–point unique: if $a(x_1) = y_1$, $a(x_2) = y_2$, and $b(x_1) = y_1$, $b(x_2) = y_2$, then of course $a = b$.

If some relational system is $n$–point homogeneous for every positive integer $n$, then it is said by Narens to be *∞–point homogeneous* (see also Narens & Luce, 1986). If some relational system is not $n$–point unique for any finite $n$, it is said to be *∞–point unique*.

It follows then, Narens (1981) shows, that relational systems giving rise to interval scales *(linear structures)* are 2–point homogeneous and 2–point unique; and those giving rise to ordinal scales *(monotonic structures)* are ∞–point homogeneous and ∞–point unique. Furthermore, a quite surprising result of Narens' research is that there are no simply ordered, unbounded, dense and continuous structures that are both $n$–point homogeneous and $n$-point unique for $2 < n < \infty$. This research demonstrates, first, the great structural gulf between scalar and linear structures (both of them I call quantitative structures) and monotonic (or ordinal) structures. Second, it shows why representationalists have identified so few scale types for structures that are at least ordinal.

Luce (1986, 1987) builds upon Narens concept of homogeneity, showing precisely what structure the automorphisms of a ratio scalable structure must have. Considering what he calls the class of *ordered relational structures* ($< X, \succcurlyeq, R_1, R_2, \ldots >$, where $X$ is a nonempty set, $\succcurlyeq$ is a simple order, and $R_1, R_2, \ldots$ are relations upon $X$), Luce distinguishes between automorphisms that do not fix any points and those that do. An automorphism, $f$, fixes a point when for some $x$ in $X$, $f(x) = x$. There will always be the automorphism that fixes every point (i.e., the automorphism $i$, such that for all $x$ in $X$, $i(x) = x$). This is called the *identity automorphism*. The identity automorphism together with all automorphisms that do not fix any points (relative to a relational structure) Luce designates *translations*. What Luce shows is that an ordered relational structure's being ratio scalable is logically equivalent to three conditions being satisfied by the set of all of its translations.

Let $O = < X, \succcurlyeq, R_1, R_2, \ldots >$ be any ordered relational structure. Let $T$ be the set of all translations upon $O$. $T$ satisfies conditions (1), (2), and (3) below, if and only if $O$ is isomorphic to a real unit structure (i.e., ratio scalable):

1. $T$ is a (mathematical) group;
2. $T$ is simply ordered and Archimedean;
3. $T$ is one–point homogeneous (what Luce calls, simply, *homogeneous*).

Let me explain each of these conditions in detail and, also, what Luce means by a real unit structure.

A mathematical group is a special kind of algebraic structure. It consists of a set, $A$, a binary operation, $*$, on $A$, and an element, $e$, of $A$ (the identity element) such that,

(i) for all $a$ in $A$, $a * e = e * a = a$;
(ii) for all $a,b$, and $c$ in $A$, $(a * b) * c = a * (b * c)$; and
(iii) for each $a$ in $A$ there exists $b$ in $A$ such that $a * b = e$.

So for $T$ to be a mathematical group there must be an operation on it and an identity element within it satisfying (i), (ii), and (iii). The operation is that of function composition. Let $s$ and $t$ be any two elements of $T$. $s$ maps each element of $X$ into another and so does $t$. Relative to $s$ and $t$ we can define another element of $T$, $r$, as follows: for any $x$ in $X$,

$$r(x) = y \text{ if and only if } s(x) = z \text{ and } t(z) = y.$$

That is, $r$ is the composition of $s$ and $t$ (written: $r = s * t$). This identifies the necessary operation. The identity element is just the identity translation, $i$, mentioned above. So condition (1) is actually saying that $< T, *, i >$ is a group, i.e.,

(i) for all $t$ in $T$, $t * i = i * t = t$;
(ii) for all $r$, $s$, and $t$ in $T$, $(r * s) * t = r* (s * t)$; and
(iii) for each $t$ in $T$ there exists $s$ in $T$ such that $t * s = i$.

Condition 2 states that there is a simple order on the elements of $T$. This may be defined relative to the order on $X$ for some range of $X$'s values. That is, for any $s$ and $t$ in $T$,

$$s \geqslant t \text{ if and only if for some fixed } y \text{ in } X,$$

$$s(x) \geqslant t(x) \text{ for all } x \text{ in } X \text{ such that } x \geqslant y.$$

However, if $O$ is ratio scalable then the translations in $T$ do not cross (i.e., if for any $x$ in $X$, $s(x) \geqslant t(x)$ then for all $x$ in $X$, $s(x) \geqslant t(x)$ (see Luce, 1987), and so the order on elements of $T$ applies across all values of $X$.

The simple order on $T$ is Archimedean in this sense: if any $s$ and $t$ in $T$ are such that $s > i$, then for some positive integer, $n$, $s^n > t$ (where $s^n$ means $n$ successive applications of $s$ i.e., $s^1(x) = s(x)$ and $s^{n+1}(x) = s(s^n(x))$, or $s^1 = s$ and $s^{n+1} = s^n * s$).

If $T$ satisfies (1) and (2) then it is an Archimedean ordered group and is isomorphic to a subgroup of the real numbers (by Hölder's theorem (see Krantz et al., 1971 p. 53). Furthermore, if $T$ is 1–point homogeneous, then $O$ has a numerical representation in which each element of $T$ maps into multiplication by a positive constant. That is, $O$ is ratio scalable and $T$ corresponds to the class of positive similarities transformations. Luce refers to any $O$ having this structure as a *unit structure*.

By a *real unit structure* Luce means a numerical relational system whose domain, $R$, is a subset of the positive real numbers, whose relations are $\geqslant$ and

$R_1, R_2, \ldots$ and it is such that there is some $T'$ (a proper subset of the positive reals) where

(i) $T'$ is a group (with multiplication as the operation);
(ii) $T'$ maps $R$ into $R$ (i.e., for each $r$ in $R$ and $t'$ in $T'$, $t'r$ is in $R$);
(iii) $T'$ restricted to $R$ is the set of translations of this structure.

So a real unit structure is a unit structure of real numbers.

The significance of Luce's work for the theory of measurement proposed in this book is that it specifies what it is for a variable to be quantitative: a variable whose values are simply ordered is quantitative if and only if its translations are 1–point homogeneous and constitute an Archimedean simply ordered group.

A second advantage of Luce's formulation is that it enables *ratios of values* of a quantitative variable to be defined in a more general way than was done in Chapter 2. There ratios were defined via additivity. Of course, all quantitative variables must be additive (in the sense that additive relations are taken to hold between values of the variable). However, additive relations may not be directly evident (i.e., extensive measurement may not be possible). In such cases it may be beneficial to have a definition of ratios that is independent of additivity. Apart from that, it is a conceptual advance to be able to define ratios relative to the empirical relational system.

The way in which ratios may be defined using Luce's result is as follows. Let $O = \langle X, \succsim, R_1, R_2, \ldots \rangle$ be an ordered relational structure whose translations are 1–point homogeneous and constitute an Archimedean simply ordered group. Then for any $w$, $x$, $y$, and $z$ in $X$, $w/x \succsim y/z$ if and only if $s \succsim t$, (where $s$ and $t$ are those translations in $T$ such that $s(x) = w$ and $t(z) = y$). Each translation in $T$ is really an equivalence class of ratios. That is, for any $t$ in $T$, $t = \{x/y \mid t(y) = x\}$.

This makes sense once it is recognized that within a unit structure each translation "expands" or "contracts" the structure by some fixed proportion. There must then be some interpretation of conditions (1), (2), and (3), above (for $O$ to be a unit structure) that applies directly to ratios. Such an interpretation would not only be of theoretical interest. It could be applied to those instances where data consists of (or may be interpreted as consisting of) an order on ratios of elements of $X$ (as, for example, in some interpretations of Stevens' method of magnitude estimation).

Because an ordering on ratios is a special case of an ordering on the Cartesian product of $X$ with itself, it follows that an ordering on ratios is ratio scalable (i.e., is a unit structure or quantitative) if and only if it is a weak order satisfying double cancellation, solvability and the Archimedean condition. Here then we have an interpretation of Luce's result about translations at the level of ratios, and it turns out to be a special instance of conjoint measurement. Given the role of both ratios and conjoint measurement in this book, this is an interesting conclusion. (Note, of course, that the interval scale is the special case where $X$ is a set of differences).

As already mentioned, this observation about ratios could be applied to the method of magnitude estimation or, more directly, to ordinal judgments of relative magnitude. One magnitude estimation procedure involves the experimenter assigning some number, say 100, to a standard stimulus, and then instructing the subject to assign numbers to other stimuli in such a way that the ratios of these numbers to 100 express the magnitude of the stimuli to that of the standard (relative to some specified attribute). Order relations between such numerical ratios could easily be used to test cancellation conditions on the relative magnitudes (or ratios) of the stimuli. Alternatively, subjects could be instructed to order stimulus ratios directly. Either way the hypothesis that human judgments about some attribute are quantitative could be tested.

## CONCLUSION

As must be obvious by now, the science of psychology is still a long way from developing procedures that may legitimately be described as measurement procedures. However, despite Pythagorian cries to the contrary, this does not impugn psychology's status as a science. Its status as a science rests solely on its use of the methods of observation, hypothesis, and deduction. It needs no more to be given that status and in this it is no different to any other science. Psychological measurement will only ever be a reality if some psychological variables are quantitative and that issue is an empirical one and must be settled by experimental research. What has been considered in this book are the kinds of experimental evidence that will support (or, alternatively, falsify) the hypothesis that some psychological variable is quantitative. The theory of conjoint measurement provides a method whereby such evidence may be collected.

In this chapter a number of developments that will enhance the quest for measurement in psychology have been looked at. The primary need is for the development of techniques of stimulus control. This is necessary not only for any application of conjoint measurement theory but also for that special application, the construction of standard sequences. It is this, more than anything else, that will establish psychological measurement. In the absence of such sequences legitimate doubts must remain.

The other developments considered relate to extending the theory and applications of conjoint measurement. This is necessary if the full range of quantitative theories used within psychology are to be brought within its scope.

Beyond these needs there lies another: the need to struggle against the mistaken belief that psychological measurement already exists. This illusion is based on the false views of measurement prevalent within psychology. That entrenched illusion is now the major obstacle in the way of those who would sooner test the reality, than accept the myth of psychological measurement.

# Appendix 1

# The Theory of Order

Quantification in psychology is distinguished from that in physics by the extent to which it has been attempted from a purely ordinal base. Order, of course, is one of the characteristics of quantity. Within psychology it has sometimes been assumed that where there is order, there must also be quantity. Thus psychologists have postulated a number of quantitative theories to explain ordinal effects such as the ones considered in this book. Although this approach has not yet been resoundingly successful in establishing psychological measurement on a sure footing, it has given rise to some interesting theories, some widely used techniques (especially multidimensional scaling), and one important discovery, the theory of conjoint measurement. Through this theory it has been discovered that measurement can be achieved upon a purely ordinal base.

## THE CONCEPT OF ORDER

An order on a class of entities is a relation that lines them up so that each entity is earlier or later than each other. Consider, for example, the points on the line in Fig. 1. They are ordered from left to right as *A*, *B*, *C*, *D*, *E*, *F*, *G*, and *H*. Any order is a relational system and there are a number of different ways that it can be described. One of the simplest is to characterize the order in terms of the relations holding between the pairs of entities. One such relation in Fig. 1 is that

FIG. 1. An illustration of an order: the eight points, *A, B, C, D, E, F, G,* and *H* are ordered from left to right along a line.

TABLE 1
Some Properties of Binary Relations

A relation, $R$, is *transitive* upon a class if and only if, for every $x$, $y$ and $z$ in that class, if $R(x,y)$ and $R(y,z)$ then $R(x,z)$.
e.g., the relation of being an ancestor of upon the class of all people is transitive.

A relation, $R$, is *intransitive* upon a class if and only if, for every $x$, $y$ and $z$ in that class, if $R(x,y)$ and $R(y,z)$ then not $R(x,z)$.
e.g., the relation of being the mother of upon the class of all people is intransitive.

A relation, $R$, is *symmetric* upon a class if and only if, for every $x$ and $y$ in that class, if $R(x,y)$ then $R(y,x)$.
e.g., the relation of being a sibling of upon the class of all people is symmetric.

A relation, $R$, is *asymmetric* upon a class if and only if, for every $x$ and $y$ in that class, if $R(x,y)$ then not $R(y,x)$.
e.g., the relation of being the father of upon the class of all people is asymmetric.

A relation, $R$, is *antisymmetric* upon a class if and only if, for every $x$ and $y$ in that class, if $R(x,y)$ and $R(y,x)$ then $x=y$ (i.e., $x$ is identical to $y$).
e.g., the relation of being at least as great as upon the real numbers is antisymmetric.

A relation, $R$, is *reflexive* upon a class if and only if, for every $x$ in that class, $R(x,x)$.
e.g., the relation of being as tall as upon the class of all people is reflexive.

A relation, $R$, is *irreflexive* upon a class if and only if, for every $x$ in that class, not $R(x,x)$.
e.g., the relation of being the brother of upon the class of all people is irreflexive.

A relation, $R$, is *strongly connected* upon a class if and only if, for every $x$ and $y$ in that class, either $R(x,y)$ or $R(y,x)$.
e.g., the relation of being at least as great as upon the natural numbers is strongly connected.

A relation, $R$, is *connected* upon a class if and only if, for every $x$ and $y$ in that class such that $x \neq y$, either $R(x,y)$ or $R(y,x)$.
e.g., the relation of being less than upon the natural numbers is connected.

of being to the left of: *A* is to the left of *B; B* is to the left of *C;* and so on. This relation orders all eight points and it does so because it possesses certain properties. It is transitive, asymmetric and connected (these and other important properties of binary relations are defined in Table 1). Any relation that is transitive, asymmetric, and connected on a particular class of entities orders the members of that class.

A logically equivalent description of this relation of being to the left of is to characterize it as being transitive, irreflexive, and connected. This is because any transitive and asymmetric relation is also transitive and irreflexive, and vice versa. So any relation that is transitive, irreflexive, and connected on a class also orders the members of that class.

In chapter 3 the fact that the values of a quantitative variable are ordered was expressed, not by referring to a relation that was transitive, asymmetric (or irreflexive), and connected, but by referring to one that was transitive, antisymmetric, and strongly connected (in that case the relation of being at least as great as). This again, is simply an alternative way of describing an order. In the case of Fig. 1 the order could also be described in terms of the relation of not being to the right of, a relation that is transitive, antisymmetric, and strongly connected. That is, a class is ordered by a transitive, asymmetric, and connected relation if and only if it is ordered by a transitive, antisymmetric, and strongly connected relation. To take another example, the real numbers are ordered by both $>$ (which is transitive, asymmetric, and connected) and $\geqslant$ (which is transitive, antisymmetric, and strongly connected).

Despite the fact that the structure described by reference to each kind of relation is the same (viz., an order) the relations themselves are given different names. Transitive, antisymmetric, and strongly connected relations are known as *simple orders* and transitive, asymmetric (or irreflexive), and connected relations are known as *strict simple orders* (cf. Suppes, 1957 & Burington, 1965).

Orders are highly prized natural structures because of their simplicity. So it is not surprising that some structures that are not orders, should be assessed in terms of their proximity to an order. Some that have been identified are weak orders, partial orders, and quasi–orders.

Weak orders may be illustrated by extending Fig. 1 so that more than one point occurs at some of the positions going from left to right. This is done in Fig. 2. Such a system of points is not an order because neither of the two relations considered (being to the left of and not being to the right of) possess the necessary properties. Being to the left of is no longer connected, and not being to the right of is no longer antisymmetric. However, the relation of not being to the right of

FIG. 2. An illustration of a weak order: the relation of not being to the right of on this set of points is both transitive and strongly connected.

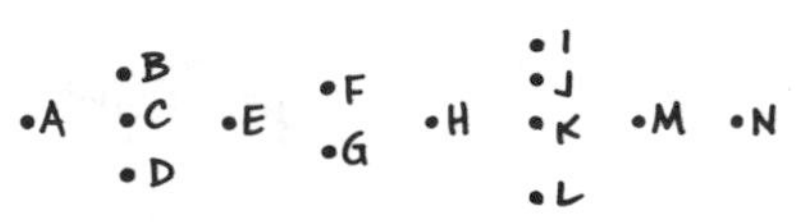

is transitive, and strongly connected, and it is these two properties which characterize a weak order.

The great beauty of a weak order is illustrated in Fig. 3. If the points in Fig. 2 are grouped according to their position going from left to right, then the resulting set of groups is an order. That is, any two points, $x$ and $y$, belong to the same *equivalence class* if and only if $x$ is not to the right of $y$ and $y$ is not to the right of $x$. These equivalence classes are exhaustive (every point belongs to one) and discrete (every point belongs to only one), and they stand in the following relation to each other: group $X$ is not to the right of group $Y$, if and only if each member of $X$ is not to the right of any member of $Y$. This relation of one group not being to the right of another is transitive, antisymmetric, and strongly connected. Hence, it constitutes an order.

This reduction of a weak order to an order may be expressed formally as follows. Let $R$ be any transitive and strongly connected relation on a class (i.e., $R$ is a weak order). A relation, $E$, definable in terms of $R$ must then exist as follows: for any $x$ and $y$ in the class,

$$E(x,y) \text{ if and only if } R(x,y) \text{ and } R(y,x).$$

$E$ is an equivalence relation (i.e., it is transitive, asymmetric, and reflexive) and pairs of objects standing in this relation belong to the same equivalence class. Objects $x$'s equivalence class, $[x]$, is the set of all things $y$ such that $E(x,y)$. Equivalence classes stand in a relation $R^*$ to one another as follows:

$$R^*([x], [y]) \text{ if and only if } R(x,y).$$

$R^*$ upon the class of equivalence classes is a simple order. Because a weak order always reduces to a simple order in this fashion it is often called a *preorder*. From the logical point of view, having a weak order is as good as having an order.

This is not generally so with partial orders. The relation of being to the left of upon the points of Fig. 2 is transitive and asymmetric (though it is not connected) and so is, what is called, a *strict partial order*. Of course, in this particular example, the equivalence relation and corresponding equivalence classes may also be defined by reference to this relation. The equivalence relation holds between points that are indifferent to each other with respect to the relation of being to the left of (e.g., points $B$ and $C$). That is, indifference with respect to this relation is an equivalence relation, but in general this is not so for transitive and asymmetric relations.

Let $R$ be any transitive and asymmetric relation. Indifference with respect to $R(I)$ is as follows: for any $x$ and $y$ in the class,

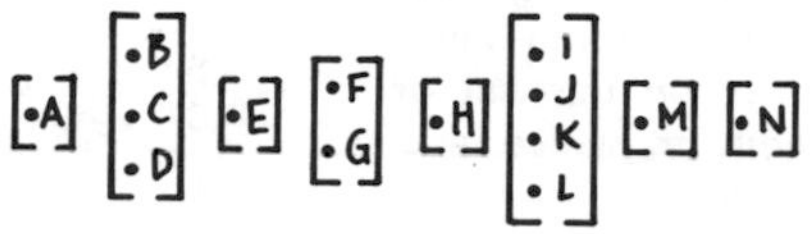

FIG. 3. When the points in Fig. 2 are grouped together the resulting groups constitute an order.

[•A] [•B •C •D] [•E] [•F •G] [•H] [•I •J •K •L] [•M] [•N]

$$I(x,y) \text{ if and only if not } R(x,y) \text{ and not } R(y,x).$$

It does not follow from the properties of $R$ that such an indifference relation must be an equivalence relation. Consider a family tree. The relation of being an ancestor of is transitive, asymmetric and so, a strict partial order. A hypothetical family tree is illustrated in Fig. 4. In that figure, an arrow from $X$ to $Y$ indicates that $X$ is an ancestor of $Y$. Now $B$ and $G$ are indifferent with respect to this relation (neither is the ancestor of the other) as are $G$ and $E$, but $B$ and $E$ are not. Hence, the indifference relation is not transitive. Of course as we have seen, in special cases it may be transitive, but in general it need not be. When it is, the strict partial order is equivalent to a weak order. When it is not, the structure may still closely approximate an order, as is seen in the cases of the *semiorder* and *interval order*.

Semiorders and interval orders are special cases of strict partial orders. Suppose that a relation, $R$, is irreflexive upon a class of objects. Then $R$ is a semiorder if and only if, for any $x$, $y$, $z$, and $w$ in the class

(i) if $R(x,y)$ and $R(z,w)$, then $R(x,w)$ or $R(z,y)$ and
(ii) if $R(x,y)$ and $R(y,z)$, then $R(x,w)$ or $R(w,z)$.

$R$ is an interval order if and only if (i) is true. An irreflexive relation that satisfies (i) must also be transitive (to see this let $y = z$), and any transitive and irreflexive relation is asymmetric. So if $R$ is an interval order (and if it is a semiorder it is an interval order), then it must be both transitive and asymmetric. Hence, semiorders and interval orders are strict partial orders.

A simple example of a semiorder might be an ordering of, say, a set of weights by a person. Since small differences between weights are not discernable, pairs of indistinguishable but different weights may be included in the set relative to any judge. Suppose that the relation of one weight being judged greater than another ($R$) is irreflexive and transitive. Also, suppose that there exists a weight increment, $e$, such that for any weights, $x$ and $y$, in the set, $R(x,y)$ if and only if $x \geqslant y + e$. ($e$ is the just noticeable difference (jnd) between weights). Then, of course, (i) and (ii) are true and so $R$ is a semiorder on the weights. On the other hand, if the magnitude of the jnd is relative to the weight involved, so that each weight, $x$, has its own particular jnd, $e_x$, then $R(x,y)$ if and only if $x \geqslant y + e_y$.

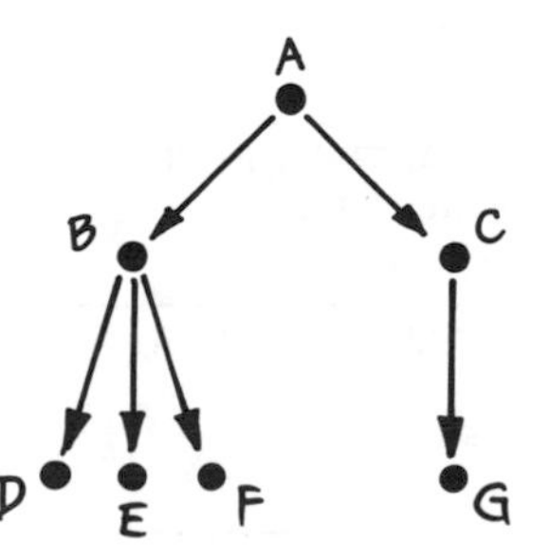


FIG. 4. A hypothetical family tree illustrating intransitive indifference.

In this case (i) is true but (ii) false and so $R$ is an interval order. Fishburn (1970) and Roberts (1976) give more details on these kinds of structures.

To each strict partial order there corresponds a partial order and conversely. A partial order is a relation that is transitive, antisymmetric, and reflexive. It is simply an alternative characterization of the same kind of structure as a strict partial order. If a relation, $R$, is a strict partial order than the disjunction of $R$ and the identity relation constitutes a partial order. For example, the composite relation of being an ancestor of or identical with on the family tree in Fig. 4 is a partial order.

Table 2 summarizes these ordinal structures. Within each row the structures characterized are equivalent. They differ only with respect to the relation selected to describe the structure. Row A contains the orders proper; row B, those structures that may be reduced to an order on equivalence classes; and row C, those structures that only approximate an order.

Psychologists have taken an interest in orders largely because of the association between orders and quantity. Obviously, quantity entails order. This, together with the fact that some physical quantities were initially identified only ordinally (e.g., temperature) has encouraged psychologists to treat order as a sign of quantity. This treatment is slightly presumptuous for two reasons. First, order alone does not entail quantity. Second, ordinal structures do not necessarily require quantitative explanation. Some of the conditions under which ordinal structures do require quantitative explanation are discussed in chapter 4.

## A PSYCHOLOGICAL EXAMPLE OF ORDINAL STRUCTURE

The typical psychological test of intellectual performance consists of a set of questions or problems (called "items" in the jargon of psychometrics). The person doing the test produces answers or solutions (called "responses"), and if these are evaluated as being either correct or incorrect the items are called "dichotomous." The standard procedure at this point is to count the number of correct

TABLE 2
A Summary of Ordinal Structures

| | | |
|---|---|---|
| A | STRICT SIMPLE ORDER<br>transitive<br>asymmetric<br>connected | SIMPLE ORDER<br>transitive<br>antisymmetric<br>strongly connected |
| B | STRICT PARTIAL ORDER<br>WITH TRANSITIVE<br>INDIFFERENCE | WEAK ORDER<br>transitive<br>strongly connected |
| C | STRICT PARTIAL ORDER<br>transitive<br>asymmetric | PARTIAL ORDER<br>transitive<br>antisymmetric<br>reflexive |

responses. This number is called the person's "total score" on the test. The total score is often converted to some kind of "transformed score" (e.g., an IQ or $z$ score) for the purpose of enabling comparisons between peoples' performances on the test. In the following example we depart from this time–honored path to follow one pioneered by L. Guttman (1944). This bases comparisons on response patterns rather than on total scores.

Each person's performance on a set of dichotomous items may be described as a sequence of ones and/or zeroes. If the response to item $i$ is correct then a "1" is placed in the $i$th position of the sequence; otherwise a "0" is placed in that position. This sequence of ones and/or zeroes describes the person's pattern of correct and incorrect responses. It is what we will call that person's "response pattern". If there are $n$ dichotomous items in a test then the number of different possible response patterns is $2^n$. For a three item test $2^n = 8$, and for this case the different possible response patterns are listed in Table 3.

Each response pattern describes a particular kind of performance on the test. Any two people having the same response pattern, have performed equivalently in the sense that they have responded correctly to precisely the same items. Any two people obtaining different response patterns, have performed differently in the sense that they have not responded correctly to the same items. This is true even when they have the same total score (e.g., if one's response pattern was 011 and the other's was 110). So the use of total scores as a basis for comparisons is not as informative as the use of response patterns.

Response patterns stand in a fairly obvious relation to one another. Each response pattern indicates a certain quality of performance. The quality of one response pattern may be superior to that of another in the following kind of way. A person who obtains response pattern 7 (in Table 3) has performed better than a person who obtains response pattern 5, simply because the first person not only responds correctly to every item that the second person gets correct, but also gets another item correct as well. By way of contrast, the performance of a person

TABLE 3
The Full Set of Eight Response Patterns Possible With Three Dichotomous Items

| | | *Items* | | |
|---|---|---|---|---|
| | | 1 | 2 | 3 |
| *Response Patterns* | 1 | 0 | 0 | 0 |
| | 2 | 0 | 0 | 1 |
| | 3 | 0 | 1 | 0 |
| | 4 | 0 | 1 | 1 |
| | 5 | 1 | 0 | 0 |
| | 6 | 1 | 0 | 1 |
| | 7 | 1 | 1 | 0 |
| | 8 | 1 | 1 | 1 |

who obtains the pattern 110 is not superior to the performance of a person who obtains the pattern 001, since neither is correct on any item correctly answered by the other. In terms of this relation they are indifferent. The relation involved here (let us call it "$R_1$") may be defined as follows: the quality of performance of a response pattern, *i*, is superior to the quality of performance of a response pattern, *j*, if and only if all items correct in *j* are correct in *i* and at least one item correct in *i* is not correct in *j*. The eight response patterns in Table 3 related by $R_1$ are shown in Fig. 5. In that figure a response pattern is superior to another if and only if an arrow points from it to the other.

It follows from the definition of this relation that it is transitive and asymmetric. Therefore, the set of all response patterns on an *n* item test related by $R_1$ is a strict partial order. Corresponding to this strict partial order there must be a partial order. This involves a slightly different relation ($R_2$) defined as follows: the quality of performance of a response pattern, *i*, is at least as good as the quality of performance of a response pattern, *j*, if and only if all items correct in *j* are correct in *i*. By definition, $R_2$ is transitive, antisymmetric and reflexive.

Does $R_1$ on the set of all possible response patterns for some test constitute either an interval order or a semiorder? The structure in Fig. 5 is a semiorder (and, hence, an interval order), so obviously, the set of all response patterns in a three item test related by $R_1$ constitutes a semiorder. However, for a four item test this is not so. The set of all possible response patterns for a four item test is listed in Table 4 and their structure according to $R_1$ is shown in Fig. 6. If this structure is an interval order, then any two ordered pairs of response patterns may be chosen, such as 8 and 6, and 15 and 11, and it must follow that either $R_1(8,11)$ or $R_1(15,6)$. Inspection of Fig. 6 shows that neither of these relations exist and, so, the set of all possible response patterns on a four item test is not an interval order and therefore not a semiorder.

Also, inspection of Fig. 5 shows that on a three item test, indifference with respect to $R_1$ is not transitive: response patterns 4 and 7 are indifferent, as are 4 and 5; but 7 and 5 are not. Hence, the set of all possible response patterns on a three item test related by $R_1$ is not a strict partial order with transitive indifference. Neither is $R_2$ strongly connected on this set. Therefore, related by $R_2$ it is not a weak order.

The fact that the set of all possible response patterns together with $R_1$ is not

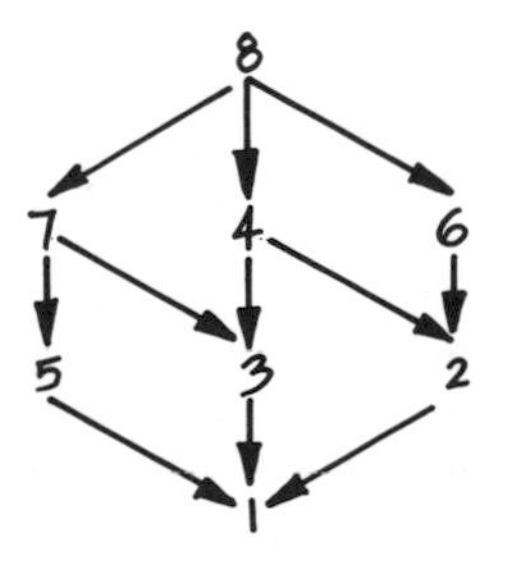


FIG. 5. A representation of the strict partial order imposed by $R_1$ on the response patterns in Table 3.

TABLE 4
The Full Set of Sixteen Response Patterns Possible With Four Dichotomous Items

| *Response Patterns* | *Items* 1 | 2 | 3 | 4 |
|---|---|---|---|---|
| 1 | 0 | 0 | 0 | 0 |
| 2 | 0 | 0 | 0 | 1 |
| 3 | 0 | 0 | 1 | 0 |
| 4 | 0 | 0 | 1 | 1 |
| 5 | 0 | 1 | 0 | 0 |
| 6 | 0 | 1 | 0 | 1 |
| 7 | 0 | 1 | 1 | 0 |
| 8 | 0 | 1 | 1 | 1 |
| 9 | 1 | 0 | 0 | 0 |
| 10 | 1 | 0 | 0 | 1 |
| 11 | 1 | 0 | 1 | 0 |
| 12 | 1 | 0 | 1 | 1 |
| 13 | 1 | 1 | 0 | 0 |
| 14 | 1 | 1 | 0 | 1 |
| 15 | 1 | 1 | 1 | 0 |
| 16 | 1 | 1 | 1 | 1 |

even an interval order once the number of items exceeds three, explains why most mental test theorists have preferred total scores as the basis for any comparisons. Most current tests possess at least thirty items, making the strict partial order on the response patterns quite complex. This complexity reduces somewhat if the actual, rather than possible, response patterns are considered. Guttman's aim was to construct tests in which the set of actual response patterns ordered by $R_1$ was a strict simple order. This happens whenever the set of actual response patterns manifests a distinctive cumulative pattern. This pattern is illustrated in Table 5 for the case of the six item test.

If the set of actual response patterns includes nothing beyond these (although it need not include all of them) then $R_1$ on these patterns is a strict simple order. Such a set of response patterns is known as a Guttman scale within the

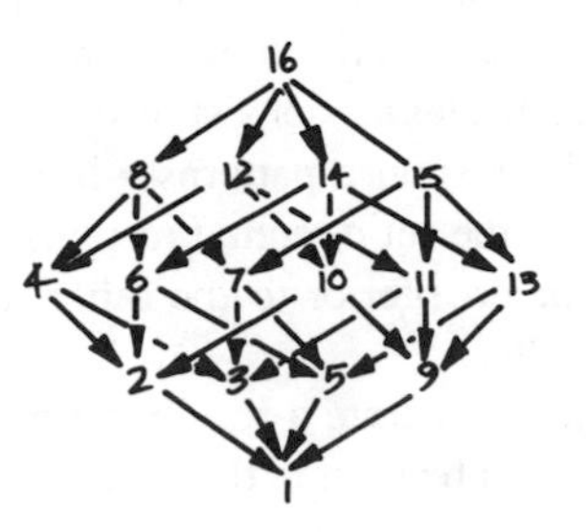


FIG. 6. A representation of the strict partial order imposed by $R_1$ upon the response patterns in Table 4.

TABLE 5
The Distinctive Cumulative Pattern Manifested by a Guttman Scale: A Set of Response Patterns Upon Which $R_1$ Imposes a Strict Simple Order

| | | Items | | | | | |
|---|---|---|---|---|---|---|---|
| | | 1 | 2 | 3 | 4 | 5 | 6 |
| *Response Patterns* | 1 | 0 | 0 | 0 | 0 | 0 | 0 |
| | 2 | 0 | 0 | 0 | 0 | 0 | 1 |
| | 3 | 0 | 0 | 0 | 0 | 1 | 1 |
| | 4 | 0 | 0 | 0 | 1 | 1 | 1 |
| | 5 | 0 | 0 | 1 | 1 | 1 | 1 |
| | 6 | 0 | 1 | 1 | 1 | 1 | 1 |
| | 7 | 1 | 1 | 1 | 1 | 1 | 1 |

psychometric literature. A Guttman scale is any set of response patterns simply ordered by $R_2$.

Guttman scales containing even a moderate number of items have proved difficult to construct. The consensus amongst mental test theorists is that they are impractical (e.g., the discussion by Nunnally, 1967). This view ignores the fact that our knowledge of the relevant attributes of test items is still quite poor. If the item attributes determining performance were known, then the possibility of constructing Guttman scales could be accurately assessed. In the absence of that knowledge the Guttman scale concept must not be dismissed, for Guttman scales make use of much more of the available information on test performance than does the use of total scores. In going from observed performance (i.e., response patterns) to total score, information is lost. Hence, the use of Guttman scales is much more efficient than the currently standard procedure.

The Guttman scale is not the only structure of interest in this context. If, for example, a set of actual response patterns related by $R_1$ is a strict partial order with transitive indifference then, by the process of reduction outlined above, a simple order would result. This is illustrated for a six item test in (a) in Fig. 7. Indifference with respect to $R_1$ occurs at three levels where there is a single indifferent pair. This makes indifference an equivalence relation (even if a degenerate one). The relation composed of the disjunction of $R_1$ and indifference weakly orders this set of response patterns. The relation in this case is: the quality of response pattern $x$ is either superior or indifferent to the quality of response pattern $y$. The three equivalence classes consist of the three pairs of mutually indifferent response patterns. The response patterns within each pair are equivalent in the sense that whatever (in the set of actual response patterns) is superior or inferior to one is also superior or inferior to the other. So a simple order on classes of response patterns results.

(b) and (c) in Fig. 7 illustrate a semiorder and an interval order respectively for a six item test. As can be seen in these cases, the number of response patterns

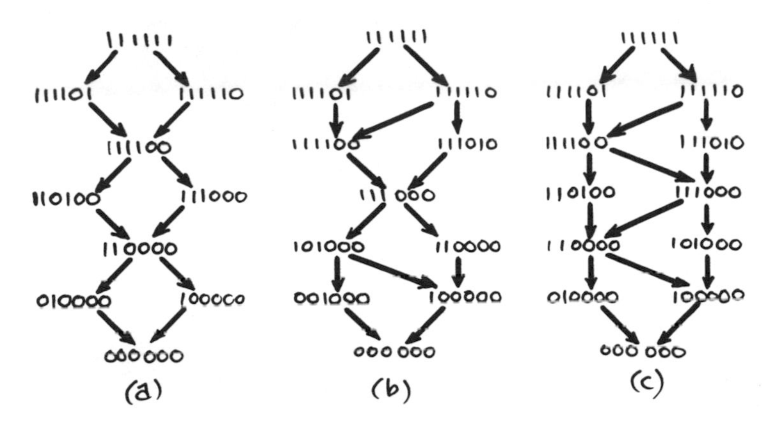


FIG. 7. An illustration of (a) a weak order, (b) a semiorder, and (c) an interval order for a six item test.

permitted progressively increases. A Guttman scale of six items allows only seven response patterns; an interval order permits twelve. In our present state of ignorance about the relevant item attributes these approximations to order may be more practical options than the Guttman scale itself.

# References


Adams, E. W. (1966). On the nature and purpose of measurement. *Synthese, 16,* 125–169.

Adams, E. W. (1979). Measurement theory. In P. D. Asquith & H. E. Kyburg (Eds.), *Current issues in the philosophy of science* (pp. 207–227). East Lansing, MI: Philosophy of Science Association.

Adams, E. W., Fagot, R. F., & Robinson, R. E. (1965). A theory of appropriate statistics. *Psychometrika, 30,* 99–127.

Adler, H. E. (1980). Vicissitudes of Fechnerian psychophysics in America. In R. W. Rieber & K. Salzinger (Eds.), *Psychology: Theoretical-historical perspectives* (pp. 11–23). New York: Academic Press.

Aristotle. (1941a). Categoriae (E. M. Edghill, Trans.) In R. McKeon (Ed.), *The basic works of Aristotle* (pp. 7–37). New York: Random House.

Aristotle. (1941b). Metaphysics. (W. D. Ross, Trans.) In R. McKeon (Ed.), *The basic works of Aristotle* (pp. 689–926). New York: Random House.

Baird, J. C. & Noma, E. (1978). *Fundamentals of scaling and psychophysics*. New York: Wiley.

Baldwin, J. M. (1902). *Dictionary of philosophy and psychology* (vol. 2). London: Macmillan.

Bergmann, G. & Spence, K. W. (1941). Operationism and theory in psychology. *Psychological Review, 48,* 1–14.

Bergmann, G., & Spence, K. W. (1944). The logic of psychophysical measurement. *Psychological Review, 51,* 1–24.

Bartlett, R. J. (1940). Measurement in psychology. *Advancement of Science, 1,* 422–441.

Beals, R., Krantz, D. H., & Tversky, A. (1968). Foundations of multidimensional scaling. *Psychological Review, 75,* 127–142.

Birkhoff, G., & MacLane, S. (1965). *A survey of modern algebra*. New York: Macmillan.

Boring, E. G. (1929). *A history of experimental psychology*. New York: Century.

Boring, E. G. (1945). The use of operational definitions in science. *Psychological Review, 52,* 243–245.

Bostock, D. (1979). *Logic and arithmetic: Vol. 2, Rational and irrational numbers*. Oxford, England: Clarendon.

Brentano, F. (1874). *Psychology from an empirical standpoint*. (English translation, 1973). New York: Humanities.

Bridgman, P. W. (1927). *The logic of modern physics*. New York: Macmillan.

Bridgman, P. W. (1938). Operational analysis. *Philosophy of Science, 5,* 114–131.

Bridgman, P. W. (1950). *Reflections of a physicist*. New York: Philosophical Library.

Burington, R. S. (1965). *Handbook of mathematical tables and formulas*. New York: McGraw-Hill.

Burke, C. J. (1953). Additive scales and statistics. *Psychological Review, 60,* 73–75.

Byerley, H. C. (1974). Realist foundations of measurement. In K. F. Schaffner & R. S. Cohen (Eds.), *P.S.A. 1972,* (pp. 375–384). Dordrecht-Holland: Reidel.

Campbell, N. R. (1920). *Physics, the elements*. Cambridge: Cambridge University Press.

Carnap, R. (1966). *Philosophical foundations of physics*. New York: Basic Books.

Carroll, J. D., & Chang, J. J. (1970). Analysis of individual differences in multidimensional scaling via an N-way generalization of 'Eckart-Young' decomposition. *Psychometrika, 35,* 283–319.

Carroll, J. D., & Wish, M. (1974). Multidimensional perceptual models and measurement methods. In E. C. Carterette & M. P. Friedman (Eds.) *Handbook of perception* (Vol. 2, pp. 391–447). New York: Academic Press.

Cattell, J. McK. (1890). Mental tests and measurements. *Mind, 15,* 373–380.

Cattell, R. B. (1971). *Abilities: Their growth and action*. Boston: Houghton, Mifflin.

Cliff, N. (1982). What is and isn't measurement. In G. Keren (Ed.), *Statistical and methodological issues in psychology and social sciences research* (pp. 3–38). Hillsdale, NJ: Lawrence Erlbaum Associates.

Cohen, M. R., & Nagel, E. (1934). *An Introduction to logic and scientific method*. London: Routledge & Kegan Paul.

Comrey, A. L. (1950). An operational approach to some problems in psychological measurement. *Psychological Review, 57,* 217–228.

Coombs, C. H. (1950). Psychological scaling without a unit of measurement. *Psychological Review, 57,* 145–158.

Coombs, C. H. (1964). *A theory of data*. New York: Wiley.

Coombs, C. H., Dawes, R. M., & Tversky, A. (1970). *Mathematical psychology: an elementary introduction*. Englewood Cliff, NJ: Prentice Hall.

Coombs, C. H., & Huang, L. C. (1970). Polynomial psychophysics of risk. *Journal of Mathematical Psychology, 7,* 317–338.

Coombs, C. H., Raiffa, H. & Thrall, R. M. (1954). Some views on mathematical models and measurement theory. *Psychological Review, 61,* 132–144.

Dawes, R. M. (1972). *Fundamentals of attitude measurement*. New York: Wiley.

Dedekind, R. (1909). *Essays on the theory of numbers*. Chicago: Open Court.

Dingle, H. (1950). A theory of measurement. *British Journal of the Philosophy of Science, 1,* 5–26.

Drake, S. (1957). *Discoveries and opinions of Galileo*. New York: Doubleday.

Ebbinghaus, H. (1908). *Psychology: an elementary textbook*. (M. Meyer, Trans.). Boston: Heath.

Ellis, B. (1966). *Basic concepts of measurement*. Cambridge: Cambridge University Press.

Euclid, (1908). *Elements, Book V*. In *The Thirteen books of Euclid's elements,* Vol. 2. (T. L. Heath, Trans.) Cambridge: Cambridge University Press.

Eysenck, H. J. (1973). *The Measurement of intelligence*. Lancaster: Medical and Technical.

Falmagne, J. C. (1986). Psychophysical measurement and theory. In K. R. Boff, L. Kaufman, & J. P. Thomas (Eds.), *Handbook of perception and human performance* (Vol. 1, pp. 1–65). New York: Wiley.

Fechner, G. T. (1860). *Elemente der psychophysik*. Leipzig, Breitkopf & Hartel.

Field, H. (1980). *Science without numbers*. Oxford, England: Basil Blackwell.

Fishbein, M. (1967). A Behavior theory approach to the relations between beliefs about an object and the attitude toward the object. In M. Fishbein (Ed.), *Readings in attitude theory and measurement* (pp. 389–400). New York: Wiley.

Fishburn, P. C. (1970). *Utility theory for decision making*. New York: Wiley.

Forrest, P., & Armstrong, D. M. (1987). The nature of number. *Philosophical Papers, 16,* 165–186.

Fraser, C. O. (1980). Measurement in psychology. *British Journal of Psychology, 71,* 23–34.

Frege, G. (1884). *Die Grundlagen der Arithmetik*. (Reprinted with J. L. Austin, Trans.) as *The Foundations of arithmetic*. Oxford: Blackwell and Mott. 1950.

Freud, S. (1895). A project for a scientific psychology. *Standard edition of the complete psychological works of Sigmund Freud,* Vol. 1, pp. 283–398). London: Hogarth.

Galton, F. (1879). Psychometric experiments. *Brain, 2,* 147–162.

Green, B. F. (1954). Attitude measurement. In *Handbook of social psychology,* Vol. 1. (pp. 335–369). Reading, MA: Addison-Wesley.

Guilford, J. P. (1954). *Psychometric methods*. New York: McGraw Hill.

Guttman, L. (1944). A basis for scaling qualitative data. *American Sociological Review, 9,* 139–150.

Guttman, L. (1968). A general non-metric technique for finding the smallest coordinate space for a configuration of points. *Psychometrika, 33,* 469–506.

Hacking, I. (1983). *Representing and intervening*. Cambridge: Cambridge University Press.

Helmholtz, H. V. (1887). Numbering and measuring from an epistemological viewpoint. (Reprinted in *Hermann von Helmholtz: Epistemological writings,* P. Hertz & M. Schlick (Eds.), *Boston studies in the philosophy of science,* Vol. 37, pp. 72–114.) Dordrecht-Holland, Reidel, 1977.

Herbart, J. F. (1816). *A textbook of psychology*. (M. K. Smith, Trans.), New York: Appleton.

Holder, O. (1901). Die axiome der qualitat und die lehre vom mass. *Berichte der Sachsischen Gesellschaft der Wissenschaften, Mathematische-Physicke Klasse, 53,* 1–64.

Hume, D. (1888). *A treatise of human nature*. (L. A. Selby-Bigge, Ed.), London: Oxford University Press.

Hunt, E. (1980). Intelligence as an information-processing concept. *British Journal of Psychology, 71,* 449–474.

Jevons, W. S. (1873). *The principles of science*. (Reprinted New York: Dover, 1958).

Johnson, H. M. (1936). Pseudo-mathematics in the mental and social sciences. *American Journal of Psychology, 48,* 342–351.

Kant, I. (1786). *Metaphysical foundations of natural science*. (J. Ellington Trans. 1970). Indianapolis: Bobbs-Merrill.

Katz, D., & Stotland, E. (1959). A preliminary statement to a theory of attitude structure and change. In S. Koch (Ed.), *Psychology: a study of a science* (Vol. 3, pp. 423–475). New York: McGraw Hill.

Kitcher, P. (1983). *The nature of mathematical knowledge*. Oxford: Oxford University Press.

Krantz, D. H. (1968). A survey of measurement theory. In G. B. Dantzig & A. F. Veinott (Eds.), *Mathematics of the decision sciences, part 2* (pp. 314–350). American Mathematical Society. RI: Providence.

Krantz, D. H. (1972). A theory of magnitude estimation and cross modality matching. *Journal of Mathematical Psychology, 9,* 168–199.

Krantz, D. H., Luce, R. D., Suppes, P., & Tversky, A. (1971). *Foundations of measurement, Vol. 1*. New York: Academic Press.

Krantz, D. H., & Tversky, A. (1971). Conjoint measurement analysis of composition rules in psychology. *Psychological Review, 78,* 151–169.

Krantz, D. H., & Tversky, A. (1975). Similarity of rectangles: an analysis of subjective dimensions. *Journal of Mathematical Psychology, 12,* 4–34.

Kruskal, J. B. (1964a) Multidimensional scaling by optimizing goodness of fit to a nonmetric hypothesis. *Psychometrika, 29,* 1–27.

Kruskal, J. B. (1964b) Nonmetric multidimensional scaling: a numerical method. *Psychometrika, 29,* 115–129.

Kuhn, T. S. (1961). The function of measurement in modern physical science. In H. Woolf (Ed.), *Quantification* (pp. 31–63). New York: Bobbs-Merrill.

Kulpe, O. (1895). *Outline of psychology*. London: Sonnenschein.

Lear, J. (1982). Aristotle's philosophy of mathematics. *Philosophical Review, 91,* 161–192.

Levelt, W. J., Riemersma, J. B., & Bunt, A. A. (1972). Binaural additivity of loudness. *British Journal of Mathematical and Statistical Psychology, 25,* 51–68.

Lindquist, F. (1951). *Educational measurement*. Washington, DC: American Council of Education.

Lord, F. M. (1953). On the statistical treatment of football numbers. *American Psychologist, 8,* 750–751.

Lorge, I. (1951). The fundamental nature of measurement. In F. Lindquist (Ed.), *Educational measurement* (pp. 533–559). Washington, DC: American Council of Education.

Luce, R. D. (1959). *Individual choice behavior*. New York: Wiley.

Luce, R. D. (1977). Thurstone's discriminal processes fifty years later. *Psychometrika, 42,* 461–489.

Luce, R. D. (1979). Suppes' contribution to the theory of measurement. In R. J. Bogdan (Ed.), *Patrick Suppes,* Dordrecht-Holland: Reidel, (pp. 93–110).

Luce, R. D. (1986). Uniqueness and homogeneity of ordered relational structures. *Journal of Mathematical Psychology, 30,* 391–415.

Luce, R. D. (1987). Measurement structures with Archimedean ordered translation groups. *Order, 4,* 165–189.

Luce, R. D., & Tukey, J. W. (1964). Simultaneous conjoint measurement: a new type of fundamental measurement. *Journal of Mathematical Psychology, 1,* 1–27.

Maze, J. R. (1973). The concept of attitude. *Inquiry, 16,* 168–205.

McCall, W. (1923). *How to measure in education*. New York: Macmillan.

McClelland, G., & Coombs, C. H. (1975). Ordmet: a general algorithm for constructing all numerical solutions to ordered metric data. *Psychometrika, 40,* 269–290.

McEvoy, J. (1982). *The philosophy of Robert Grosseteste*. Oxford: Clarendon Press.

McGregor, D. (1935). Scientific measurement and psychology. *Psychological Review, 42,* 246–266.

Merton, R. K., Sills, D. L., & Stigler, S. M. (1984). The Kelvin dictum and social science: an excursion into the history of an idea. *Journal of the History of Behavioral Sciences, 20,* 319–331.

Michell, J. (1986). Measurement scales and statistics: a clash of paradigms. *Psychological Bulletin, 100,* 398–407.

Michell, J. (1988). Some problems in testing the double cancellation condition in conjoint measurement. *Journal of Mathematical Psychology, 32,* 466–473.

Mill, J. S. (1843). *A system of logic*. (Reprinted in *Collected works of John Stuart Mill,* Vol. 7, J. M. Robson, Ed.). Toronto: University of Toronto Press. 1973.

Narens, L. (1981). On the scales of measurement. *Journal of Mathematical Psychology, 24,* 249–275.

Narens, L. (1985). *Abstract measurement theory*. Cambridge, MA: MIT Press.

Narens, L., & Luce, R. D. (1986). Measurement: the theory of numerical assignments. *Psychological Bulletin, 99,* 166–180.

Newman, E. B. (1974). On the origin of 'scales of measurement'. In H. R. Moskowitz et al. (Eds.), *Sensation and measurement* (pp. 137–145). Dordrecht-Holland: Reidel.

Newton, I. (1728). Universal arithmetic: or, a treatise of arithmetical composition and resolution. In D. T. Whiteside (Ed.), *The mathematical works of Isaac Newton,* (Vol. 2, pp. 3–134). (1967). New York: Johnson Reprint Corp.

Nietzsche, F. (1968). *The will to power*. (W. Kaufmann & R. J. Hollingdale, Trans.) New York: Random House.

Nunnally, J. C. (1967). *Psychometric theory*. New York: McGraw-Hill.

O'Neil, W. M. (1969). *Fact and theory*. Sydney: Sydney University Press.

Oresme, N. (1968). *Tractatus de Configurationibus qualitatum et Motuum*. In M. Clagett (Ed. & Trans.) *Nicole Oresme and the medieval geometry of qualities and motions*. Wisconsin: University Press.

Pap, A. (1962). *An Introduction to the philosophy of science*. London: Eyre and Spottiswoode.

Pearson, K. (1978). *The history of statistics in the seventeenth and eighteenth centuries*. London: Griffin.

Perline, R., Wright, B. D., & Wainer, H. (1979). The Rasch model as additive conjoint measurement. *Applied Psychological Measurement, 3,* 237–255.

Pollatsek, A., & Tversky, A. (1970). A theory of risk. *Journal of Mathematical Psychology, 7,* 540–553.

Reese, T. W. (1943). The application of the theory of physical measurement to the measurement of psychological magnitudes, with three experimental examples. *Psychological Monographs, 55,* 1–89.

Rokeach, M. (1968). The nature of attitudes. In D. L. Sills (Ed.), *International encyclopedia of the social sciences, Vol. 1,* (pp. 449–458), New York: Collier & Macmillan.

Roberts, F. S. (1976). *Discrete mathematical models:* Englewood Cliffs, NJ: Prentice-Hall.

Roberts, F. S. (1979). *Measurement theory.* Reading, MA: Addison-Wesley.

Rozeboom, W. W. (1966). Scaling theory and the nature of measurement. *Synthese, 16,* 170–233.

Russell, B. (1903). *Principles of mathematics.* Cambridge: Cambridge University Press.

Russell, L. J. (1928). Review of Bridgman's 'The Logic of Modern Physics'. *Mind, 37,* 355–361.

Scott, D. (1964). Measurement models and linear inequalities. *Journal of Mathematical Psychology, 1,* 233–247.

Shaw, M. E., & Wright, J. M. (1967). *Scales for the measurement of attitudes.* New York: McGraw-Hill.

Shepard, R. N. (1962a). Analysis of proximities: multidimensional scaling with an unknown distance function. I. *Psychometrika, 27,* 125–140.

Shepard, R. N. (1962b). Analysis of proximities: multidimensional scaling with an unknown distance function. II. *Psychometrika, 27,* 219–246.

Smith, B. O. (1938). *Logical aspects of educational measurement.* New York: Columbia University Press.

Spearman, C. (1904). General intelligence, objectively determined and measured. *American Journal of Psychology, 15,* 201–293.

Spearman, C. (1937). *Psychology down the ages,* Vol. 1. London: Macmillan.

Stevens, S. S. (1935a). The operational definition of psychological terms. *Psychological Review, 42,* 517–527.

Stevens, S. S. (1935b). The operational basis of psychology. *American Journal of Psychology, 47,* 323–330.

Stevens, S. S. (1939). Psychology and the science of science. *Psychological Bulletin, 36,* 221–263.

Stevens, S. S. (1946). On the theory of scales of measurement. *Science, 103,* 667–680.

Stevens, S. S. (1951). Mathematics, measurement and psychophysics. In S. S. Stevens (Ed.), *Handbook of experimental psychology* (pp. 1–49). New York: Wiley.

Stevens, S. S. (1959). Measurement, psychophysics and utility. In C. W. Churchman, & P. Ratoosh (Eds.), *Measurement: definition and theories* (pp. 18–63). New York: Wiley.

Stevens, S. S. (1974). S. S. Stevens. In G. Lindzey (Ed.) *A History of psychology in autobiography,* (Vol. VI, pp. 393–420). Englewood Cliffs, NJ: Prentice Hall.

Stevens, S. S. (1986). *Psychophysics: Introduction to its perceptual, neural, and social prospects.* Second Edition. New Brunswick, NJ: Transaction Books.

Suppes, P. (1957). *Introduction to logic.* Princeton, NJ: Von Nostrand.

Suppes, P. (1959). Measurement, empirical meaningfulness and three-valued logic. In C. W. Churchman & P. Ratoosh (Eds.), *Measurement: definition and theories* (pp. 129–143). New York: Wiley.

Suppes, P. (1979). "Replies." In R. J. Bogdan (Ed.), *Patrick Suppes* (pp. 207–232). Dordrecht-Holland: Reidel.

Suppes, P., & Zinnes, J. (1963). Basic measurement theory. In R. D. Luce, R. R. Bush, & E. H. Galanter (Eds.), *Handbook of mathematical psychology* (Vol. 1, pp. 1–76). New York: Wiley.

Thomas, L. G. (1942). Mental tests as instruments of science. *Psychological Monographs, 54.*

Thomson, W. (1891). *Popular lectures and addresses* (Vol. 1). London: Macmillan.

Thurstone, L. L. (1927a). A law of comparative judgment. *Psychological Review, 34,* 278–286.

Thurstone, L. L. (1927b). Psychophysical analysis. *American Journal of Psychology, 38,* 368–389.

Thurstone, L. L. (1927c). Three psychophysical laws. *Psychological Review, 34,* 424–432.

Thurstone, L. L. (1927d). The method of paired comparisons for social values. *Journal of Abnormal and social psychology, 21,* 384–400.

Thurstone, L. L. (1931). The measurement of social attitudes. *Journal of Abnormal and Social Psychology, 26,* 249–269.

Thurstone, L. L. (1935). *Vectors of Mind*. Chicago: University of Chicago Press.

Thurstone, L. L. (1947). *Multiple factor analysis*. Chicago: University of Chicago Press.

Thurstone, L. L. & Chave, E. J. (1929). *The measurement of attitudes*. Chicago: University of Chicago Press.

Titchener, E. B. (1905). *Experimental psychology* (Vols. 1–3). New York: Macmillan.

Torgerson, W. S. (1958). *Theory and methods of scaling*. New York: Wiley.

Tversky, A. (1967a). A general theory of polynomial conjoint measurement. *Journal of Mathematical Psychology, 4,* 1–20.

Tversky, A. (1967b). Additivity, utility and subjective probability. *Journal of Mathematical Psychology, 4,* 175–201.

Tversky, A. (1977). Features of similarity. *Psychological Review, 84,* 327–352.

Tversky, A. & Gati, I. (1978). Studies of similarity. In E. Rosch & B. Lloyd (Eds.), *Cognition and Categorization* (pp. 79–98). Hillsdale, NJ: Lawrence Erlbaum Associates.

Tversky, A., & Gati, I. (1982). Similarity, separability and the triangle inequality. *Psychological Review, 89,* 123–154.

Tversky, A., & Krantz, D. H. (1969). Similarity of schematic faces: a test of inter-dimensional additivity. *Perception and Psychophysics, 5,* 125–128.

Tversky, A., & Krantz, D. H. (1970). The dimensional representation of the metric structure of similarity data. *Journal of Mathematical Psychology, 7,* 572–597.

van der Ven, A.H.G.S. (1980). *Introduction to Scaling*. New York: Wiley.

Wender, K. (1971). A test of independence of dimensions in multidimensional scaling. *Perception and Psychophysics, 10,* 30–32.

Wiener-Ehrlich, W. K. (1978). Dimensional and metric structures in multidimensional stimuli. *Perception and Psychophysics, 24,* 399–414.

Wish, M., Deutsch, M., & Biener, L. (1970). Differences in conceptual structures of nations: an exploratory study. *Journal of Personality and Social Psychology, 16,* 361–373.

Wundt, W. M. (1873). *Principles of physiological psychology*. New York: Macmillan.

Young, F. W. (1984). Scaling. *Annual Review of Psychology, 35,* 55–81.

Yule, G. U., & Kendall, M. G. (1911). *An introduction to the theory of statistics*. London: Griffin.

# Author Index

## F



## G



## H



## J



## K



## L



## M



## N



## O



## P

# Subject Index

## A



## C



## D

## E



## F



## G



## H



## I



## J



## K



## L



## M



## N

## O



## P



## Q



## R



## S



## T



## U

## V



## W